Irish Mormons

Irish Mormons

Reconciling Identity in Global Mormonism

HAZEL O'BRIEN

UNIVERSITY OF
ILLINOIS PRESS
Urbana, Chicago, and Springfield

Some material appearing in this book was previously published in:

O'Brien, H. (2019). The marginality of "Irish Mormonism":
Confronting intersections of religion, race, and nation. *Journal of
the British Association for the Study of Religions 21*, 52–75
doi: https://doi.org/10.18792/jbasr.v21i0.40.

O'Brien, H. (2020). Institutional gender negotiations in Irish Mormon
congregations. In A. Hoyt & T. G. Petrey (Eds.), *The Routledge
handbook of gender and Mormonism* (405–419). Routledge.
https://doi.org/10.4324/9781351181600-32.

Halford, A., & O'Brien, H. (2020). Contemporary issues for the Church
of Jesus Christ of Latter-day Saints in Ireland and the United Kingdom.
In G. R. Shepherd, G. A. Shepherd, & R. T. Cragun (Eds.), *The Palgrave
handbook of global Mormonism* (475–503). Palgrave Macmillan.
https://doi.org/10.1007/978-3-030-52616-0_18.

Cataloging data available from the Library of Congress

ISBN 9780252045073 (hardcover)
ISBN 9780252087202 (paperback)
ISBN 9780252054396 (ebook)

For Tishy

Contents

Acknowledgments   ix

Introduction: Positioning Mormonism within Irish Religions   1

1 Religion in Contemporary Ireland   25

2 The Challenges of Belonging in Modern Mormonism   47

3 They All Seem Very Nice but It's a Bit Weird Isn't It?   67

4 Their Ancestors Are Watching Them   87

5 Irish-Irish and Mormon-Irish   113

6 We Preach That Culture   135

Conclusion: Reflections for the Future   165

Notes   181

Bibliography   187

Index   205

Acknowledgments

I would like to give a heartfelt thanks to the following individuals without whom this book could not have been produced. Professor Katharine Tyler of the University of Exeter for her outstanding supervision; I am both lucky and grateful to have been supported by such a mentor. Professor Douglas Davies of the University of Durham and Professor Emeritus Grace Davie of University of Exeter for their helpful advice and criticism. Professor Laurie Maffly-Kipp of Washington University–St. Louis and Dr. Kate Holbrook of the Church History Department of the Church of Jesus Christ of Latter-day Saints have supported my scholarship since they first included me in BYU Maxwell Institute's "Consultation on Latter-day Saint Women" in 2019. I am so grateful for all their advice and guidance. I will always remember Kate's kindness, may she rest in peace.

This book would quite literally not have happened were it not for my colleagues in the "Consultation on Latter-day Saint Women" gathering who encouraged me to publish a monograph at a time when such a task felt overwhelming. These women have become my friends, and I am the better for their friendship. My thanks to my editor at the University of Illinois Press, Alison Syring Bassford, whose enthusiasm about this book from the early proposal stage onward helped me enormously throughout the publication process. I am very grateful for the careful work of the book's reviewers; their insightful feedback has improved the book immeasurably. I also appreciate the support offered by South East Technological University's Research Connexions funding, which facilitated the completion of this book project.

Finally, I thank my family. My beloved parents, John and Anne, gave me a love of learning and an appreciation of the importance of education that I carry with me to this day. My sister Rachelle's comments on earlier versions of this project have been invaluable. My husband, Keith, has kept patience and good humor throughout the years it has taken to bring this project to fruition. I am grateful for his unwavering love and support. He tells me to persevere, so I do.

Irish Mormons

Positioning Mormonism within Irish Religions

My grandmother Tishy loved Padre Pio. As a typical elderly Irish Catholic woman in the twentieth century, she had religious medals and prayer cards of all kinds but those of the Catholic saint Padre Pio were her favorite. She kept one Padre Pio prayer card under her pillow, another by her armchair, another in her purse, and more scattered around the house. In her home you never knew where or when you might encounter Padre Pio. I was not surprised, then, to hear recently a dear friend of mine mention his own grandmother's love of St. Anthony. Like my own grandmother, her affection for St. Anthony seems to have been strong enough to defy death, as many years after her passing my friend and his family still recall her love of St. Anthony as we might recall any other passions that our loved ones embraced in life. My friend and I were baptized Catholic in Ireland,[1] we went to Catholic schools, we received the sacraments, but in adulthood we do not consider ourselves religious. There is little social penalty for this. This experience of Irish Catholicism, common among our generation, is very different to that of our grandmothers. Our families' experiences of Irish religion have changed dramatically in just two generations.

What happened in Ireland to generate this shift? As I came of age in the late 1990s, I emerged into a society that was transforming itself. The Celtic Tiger of the late 1990s and early 2000s brought unparalleled economic growth, which reformed and restructured the country, accelerated social liberalization, and increased religious and ethnic diversity—including increases in those who were nonreligious. This diversity, driven by mass immigration, began to challenge homogenous understandings of Irishness and Irish religion. These changes meant that a decline of Irish Catholicism occurred simultaneous to the growth of small religions, and the establishment in Ireland of world religions that had never been seen before in any significant numbers. The country of my adulthood felt very different from the country I grew up in as a child.

Justification and Scope

My core motivation for the research that informed this book was to try to understand this religious landscape and to illustrate the complexity of Irish religious identity in the contemporary age. When contemplating modern Irish society, I ask myself plenty of questions, the same questions that have informed the writing of this book. What does it mean to be religious in twenty-first-century Ireland? How does rapid social change affect the relationship between religious and national identities? Can religious tradition be sustained in times of societal instability? What is the relationship between Ireland's minority religions and the dominant religion of Catholicism?

It was clear to me that the situation in Ireland was complex, and that below sometimes-superficial constructions of Irish identity there was great nuance. As I considered these ideas, I became fascinated by the invisibility of much of Ireland's religious diversity. Ireland is overwhelmingly White, Irish, and Catholic. Many small or new religions are known as migrant religions due to their immigration-fueled growth, and many of the adherents of these religions are not Irish, or White. Ireland's long history of racializing religions has become further entrenched as Ireland's diversity has increased.

Through "racialized religion" I refer to multiple interconnected phenomena. First, at an individual level, people's actions are primarily attributed to their religious identity when they are White, but when they are not White these are attributed to their racial identity (Yukich and Edgell, 2020). This causes the intersections of race and religion to be overlooked for White religious adherents. Second, at a societal level I refer to the process through which "White racial superiority and Christian religious superiority have augmented and magnified each other" (Joshi, 2020, p. 5) within majority-White Christian countries. Third, I refer to the association in the Global North of certain religions, such as Islam, with migrant populations, and the association of migration itself with non-White groups. This phenomenon, common in many European countries (including Ireland), has the effect of homogenizing and stereotyping diverse religious groups (Es, 2019). As noted by Theodore Vial (2016, p. 1), "the category of religion is always already a racialized category, even when race is not explicitly under discussion."

In Ireland, these interconnecting processes have meant that for much of the twenty-first century Catholics have been assumed to be White and Irish, and other religions have often been presumed to be "'foreign.'" I knew that this picture was too simplistic; for example, for many years Ireland's largest religious minority has been adherents of the Church of Ireland, a form of Anglicanism that is predominantly White Irish. As ethnic diversity has increased in Ireland, Irish Catholicism has become more diverse, and as the power of the Catholic Church in Ireland has declined, more White Irish are also to be found within other religions. As I began the research that has informed this project, it seemed to me that there was a perception about religion in Ireland, reproduced through dominant discourse and popular culture, that sometimes did not match the contemporary reality. Catholicism was continuing to be constructed as White and uniquely Irish, with the result that racialized migrant religions came to be seen to represent all other religions, and the White Irish membership of these religions and other religions was ignored. Racial and ethnic minorities, both Irish and migrant, continued to be portrayed as unusual, when in reality their presence was increasing in most parts of the country and rapidly increasing in urban areas.

Within popular culture, one of Ireland's most successful TV shows was the late 1990s situation comedy *Father Ted*. It followed the trials and tribulations of two Catholic priests in rural Ireland and illuminated these kinds of cultural presumptions, often using comedy to critique Irish culture just as the Celtic Tiger—the economic boom that socially transformed Ireland—was moving into high gear. The show remained part of the fabric of popular culture in Ireland for many years after it ended thanks to its great popularity and endless repeats. Many phrases from the show entered the Irish cultural milieu including one of its most well known, "I hear you're a racist now, Father," a quote from an episode where the eponymous character is caught by a Chinese family making racist jokes (Are you right there Father Ted? 1998). In a biting critique of Irish attitudes and behavior toward those considered to be outsiders at the end of the twentieth century, Father Ted is distressed not because he was racist, but that he had been so publicly caught out being racist. In that same episode, the power of the Irish Catholic Church in shaping societal attitudes is comedically alluded to when a character asks Father Ted, "Should we all be racist now? What's the official line the [Catholic] church is taking on this?" *Father Ted* is of course a sitcom, and as such we cannot read too much into its content. Additionally, its creators have claimed they envisaged the characters as caricatures of common stereotypes about the Irish, rather than representative of any sort of social realism. Yet, it has also been noted that the allocation of the show's starring role to Dermot Morgan, an Irish comic well known to Irish audiences for his biting satire of the Irish Catholic Church, worked as a signifier to the audience that the show was perhaps, after all, a commentary on Irish Catholicism and Irish society more generally (McGonigle, 2012).

Increasing racial and ethnic diversity and social change has also been a point of exploration for Irish social research. Recent scholarship on Irish religions has often focused upon migrant religions and the racialized religious experience. This is necessary work, but it does contribute to a wider societal phenomenon where the consequences of Irish Catholicism's changing demographics are overlooked and where the experience of White Irish adherents within minority religions is made less visible. The invisibility of many minority religions in Ireland works as a form of exclusion, ensuring that only Catholicism remains accepted as "Irish religion" in Ireland. I wondered what might be the experience of those who do belong to a minority religion, but who are also White and Irish? What does this invisibility do to their sense of self, their understanding of their place in the nation-state, and how does it shape their religiosity?

This book centers itself around the experiences of Mormons in Ireland.[2] They are members of the Church of Jesus Christ of Latter-day Saints (referred to throughout this book as the CoJCoLDS, the Church, or the LDS Church),[3] and include those who are Irish-born and those who consider Ireland home. An obvious question might be "Why Mormonism?" How can Mormonism help us to answer the questions I lay out above? Scholars have commented on how Islam, Pentecostalism, Judaism, Buddhism, new religious movements (NRMs), New Age spiritualities, and others have developed in an Irish context. What can a study of Mormonism in Ireland add to this picture?

Mormonism in Utah has, much like Catholicism in Ireland, shaped the state and influenced its development. Such is its influence that outsiders associate Utah with Mormonism just as they do Ireland with Catholicism. Mormonism, like Irish society, has historically been majority White but recently the Church as an organization and its culture has been undergoing significant change, which is increasing the diversity of the Church and highlighting divergences and dislocations in the experience of being Mormon across the globe. Ireland, and Irish Catholicism, have found themselves facing similar transformations. Though the history of Mormonism as a religion and Ireland as a country have clearly been very different, they share the contemporary experience of a fragmentation of collective identity.

Ireland and Mormonism both have a relationship to colonization and colonialism. As this book illustrates, Irish society has been shaped by its own past experiences of colonialism, which, like Mormonism, have shaped attitudes toward the Other and formulated collective conceptions of belonging in Ireland. In Ireland, its history as a colonized nation under the British Empire shaped cultural attitudes toward outsiders. Ireland's contemporary role in the European Union (EU) means that it is now complicit in maintaining restrictive policies toward migrants from outside of the EU, many of whom are not White. Meanwhile, Mormon culture has also been affected by historical legacies and contemporary policies. As Gina Colvin and Joanna Brooks (2018b, p. 7) note, "Mormonism's rise in the nineteenth century and its global growth in the twentieth century also took place within the context of colonization and neo-colonization and drew from colonialist and neocolonialist ideas and attitudes." Modern Mormonism is infused with the colonial legacies of its past with consequences that are still relevant today.

Mormonism and Ireland also share the experience of being inescapably influenced by globalization. Mormonism's international expansion into a global religion and Ireland's modernization into a global economy both accelerated in the late twentieth century, leading them to be faced with the opportunities and challenges of globalization at a broadly similar point in history. Jehu Hanciles (2015, p. 41) argues that the effects of globalization on contemporary religions mean that to understand a global religion we must explore "cultural adaptation, translatability of its core message and vision, diversity of forms, and the shaping of identity outside its original context, as well as the nature and inclusiveness of its outreach." We can also consider many of these ideas when examining Irish social change as a result of globalization. Through Mormonism, this book explores the cultural adaptability of Irishness, the diversity of its forms, and the shaping of Irish identity outside its original context.

Finally, both Mormonism and Ireland are navigating the consequences of secularization. Rapid declines in Irish religiosity are mirrored in many parts of the world that once sustained the LDS Church. This is evident particularly in Europe. The United Kingdom and Nordic countries were once celebrated as regions that supported the early Church, through its "pioneers" who traveled to Utah to build Zion and through Church members who in the nineteenth century began the process of developing a global church by remaining in their own countries. Yet these countries are now often associated with a secularization process that is transforming how religion is experienced, and all religions including Mormonism must adapt to this changing environment. A study of Mormonism in Ireland, then, offers the opportunity to better understand the legacies of colonialism, the effects of rapid social and cultural change as a result of globalization and secularization, and the mechanisms through which a collective understanding of belonging is sustained in the face of disorder.

As my interest in Irish Mormonism grew, I came to understand how the experiences and identities of contemporary Irish Mormons are intimately shaped by the history of the CoJCoLDS in the United States, and by the development of the religion more recently into a global powerhouse. In recent years the work of global Mormon studies has made it inescapably clear that the future of the Church lies outside of the United States, emphasizing the urgency of better understanding the nature of the Church and the lives of its adherents outside of a US milieu. In contemplating the gravitational pull of the Church's headquarters and spiritual home of Utah, historian Laurie Maffly-Kipp (2017, p. 5) asks, "What would it mean, then, to focus both on the forces that draw Mormons toward a center and also on the movements toward and around the borders and peripheries that occasionally intersect with, complicate, and confound that attractional impulse? If we drop for the moment the force field exerted by the gravitational pull of Zion, what do we see? What are Mormons doing? Where is Mormonism present?" Given the global transformation of the Church and the scale of the impact this will have on the religion in coming generations, it is vital to explore precisely what Maffly-Kipp asks—the movements toward and around the borders of Mormonism. Thus, the research that informs this book developed as one of dual interests: Mormonism as a case study for understanding contemporary Irish religion, and Irish Mormons as a case study for understanding contemporary Mormonism.

In reflecting upon the "translocative" nature of Mormonism, Thomas Tweed (2014, p. 28) asks, "How do we tell a coherent tale about religious history with multiple beginnings and multiple locales?" and starts his answer with "I'm not sure." Truthfully, I'm not sure either, but a good place to start may be to tell a coherent tale about just one element of those multiple beginnings and multiple locales. In the case of this book, that element is Irish Mormonism and its complicated relationship to Irish society and Irish people, and to Mormonism itself. This book primarily seeks to examine the place of Mormons in contemporary Ireland, their experiences of inclusion and exclusion, and the complicated nuances of belonging that shape their collective and individual identities.

By focusing on Mormons in Ireland, this book describes the experience of contemporary Mormons in their relationship to the dominant White Irish Catholic population in Ireland, and to the CoJCoLDS, now a global religion with a continuing US focus. It explores the interconnections between Irishness and Catholicism, and between Mormonism and Americanism, with Whiteness serving as a mediator between all these categories. These interconnections illustrate how belonging is sustained not solely in religious terms, but also through race, ethnicity, nationality, language, and culture. I argue throughout this book that Irish Mormons are adapting a collective memory of Irishness and of Mormonism to create a sense of belonging for themselves in spite of their marginalized positions on the outskirts of both "Irish" and "Mormon." Although Mormonism has typically not been part of Ireland's religious memory, Irish Mormons are variously working to ensure that collective understandings of Irish religion expand beyond Catholicism. Similarly, Mormonism has a strong pull toward Utah and the wider United States. This focus has marginalized Mormon adherents based outside of the United States and particularly those beyond the Global North. Though large numbers of adherents immigrated to the United States to practice Mormonism in the nineteenth century, contemporary research has shown that some members outside the United States now feel isolated because of the Church's US focus (Hwang Chen, 2014; Hansen, Noot, & Mema, 2016). I show in this book how Irish Mormons, like Mormons in many parts of the world, are challenging dominant constructions of Mormonism to ensure they can insert themselves into Mormonism's powerful religious and cultural lineage.

When examining Mormonism's specific conditions in Ireland as a predominantly White Irish and relatively invisible minority religion, I found interesting insights into how Irish Mormonism appears to hide in plain sight. In 2022, the Republic of Ireland had thirteen LDS congregations; five wards and eight branches.[4] These are divided between one stake and one district.[5] Few of the congregations attend church in purpose-built meetinghouses, and there is no temple in either the Republic or Northern Ireland. Irish members usually travel to Preston, England, for temple visits. According to 2019 Church figures, there were 3,985 members in Ireland, 0.078 percent of the population (Stewart & Martinich, n.d.). However, this is likely to be a significant overestimation, as the Church does not remove inactive members from its rolls. Up to 80 percent of the membership in Europe may be inactive (Decoo, 2015). Ireland's Central Statistics Office shows that in 2016, the Mormon population was 0.03 percent of the general population with 1,332 members self-identifying as such (Central Statistics Office, 2017b). It is commonly accepted that the largest congregation is a ward in Dublin where an average of 150 attend each week. Other congregations often have anywhere from 20 to 80 regularly attending members and numbers often drop below this during holidays. The small number of members in Ireland, and the lack of a temple and purpose-built church buildings, adds to the low level of visibility of Mormonism in Ireland, and this compounds the lack of knowledge that Irish people have about the religion more generally.

If my own coming of age was in the late 1990s, it could be argued that the coming of age for the LDS Church in Ireland also occurred around this time. In 1995, the number of congregations grew to their highest number of fifteen, and one of the two districts became a stake. Membership numbers had been steadily increasing since the late 1970s—but progress was short-lived. By 1997, the number of congregations was back down to twelve, and by 2010 the Ireland mission had been subsumed into the Scotland and Ireland mission. Recently, some increases in Mormon membership are again evident. Notably, Irish Church membership figures broke the 4,000 barrier in 2018, though dropping to less than this the following year (Stewart & Martinich, n.d.). The Church in Ireland recognizes its slow growth of membership, even in comparison to other European countries where it is commonly accepted that membership is at best stagnating, and often in decline. It has been observed that "for some years the Ireland Dublin mission was the lowest baptizing mission in the world," though Eastern European missions now tend to take this position (Stewart & Martinich, n.d). The most pressing issue regarding growth for the Church in Ireland, as in other European countries, is not gaining converts, but keeping them. Reports from Ireland indicate that 82 percent of the 3,985 church-reported members may be inactive, leaving an active membership of just 700 people (Stewart & Martinich, n.d.). These Mormons live on the margins of Irish society, so small in number to be almost invisible, yet so deeply a part of Irish society that their influence is inseparable from it.

Doing Research in Appleby and Sweetwater

For the research behind this book, I spent a year engaging in participant observation and conducting interviews within two Mormon congregations, which I have named Sweetwater and Appleby. Appleby is situated about 180 kilometers away from Sweetwater. Appleby is the more established congregation, formed in the 1980s and with a regularly attending membership of about 70 people, though their official membership sits at about 150. Sweetwater is a newer and smaller congregation of about 30 regularly attending members, though in the summer months during my fieldwork I found that this number can fall to as low as 15 to 20. Like Appleby, their official membership is much higher than this. There is not a great deal of engagement between the two congregations, firstly because Appleby forms part of a separate Church administrative district to Sweetwater, which means that when congregations do come together, they are often split along administrative lines. Secondly, the relatively large distance between them makes it less likely that individuals might attend church at the other congregation sporadically, as when visiting family or friends. However, occasionally these visits do happen. This means that only some of each congregation have visited the other, or personally know some of the other's members. With only thirteen congregations in the country, most have at least heard of the other congregations, and have small pieces of information about congregations elsewhere. For instance, Appleby members told me in advance of my fieldwork with Sweetwater that the Sweetwater congregation was "very diverse," "transient," and they knew that the Sweetwater church building was quite small. In contrast, Sweetwater members appeared to have little knowledge of the Appleby branch other than its location.

The Appleby church building was a rented space in an office park on the outskirts of a city. The Appleby congregation have occupied multiple church buildings since the formation of the Appleby congregation in the 1970s. They have previously attended church in a house in a suburban housing development, in the function room of a hotel on the outskirts of the city, and in another office park in a more central location. The current office park where they are housed is relatively new, which is pleasing to some members who had previously attended church in the older and more industrial location prior to the move to the current premises. Some members, however, dislike the unconventional premises for church, aspiring for a purpose-built church building instead. Outside there is plenty of parking, surrounding a variety of businesses also renting spaces in the estate. During the time of my fieldwork there was a gym, various office spaces, a children's charity, and a Pentecostal church, which was mainly frequented by Black Africans. This contrasted with the mainly White Mormon congregation.

The journey to Appleby from my home in Sweetwater was a three-hour-and-twenty-minute round trip. Hence, I found traveling to church during my time in Appleby more tiring than during my time with the Sweetwater congregation. However, I was glad to have experienced this, as a key issue for the Appleby congregation was the long journeys that many members had to undertake to get to church. Appleby serves a wide and mainly rural catchment area. Many members in the congregation traveled for an hour or more to reach church on Sundays. My own commute during fieldwork meant that I better understood how the distance between church and home strongly affects the participation and wellbeing of the church members, and so although challenging, it was worthwhile.

The Appleby branch president told me that using their designated international architectural teams, the Church has converted the space into the configuration that they feel is appropriate for church meetings, and that roughly reflects church buildings internationally. Inside, the space consisted of a chapel, a series of classrooms, a kitchen, an office, a small library, toilets, and some storage space. Like Sweetwater it was clean and functional in design—as Mormon church buildings and chapels tend to be—with little of the typical decorations or adornments that one might imagine would accompany a religious space, such as a Catholic church. The Appleby church building had no permanent signage, but during my time attending church there were various posters placed on the large glass windows that front the building. They identified the name of the church, and informed passersby of assistance that the Church could offer in stopping smoking. This assistance was organized by Elder and Sister McGuire, who were based in Appleby for a year to do missionary work.[6] They had a background in volunteering in areas of addiction services, and so made assistance with stopping smoking and drinking alcohol a focus for their time on their mission in Appleby. Aside from the posters placed in the window by the elderly couple, there was little that would identify the space as religious to a passerby.

Since the time of my research the Sweetwater congregation has been moved to a building that is about a half-hour drive from Sweetwater. They now share the church building with another congregation. During my time with the Sweetwater congregation, their church building was in a central location on Sweetwater's main street. It was a single-story gray brick building with a flat roof, set back from the street along a curved path in such a way as not to be noticeable if one were passing by. There were tall black gates at the entrance to the Sweetwater building. During my fieldwork these were usually closed unless it was Sunday, or if other events were ongoing during the week. There was a sign with black letters above the gates, which said, "The Church of Jesus Christ of Latter-day Saints," and underneath that, "All Welcome." As the sign was high above the tall gates, it was difficult to see if you were passing by. There was no additional signage displaying the times of services or other useful information. On one occasion during my fieldwork I came across a Mormon couple lost on the street outside, looking for the building. When I showed them the location, they exclaimed, "Oh! We drove right past it and didn't know that it was the church."

The building was not a purpose-built church building. I grew up not far from Sweetwater and spent much of my childhood in the town. In the 1980s and 1990s, the Sweetwater church building was used as the local branch office of an Irish trade union. My father was the branch secretary of this trade union for much of his working life, and so I clearly remember spending time in the building as a child, visiting my father or waiting for him to finish work. It was a small and claustrophobic building, and although there have been some prefab extensions added since my father's days in the building, these were cramped. The inside space consisted of a narrow corridor, off which was a large room with two partitions. With the partitions open, the congregation would meet in that room for the key Sunday service each week. After this, the partitions were closed to separate the room into three smaller rooms for religious lessons. There was a small kitchen space at the back of the large room, but not separated from it. There were toilets, and two small classrooms in the prefab extension. The office for the congregation's leader was very small, about the size of a broom cupboard. During my fieldwork, the unsuitability of the building for its purpose was often discussed by members. They cited the small interior, the lack of suitable classrooms, the lack of large outside space for the children to play, and the lack of any car parking.

However, the logistics of conducting fieldwork in Sweetwater was easy for me as my home is around the corner from the church building. I found going back and forth to church in Sweetwater a simple process, which reminded me of the importance of the location of a church building in one's religious experience. I did not have to greatly concern myself with the details of traveling to church such as ensuring I had enough fuel in my car or planning my journey times. This was a contrast to my time in Appleby, which necessitated a car journey from my home to the church building of one hour and forty minutes each way on Sundays. I was glad to have experienced both scenarios, knowing how many Irish Mormons travel long distances to church. This gave me the opportunity to experience just how much a long journey changes your experience of church, and of Sundays.

My participant observation included attendance at as many church meetings and activities as I could. I also attended missionary events in church, sat in on missionaries teaching an investigator,[7] attended branch parties and social activities organized for the Relief Society. I decided before fieldwork began to introduce myself to the congregation during my first day at church. I asked permission from the branch presidents to do this, and this was granted. At the lectern in the chapel spaces of each congregation I introduced myself and briefly described my research. I explained how long

I would be attending church and what I hoped to achieve during my time. I said that I was interested in all aspects of church life, including what might be considered to be quite ordinary interactions and conversations. I felt that this transparent introduction to the congregations assisted in creating clarity among regularly attending members about what my role was. My introduction to both congregations were received very positively.

Each Sunday, I would arrive about twenty minutes early for church, which began every week with Sacrament meeting. I would use this time to chat to others who had arrived early, to make arrangements for interviews with provisional interviewees, or to sit by myself and observe what was going on around me, in typical ethnographer style. During meetings I took notes, and this was generally well received. People would joke with me about what number notebook I was on, as I was clearly filling up many of them. Following the Sacrament meeting, several other meetings ran concurrently for the time remaining. First, all adults not supervising the children in Primary attend Sunday School where the Bible and the *Book of Mormon* are studied. Then, the final hour of the day segregates the congregation by age and gender. Children remain in Primary, youth attend Young Women's and Young Men's groups, women attend Relief Society, and men attend the Elders Quorum meeting, which is usually referred to in Sweetwater and Appleby as "the Priesthood meeting." For most of my time with the congregations under study I spent the final two hours attending the Sunday School class, followed by either the Relief Society meeting or the Priesthood meeting. Since the time of my research, the weekly meeting block has been reduced by one hour. In both congregations I spent three months in Relief Society, followed by three months in Priesthood meetings to ensure I experienced both meetings in both congregations equally. I also participated in some Gospel Principles lessons at the start of my fieldwork—a class offered to investigators to ground them in the basics of doctrine.

Attending Relief Society and Priesthood meetings, which are separated by gender, I found few significant differences in content and teaching style along gender lines. I found that the men were quite open in their Priesthood meeting, providing personal examples from their lives to demonstrate a point they were making, just as the women regularly did. I did find that in both congregations, women were more likely to cry than men in the telling of a personal story or in the hearing of someone else's. However, I also observed men crying in church on multiple occasions. This was usually when giving talks to the congregation during Sacrament meeting, and often when speaking about their families or their testimony of Jesus Christ. There were gendered differences in the physical use of space. In Appleby the Priesthood meeting took place in the chapel, and the men sat with the chairs facing the front of the room in rows, as they had been laid out for previous meetings. This created a less intimate atmosphere than was evident in the Relief Society meeting, where the small room's chairs were arranged into a rough circle.

The chapel was seen as the more important room in the building, however, and the women in Relief Society did occasionally grumble that they were allocated such a small room by comparison. In Sweetwater, the Relief Society also used a circular arrangement of chairs, but the Priesthood meeting was held in such a small space that the chairs were arranged against the four walls in a vaguely circular fashion because any rearranging was almost impossible without large disruption. Therefore, there were some differences between the gendered meetings, but these were not sufficient to create drastically differing experiences, and these were heavily dictated by space. I found that it was individual personalities that most affected the diversity of teaching and learning that I observed.

Though the Church issues handbooks to guide the format and focus of lessons in Relief Society and Priesthood meetings, there are still significant differences in how meetings are experienced depending on who is present and who is teaching the lesson. Some members asked to teach a lesson will lecture the class in a traditional manner, while others use the method of facilitation that is so heavily encouraged by the Church as a teaching tool in recent years (Church of Jesus Christ of Latter-day Saints, 2016). This method focuses on asking questions that facilitate group discussion and allow the group to direct the conversation. The teacher only intermittently interjects to direct the conversation toward particular lesson-specific talking points. In short, despite a standardization of lesson material in these meetings, lessons still vary depending on who is teaching, what topics are being taught, and who is participating in the lesson.

Aside from my regular attendance at meetings, a key way that I got to know the congregational members of each branch was through social events. I also came to realize that social events were a bit of a sensitive topic, for reasons that I explore in more detail in chapter 5. The constraints of small congregations, large distances to travel to church, and the long day of meetings on Sunday, which already demanded a lot of people, meant that social life in Irish Mormonism was not as vibrant as many wished it would be. In Appleby, numerous people would travel more than an hour each way to church on a Sunday, which limited their enthusiasm for further journeys during the week. I was told by US Mormons visiting both branches that the social calendar in US wards is busier, as the size of the congregations and small distances between home and church support a busy schedule of sports, crafts, and other social events. This means that US Mormons feel they "have far more interactivity" (Elder McGuire, Appleby) within their congregations than in Ireland.

In Appleby, a good solution to the geographical spread of their membership was the commitment to the Munch and Mingle event, which took place once a month on the day of Fast and Testimony Sacrament meetings.[8] As the members would have been fasting earlier in the day, they would bring along sweets, cakes, crisps, as well as dishes such as quiche, which were easy to eat when standing. I also fasted, and brought cakes and snacks along, as I understood the communal effort of the event and I wished to commit myself to experiencing life as a Mormon as much as possible. After the three-hour meeting block was finished,[9] the members would gather in the foyer area to break their fast and to chat with their fellow members. Because this event took place directly after church, it facilitated participation by those who had a long distance to travel. The foyer was a bright, light-filled space due to large windows all around, which made it a pleasant space to gather around the long table filled with tasty food. I always enjoyed these occasions as it offered me an opportunity to get to know members that I had not yet had an opportunity to talk to, and to build upon existing relationships. The event also provided members with an opportunity to ask me about my research, asking questions such as "Why did I decide to research their religion rather than another?" or "What did I hope to achieve by my research?" The relaxed nature of Munch and Mingle meant that these questions could be asked and answered in an informal manner, building trust and rapport between me and the congregation.

During the time of my fieldwork in Sweetwater, a Munch and Mingle was never held, though since now the congregation has moved to share larger and better church facilities with another ward, they have started to develop a potluck dinner after church—a similar idea. However, Sweetwater was more likely than Appleby to organize regular Relief Society social events outside of their weekly Relief Society meeting on Sunday afternoons. These social events would often take place on a Thursday evening in the branch building from about 7 p.m. to 9 p.m. They involved events such as knitting circles, clothing swaps, and gardening workshops. Small numbers of women attended these events. For one thing the pool of available people was already reduced, due to Relief Society being a female-only organization. This meant that these events sometimes numbered just seven to nine people, including the organizers. I never encountered any male-only social events in either branch, something that belatedly struck me as fascinating.

How I wished I had thought to ask about this anomaly at the time of my research! It is possible that male-only social events were held outside of church, but if so I was unaware of this.

Appleby held an event each Wednesday evening during my time there, which I never saw replicated in Sweetwater. This was a Mormons Having Fun evening, which was open to both members and nonmembers. A night of games and conversation with a brief religious message at the start, this event was launched by Elder and Sister McGuire. The idea behind it was to give investigators a chance to become familiar with the church building, meet other members, and consolidate their relationships with the missionaries. Like other social events in both branches, Mormons Having Fun was often poorly attended, particularly by the existing members of the branch, who seemed to view it more as a missionary-investigator event. Numbers attending would average at eight, including two to four missionaries and children. By attending Mormons Having Fun, I learned that developing investigators' interest in the Church involves creating and maintaining positive relationships with missionaries and the wider congregation. For instance, a key part of Mormons Having Fun was playing team-bonding games, designed as icebreakers and to allow people to let their guard down. After an evening of imitating elephant, cat, snake, and other animal noises as part of one such game, I certainly felt as though I had made a real connection with the other participants, as we laughed our way through the deliberately silly activities. Thus, social events such as Munch and Mingle or Mormons Having Fun are an important part of building and maintaining Mormon community at a local level.

Many of these social events (with the exception of branch parties, described below, which were generally well attended) suffered from my informant Andrei's descriptor of "STP, which is Same Ten People." Andrei was one of those STP and was clearly frustrated by these dynamics. From my time in his branch I came to understand how this experience was mutually reinforcing. Few people would assist in or attend events outside of Sunday meetings due to difficulties in scheduling and work or family commitments, causing a lack of enthusiasm for social events generally, which then continued to fuel the low participation. These difficulties present clear challenges for the branches in maintaining community locally.

The other main social outlet for both branches was the holding of branch parties to celebrate various events in the calendar. Both branches held Christmas, Halloween, and St. Patrick's Day parties. The celebration of Christmas was clearly related to their Christian beliefs; St. Patrick's Day events were held to celebrate Ireland's national holiday; and Halloween celebrations are ubiquitous in Ireland, where the event originated before it became popular in the United States. Halloween is a key family event in Ireland's national calendar, with children and adults dressing up in costumes and going trick or treating. Given the family-focused values of Mormonism, it is unsurprising that Irish Mormons embrace this holiday. Parties were held in the branch buildings. Appleby normally held its parties during the day—usually on a Saturday and finishing at about 6 p.m. Sweetwater usually held their parties on Saturday evenings, finishing at about 9:30 p.m. Most social events were equally open to nonmembers as well as members, but I found that it was really only at branch parties that Church members would bring along nonmember family and friends, perhaps because branch parties were the best attended social events, and celebrated moments such as Christmas, which were also celebrated by most nonmembers in Ireland.

Social events in both branches are constrained by the facilities available to them. In Appleby, members such as the influential Murphy family, who were founding members of the branch, felt that the branch deserved a purpose-built church building. They cite their shame in bringing family and friends to the current and to previous buildings as part of their justification for this. Sue told me: "I think for me it's just the idea of being somewhere respectable. I have a little bit of snobbiness about where I go to church and not in a bad way, but I just don't want to have to walk over broken glass to get there. I just want to go somewhere that's nice that you can bring people and they are not looking at the outside going, 'what have I got myself in for.' You just want somewhere that's welcoming."

In Sweetwater, a key challenge for conducting social events was inadequate facilities, particularly the inadequate kitchen. Mormon social events often center around food. For instance, Mary Daly jokingly told me during a Munch and Mingle, "I was skinny before I was Mormon! That's how we celebrate everything, with food, because you don't drink." It is the centrality of food for Mormon social life that dictates that each congregation should have kitchen facilities in its building so that food can be cooked or heated up for social events. Sweetwater's difficulties have recently been addressed by the move of the congregation to the purpose-built church building about twenty-five minutes' drive away.

As part of my year with Mormonism I interviewed thirty congregants, fifteen from each congregation. Sixteen of the thirty interviewees are White Irish. Eight interviewees are from North America, four are from South America, one is from Africa, and one is from elsewhere in Europe.[10] The thirty interviewees incorporated sixteen women and fourteen men. At the time of the interviews they were aged from eighteen to mid-seventies, with each decade in between represented. In many cases the participants would self-describe themselves during our discussions in terms of the country of their birth or the broader region they come from: "Irish," "African," "South American." All were living in Ireland at the time of the fieldwork.

In both congregations, I asked permission to put up a flyer with my contact details on the church noticeboard asking for interviewees. During the time of my fieldwork, Appleby had a congregational newsletter and so I also placed a brief article about myself and my research there. I received no phone calls or emails, but people did approach me in church to say that they had seen my flyer or read my newsletter piece and offered themselves for interview. Others heard that a friend had been interviewed, and they too now wanted to do an interview. I estimate I gathered about three-quarters of interviewees from individuals volunteering themselves in these ways. The other interviewees came through casual conversations with members. People would ask me about my research, which would often lead into detailed discussions between us about relevant issues. Noting their interest, I would tell them I was still looking for interviewees, and if they wanted to sit for an interview with me to discuss these issues in more detail, I would be happy to explain the interview process to them. The last quarter of my interviewees were procured in this way. Although many of my interviews were self-volunteered and so were not deliberately targeted by me, I did establish a relatively diverse sample of young and old, male and female, converts and those born into the Church, and Irish and non-Irish.

Once interviews with participants were arranged, I emphasized to them that we could meet at a place where they were comfortable and at a time that suited them. I conducted interviews in a variety of places, often in the participants' homes, but also in the home of a participant's family member, in hotel foyers, restaurants, and cafes. Some were joint interviews, often when a husband and wife would invite me to their home for dinner and talk with me together. These interviews tended to be longer than single interviews, running to roughly two hours and thirty minutes or more, as both participants often wanted to contribute to the discussion or to pick up on something their partner had said. Most interviews were conducted with one participant at a time, and these were approximately one hour and forty-five minutes in length. The shortest interview was fifty minutes, and the longest was three hours. There are small numbers of LDS congregations in Ireland, and the congregations themselves are small. Many congregations are, like many locations in Ireland, the sort of place where everyone knows everyone. For this reason, I have changed the names of all the participants of this research and avoided including identifying information about participants unless it is relevant to their narrative and my analysis.

Insider-Outsider Conundrums

As time went on, I found that insider and outsider considerations came to the fore in surprising ways. Upon my arrival in Sweetwater, I had already completed six months of fieldwork in Appleby. I felt that I had a good sense of congregational life at that point and had gained an appreciation for the importance of members engaging in talks, prayers, and testimonies at the lectern in a specific way. The phrase "I say these things in the name of Jesus Christ, Amen" indicates the end of a member's talk or prayer, and I became so familiar with the phrase that it seemed to lodge itself deeply in my mind. In Sweetwater, for reasons I am still not sure of as it certainly wasn't planned, I ended my introduction to the congregation by using this phrase. At the time, I felt embarrassed about this. I feared that it would cause confusion, as I had mentioned in my introduction that I was not religious. I was afraid it might cause offence or appear arrogant in some way. In fact, though, I was told afterward by several members that using the phrase endeared me to them and made them feel that I could be trusted.

From then on, I was referred to by members as "the student" and "the researcher" in both congregations. Although many were eager to know if I might consider converting to Mormonism, and some explicitly tried to encourage this, for the most part there were few obvious attempts to encourage my conversion. This researcher role contributed to a complex experience of my status. I was often both an insider and an outsider, sometimes simultaneously, and sometimes, it felt as though I was neither. However, as the congregations became familiar with me and I became more familiar with the Church generally and the congregations specifically, there came some assumption of insider status. Although still "the researcher," my long-time presence created a familiarity with my unique position. My status as an "expert" in religion or in sociology did not serve as a barrier to inclusion; many members in the congregations had completed their own postgraduate education. Therefore, many were comfortable with the idea of the Church being studied academically. Even if they had no experience of higher education themselves, many of their friends in church did, which seemed to reassure them.

Once immersed in the Sweetwater congregation, I found that I struggled to build a strong rapport with a group of Southeast Asian members. I had desired to understand more about their experiences of life as a Mormon in

Ireland, particularly as Mormonism in Ireland is majority White. Despite many casual conversations in church and at church events, I was unable to secure an interview with any member of this group. At one point two women had arranged a time and date for a joint interview with me but they did not arrive at our prearranged location on the day, did not answer a phone call from me, and did not attend church for some weeks afterward. I knew enough of ongoing consent within research to not push this any further with them. However, I carefully made note of informal conversations in church with all members, including members of this group, and was sure to use this material in my analysis of the data, to ensure that as many viewpoints as possible were reflected in the research. As a White Irish woman, I often found it easier to form friendships with White Irish members. There was a familiarity in our encounters that came easily to me, and it is likely that this affected my rapport with other members who were not White Irish, such as the Southeast Asian members in Sweetwater.

Ruth Frankenburg argues that Whiteness is "a set of locations that are historically, socially, politically, and culturally produced, and moreover, are intrinsically linked to unfolding relations of domination" (1993, p. 6) and it is likely that my rapport with the Irish-born participants of this research, all of whom were White, was at least partly influenced by the shared experience of Whiteness that Frankenburg describes. Many Irish participants were also converts from Catholicism and so we straightforwardly found common ground in discussions of the specific nature of Irish Catholicism. In Sweetwater there were some conflicts between the Southeast Asian group and a White Irish group, which meant that there was little meaningful engagement between them. On reflection my easy familiarity with the Irish group perhaps hindered my friendships with the Southeast Asian group. This would explain their reluctance to participate in interviews with me. It is likely that the White Irish participants and I were able to find commonality within this particular "set of locations" (Frankenberg, 1993, p. 6), which as a consequence excluded those outside of those experiences. I acknowledge the ways in which this has inevitably shaped the research.

As weeks passed in both congregations, people began to treat me with less formality and more familiarity and began to confide in me the latest gossip or disagreement. I began to understand the inside jokes and the ongoing discussions within the congregations and their various subgroups. I was increasingly called upon to offer opinions, answer questions, and to say an opening or closing prayer in lessons in the same way as other members. As a nonbeliever, I always felt slightly uncomfortable saying a prayer, and was fearful that others might interpret it as disingenuous on my part.

However, it did give me the opportunity to learn the format of prayers and the patterns within it, such as praying for those not present due to illness, or praying that everyone present would travel home safely. This shift from observer to active participant assisted the research, allowing me to more fully experience life as a Mormon.

One interesting way in which insider/outsider complexities played themselves out in the course of my fieldwork is in regard to the participation described above. In reflecting upon these decisions to pray or to answer spiritual and scriptural questions, I have come to realize how my participation in church revealed insights into my own perceptions of my status and also the perceptions of the participants. In agreeing to participate in this way I hoped to better experience life as a Mormon, despite my atheist position. Yet, it may be that those who asked me to contribute might also have been hopeful that my participation might change the nature of my role in church. Mormonism's First Vision, in which founder Joseph Smith forged a personal relationship with God through prayer, is a foundational narrative within Mormonism. I found during fieldwork that members will frequently encourage each other to "pray on it" to receive wisdom as to the best approach to almost all problems. Additionally, missionaries advised prospective converts to pray to God to ascertain if the Church is true. By encouraging my active participation, members ensured that I, too, was doing as they themselves had done. I was following the model set down by Joseph Smith, in which prayer leads to wisdom regarding the truthfulness of the Church. Viewed from this perspective the positive response of the Sweetwater members to my reciting of "I say these things in the name of Jesus Christ, Amen" during my first introduction to them is part of this same phenomenon. By inadvertently using a phrase contained in Mormon prayer, I provided proof that I could be trusted. My prayerlike phrase signified to them the integrity and truthfulness of my statements and validated my presence there.

As time went on, I found that visitors from other congregations often assumed me to be a regular member and were often surprised to be told that I was not Mormon. One visitor told me that I "looked like a Mormon." I did take care to dress in a similar fashion to other women of my age during Sunday services. This often meant a long or mid-length dress, with shoulders covered. Another visitor told me that I "had the lingo and everything," a reference to my efforts to correctly understand and use the words and phrases common within Mormonism. Yet, in a variety of ways, I remained an outsider. The congregations knew that I was leaving after a set period, and often would ask me "when are you leaving us?" as a conversation starter. This conscious awareness of my temporary presence served as a reminder that I was not fully one of them. I was also always honest whenever anyone asked me about my own religious beliefs and, as a result, many knew that I was an atheist. This was generally well accepted in both congregations, but it did function as a symbolic boundary. Not only was I not a believer in their particular conception of God, but I did not believe in *any* god, and so I always felt that I was marked as different, though not in a hostile way.

Jan Shipps had a similar experience of being in, out, and neither during her almost sixty years researching Mormonism as a nonmember in the United States. Shipps (2006, p. 29) argues that she never fully became an insider, yet nor is she an outsider. She says, "fortuitous circumstances had worked to usher me into what is best described as a liminal status, into between-ness." For Shipps, the boundaries are porous, and dependent on context. She suggests that Mormonism created and maintained a complex position for her, and perhaps Mormonism has, in a similar way, made a place for me. By including me in active participation in church, accepting my presence in male-only meetings, and generally receiving me in a positive way, Irish Mormons endeavored to make me feel welcome despite my clear differences from them based on religious identifications and my researcher status.

As much time has passed between the time of my research and the present moment, I am able to look back on my time with the two communities at the heart of this book with fondness. Though always an outsider, I have kept with me a deep attachment to the people who create and sustain Mormonism. I still find myself singing Mormon hymns around the house if a melody or phrase that I happen to hear somehow sparks a memory. Yet I remain a committed atheist, a fierce nonbeliever, and at times a tough critic of the Church and its policies. I have come to embrace this complexity and, like many of the participants of my research, I find that any contradictions are reconciled within me.

Chapter Outline

Each chapter in *Irish Mormons* tells part of the story of Mormonism in Ireland. Chapter 1, "Religion in Contemporary Ireland," discusses the nature of religious change in modern Ireland and introduces Irish Mormonism within that context. By outlining the scale of economic and social change that has occurred in Ireland's recent history, this chapter explains how these changes have affected Ireland's relationship with religion and illustrates how these changes have shaped the development of Irish Mormonism. I discuss how and why Catholicism has come to hold much less influence in contemporary Irish public life, while paradoxically continuing to influence Irish people's identities and understandings of religion, and show how other religions have experienced these shifts. The chapter then moves to outline the theoretical underpinnings of the book, by explaining how an understanding of collective memory and tradition is useful to make sense of Irish religion's relationship to identity and belonging in the contemporary moment.

In the next chapter, "The Challenges of Belonging in Modern Mormonism," I illustrate the complex relationship between the global LDS Church and the local areas where it is lived. By focusing on how the Church has been experienced across Europe and in outlining some of the challenges therein, the chapter facilitates a deeper understanding of the challenges reported by Mormons in Ireland that follow later in the book. The place of the Church in Europe has been much discussed, and ideas of religion in public life, secularization, immigration, and socioeconomic factors all have their part in this story and are addressed here. The chapter examines the central debates regarding the Church's international growth and explains the challenges associated with establishing a strong presence in societies with very different cultural contexts than that of the "Mormon Culture Region" (Menig, 1965).

Chapter 3, "They All Seem Very Nice but It's a Bit Weird Isn't It?" focuses on how Mormonism is perceived by others in Irish society who aren't Mormon, and how Church members negotiate these perceptions. The chapter emphasizes that Mormonism is poorly understood in Ireland, and is viewed by those in the majority population as strange and foreign. This leads to stigmatization and marginalization—Mormons are excluded from Irish understandings of "who belongs" in Irish society. I illustrate in this chapter that although Church members who are migrants or people of color are doubly marginalized, White Irish Mormons are also excluded, holding a dual insider-outsider position in Irish society. The chapter then moves to articulate how Irish Mormons navigate this environment by showing the strategies they use to manage their minority role in everyday life.

"Their Ancestors Are Watching Them," chapter 4, shows that competing conceptions of family shape Irish Mormons' experiences of family life. On one hand, there are cultural constructs of the Irish family, heavily informed by traditional understandings of the Irish Catholic family and its relationship to the Irish nation. On the other, there are Mormon traditions concerning family, which are essential to adhere to for one's salvation, but difficult to achieve in an Irish context. This chapter illustrates the pressures faced by Irish Mormons as they try to do what is expected of them regarding Mormon family life in the context of an Irish society that has different conceptions of family. It shows the isolation faced by Ireland's many part-member families, the guilt of converts from Catholicism to Mormonism, and the worries of young Mormons in Ireland about finding a partner for their future family life.

In chapter 5, "Irish-Irish and Mormon-Irish," congregational conflicts are understood for what they are—attempts by a community made up of diverse experiences and backgrounds to shape the collective identity of the group. In the course of these conflicts, debates regarding inclusion and exclusion based on factors such as nationality, ethnicity, and religiosity arise. Through the congregation, the community comes to understand its place in the wider religion, and its place in the wider society. This chapter tells the story of congregational conflict through this lens, emphasizing that struggles to shape the congregational identity of the group take on a deep emotional meaning for members when they find themselves marginalized within the wider society for varying reasons. In this scenario the need to feel a sense of belonging within the congregation becomes all the more important. Examining these ideas in detail, I show in this chapter that increasing congregational diversity within Irish Mormonism is a source of discord, but also unity.

"We Preach That Culture," chapter 6, focuses on conceptions of Mormon culture and examines how it is understood, enacted, and challenged in an Irish milieu. I note in this chapter that Mormons in Ireland actively create a picture of Mormonism's spiritual and cultural homeland of Utah, which leads to a sense of connection with the United States, but also disunity with Mormonism's Church culture. I then move to illumine the difficult position in which North American, and specifically US Mormons in Ireland, find themselves. Immersed in diverse Irish congregations, they are confronted with the reality that a White North American worldview permeates Mormon culture. They must work to make sense of this in their daily engagements with their fellow Mormons. The chapter also shows that while there is some idealization of US Mormonism among Irish Mormons, there is also a good deal of resentment, which has the effect of hindering Irish feelings of inclusion in the worldwide Church.

The conclusion, "Reflections for the Future," synthesizes the previous chapters to emphasize that Irish Mormons use tradition, community, and identity to manage the complex experiences of inclusion and exclusion they experience as Church members in contemporary Ireland. It reminds readers of the great adaptability of modern Irish Mormonism and of the need for continuity in the midst of transformation that exists at the heart of the Irish Mormon experience. It highlights the diverse ways Mormons in Ireland make use of Irish identity, Mormon identity, and the relationship between the two to ground themselves. I conclude by offering some observations on what these experiences may tell us about the development of Mormonism as a global religion, and the challenges it faces in that transformation.

1

Religion in Contemporary Ireland

Early Irish Mormonism

This chapter seeks to set Irish Mormonism in its broader context. How has Ireland developed in ways that are similar to, and distinct from, its near neighbors? How has sudden economic growth changed Irish society and Irish culture? How have religions in Ireland been experienced throughout rapid social change? Like many European countries, Ireland is wealthy, predominantly White, and Christian. Like other European countries, it has a historically dominant religion that has shaped the collective memory of the nation, but is undergoing a secularization process that causes unexpected changes in experiences of religion. As in many European countries, early converts to Mormonism were "gathered" in Zion, leading to a weakening of the Mormon community that remained in Ireland. Similar to other European Mormons, Irish Mormons have been Othered by their society; their religion is perceived as foreign. The Church in Ireland struggles to foster growth amid a wider religious landscape that is suspicious of "new" religions and within a religious organization that exerts tight controls on how the religion is experienced locally. As elsewhere, much of Irish Mormonism's growth comes not from the majority White Irish population, but from migrants and from people of color.

Yet, there is much about Ireland and Irish Mormonism that sets them apart from other European countries in the wider region. Perhaps most notably, where much of Europe's experience of colonialism was as an oppressor, Ireland's experience was the opposite. Under British colonial control for much of its modern history, having achieved independence only in 1922, contemporary Ireland continues to navigate the lasting legacies of this experience. Colonialism, for example, is partly the cause of Ireland's ethno-nationalism as a Catholic nation-state (Cleary, 2004). In the rush to assert independence from Protestant Britain, Ireland embraced a cultural nationalism infused with Catholicism in efforts to re-create its identity as distinct from Britain, what Todd Ruane describes as a "Catholic-driven decolonizing nationalism" (Ruane, 2010, p. 129). By the 1990s the effects of this were clear. Marguerite Corish (1996, p. 139) observed, "because Irish became synonymous with being Catholic for 95 per cent of the population . . . it has proved difficult not [to] be a Catholic in Ireland, for fear of losing one's national identity." Colonialism is also the cause of partition, the division of the island of Ireland into the independent Republic of Ireland in the south and Northern Ireland, still part of the United Kingdom.

Ireland is also distinct in its experience of the potato famine of the nineteenth century, which decimated the population through death and emigration. However, as Kevin Kenny (2004) notes, Irish emigration did not begin with the Famine and nor did it cease after it. There were deeper economic and social difficulties within the country, many of which were exacerbated by colonialism. Ireland's massive population decrease made Ireland an outlier across Europe, with population falling steadily well into the twentieth century.[1] As the twentieth century progressed, Ireland continued to stand apart through its ongoing high religiosity, even as its European neighbors entered a rapid secularization process (Halman & Draulans, 2006). By the end of the twentieth and start of the twenty-first centuries Ireland's Celtic Tiger runaway economic success made it unique once more, though this was soon tempered by severe recession, as the world economy collapsed after 2008.

So, although the development of Mormonism in Ireland bears many commonalities with how Mormonism developed in many European countries, there are specific social, political, religious, and economic circumstances in an Irish context that necessitate further explanation in order to be able to fully comprehend the early development and the contemporary continuation of Irish Mormonism. In this chapter I provide an abbreviated history of the development of Mormonism in Ireland, and an analysis of the social and religious changes that has occurred in Ireland's recent history, so as to better situate the discussion of contemporary Irish Mormonism in subsequent chapters.

Before we begin to explore the experience of Mormonism in Ireland in some detail, there are points to note regarding the terminology I use for different jurisdictions across the island of Ireland during different time periods. In this section I outline the history of Mormonism in Ireland across a tumultuous political period. When Church missionaries arrived on the island of Ireland in 1840, the entire island was under the jurisdiction of Britain. Yet even then religious and social differences across the island were evident, based on different religious and political profiles in the north and south of the island. When I discuss this phenomenon during this time period, I will refer to the southern region of the island as "the south" and the northern region as "northern Ireland." I make this distinction to illustrate the different social and religious experiences in these regions both then and now. In 1922, most of the island achieved independence, ultimately becoming the Republic of Ireland, which I abbreviate in this book to "Ireland." Post-1922, the northern part of the island remained part of the United Kingdom and is known as Northern Ireland.

Brent A. Barlow's 1968 MA thesis on the history of the LDS Church in Ireland is an invaluable resource on the arrival of Mormonism to Ireland and subsequent developments during the nineteenth and twentieth century. Little else has been published that deeply informs understanding of the development of Mormonism in either Ireland (post-independence from the British) or in the south prior to independence from the British. Although there are multiple sources available that detail the emergence of Mormonism in Britain and/or the British Isles (Fielding Smith, 1950; Bloxham, Moss, & Porter, 1987; Buchanan, 1987; Cuthbert, 1987; Heaton, Albrecht, & Johnson, 1987; Thomas, 1987; Grant, 1992; Rasmussen, 2016), there are only a handful of these sources that make any more than a fleeting reference to Ireland (Barlow, 1968, 2000; Card, 1978; Harris, 1984, 1990; Allen, 1990) and some of these are only relevant in relation to more recent periods of Ireland's history (Harris, 1984, 1990; Allen, 1990). Within the literature there is little acknowledgment of how the experiences or history of the north of Ireland may not have been relevant or applicable to the experience of the south. Mormonism developed differently in the south than in northern Ireland due to social, political, and religious reasons that will be explained further below. To ignore these differences or, worse, to remain unaware of the importance of them, appears to be an oversight in terms of our understanding of the development of the Church throughout the entire region of the United Kingdom and Ireland. Part of my motivation for writing this book has been to put Ireland back into the history of Mormonism. I hope to highlight the distinctive social and political context in Ireland, which has so intimately shaped that nation-state's relationship to religion, and in the process give voice to the experience of Mormonism there.

The first official missionaries to the island of Ireland arrived in County Down, northern Ireland, in 1840 (Barlow, 1968; Card, 1978). The first missionaries did not arrive in Dublin in the south for another ten years, where they set about conducting their work of informing and converting the mainly Catholic population there. They encountered opposition, with organized anti-Mormon campaigns challenging their efforts to inform local communities about Mormonism. Barlow (1968) recounts from original sources a number of testimonies of abuse, threats, and violent mobs (Protestant as well as Catholic) who caused the missionaries in Dublin fear for their lives. Early experiences of Ireland could therefore be summed up by Tim B. Heaton and colleagues who suggest that "efforts in Ireland were not very fruitful" (Heaton, Albrecht, & Johnson, 1987, p. 121).

During this period an article published by one of the Dublin missionaries in the Mormon periodical the *Millennial Star* illumines something of interest concerning the Mormon experience in the south. The writer reported, "Things are going well in the north of Ireland. There are not so many Catholics there, and consequently, we get along better there than about Dublin" (*Millennial Star, 18*, 1856, pp. 561–562 cited in Barlow, 1968, p. 52). It appears that the Catholicism of the south was more resistant to Mormon proselytizing than the people of northern Ireland, with far greater numbers of Protestants. As early as 1865 the *Millennial Star* reported that "Ireland is a dead beat, those who desire persecution have only to declare themselves Latter-day Saints and the multitudes are more relentless in their pursuit than if they were chasing mad dogs" (*Millennial Star, 28*, 1865, p. 822, cited in Barlow, 1968, p. 62). In 1867 the Mormon mission in the whole of Ireland was officially closed, although continued attempts to gain new converts in northern Ireland from the 1880s onward were moderately successful (Barlow, 1968).

Perhaps because Barlow's (1968) work is a history of the Church in Ireland rather than a sociological study, he makes few attempts to establish why it was that a greater number of Catholics made the missionary experience more difficult in the south. One must assume that either or both the Catholic hierarchy and ordinary Catholics were inherently opposed to Mormonism and what they felt it represented. Insight on this comes from Orson Scott Card (1978), writing for Church magazine *Ensign*. He observes that Irish Catholicism was bound up with Irish nationalism at this time, and so conversions among Catholics were unsuccessful because the Mormons were viewed as "just another Protestant church—and Protestant churches were not viewed very kindly in those days" due to its links to colonialism by the Protestant British (Card, 1978).

It appears from what little has been written about missionary efforts in the south that a dominant narrative emerged: since the south was predominantly Catholic, it was less well disposed to hearing the Mormon message than the predominantly Protestant northern Ireland, Scotland, England, and Wales. Yet, it should be noted that during the nineteenth century there also existed a Mormon bias against Catholics (Grow, 2004), one that directly affected the development of the Church in Italy in similar ways to the Church in Ireland (Dursteler, 2018). Regarding a Church decision to disengage from proselytizing in Italy in the nineteenth century, Eric Dursteler (2018, p. 114) argues that the decision "was a by-product of cultural attitudes amongst the leadership and the body of the saints" toward Catholics. Thus, we must consider if similar thought processes affected decisions in Ireland, such as not venturing south for a full decade after missionaries first arrived in northern Ireland, and in essentially abandoning missionary efforts in Ireland until the 1960s despite intermittent efforts ongoing in northern Ireland. There is no doubt, however, that Ireland was certainly not very open to religions other than Catholicism, and in this respect, the dominant narrative cannot be denied. In the years following Irish independence in 1922, the Irish State implemented deliberate attempts to reassert Irish cultural identity through promotion of the Irish language, history, and its Catholic religion (Whyte, 1976). Throughout this era "Protestants, with their historical connection to processes of English colonialization and their alternative understandings of religion, were seen as tainted, foreign, and heretical" (Walsh, 2015, p. 75).

In the twentieth century, "Irish Protestants saw themselves as Irish, but in a different way from the Catholic Irish" (Ruane & Todd, 2009, p. 4). Supporting this perspective, Claudia W. Harris observed in 1990 that "the [Mormon] church is growing much more rapidly in the north than it is in the predominantly Catholic south, where religion and patriotism—being Catholic and being Irish—are intertwined, where leaving the Catholic church is almost synonymous with defecting" (Harris, 1990, p. 8). The Church's focus on northern Ireland, and the friendlier reception that Mormonism received there, has a long legacy that can still be seen to this day. According to 2017 Church figures, there are 5,345 members in Northern Ireland, much more than in Ireland even though Northern Ireland's population is one-quarter of Ireland's (Stewart et al., 2017). On this basis, I suggest that the development of Mormonism in Ireland has been directly influenced by the religious, cultural, and political meanings behind Ireland's collective understandings of the categories of Catholic and Protestant.

It was not until the 1960s that we see renewed interest from the Church in further developing missionary efforts in Ireland. In 1963, six missionaries were sent to Ireland as part of a renewed focus on Ireland on behalf of the Church. Small congregations were established outside of Dublin. By the end of 1967 there were 107 members in Ireland, half of them based outside of Dublin (Barlow, 1968). The years following up to the present day saw some success for Mormonism in terms of increased membership and establishment of new congregations. According to Church figures in 1978, Church members in Ireland constituted 0.025 percent of the general population, while in 2019 this number was 0.078 percent (Stewart & Martinich, n.d.). The only research with Mormons in Ireland in more recent times has been the work of Olivia Cosgrove (2013) and my own. Cosgrove (2013) identifies that the stigma attached to Mormonism in its earliest days in Ireland has continued to the present day. Her findings of widespread stigmatization and discrimination toward Mormons in modern Ireland confirm that Mormonism is still constructed by the majority society in negative terms, and is seen to be a threat to established perceptions of religion in Ireland. These findings confirm similar research in other European countries.

Data on minority religions in Ireland shows that the majority of LDS Church membership in Ireland is, like Catholic membership, majority White Irish (Central Statistics Office, 2017b). However, other commonalities between Catholicism and Mormonism have also intrigued me. Both have a spiritual and administrative center that guides and controls the religious experience of its adherents worldwide. Both are patriarchal and hierarchical religions that emphasize the importance of family. Yet, Mormons in Ireland live their faith in the shadow of another. Catholicism dominates the religious landscape in Ireland, forcing adherents of Mormonism and other minority religions to exist in a society that is historically structured and culturally entangled with another religious tradition.

Irish Mormonism within Contemporary Ireland

It is beyond the scope of this book to provide a historical overview of all of Ireland's changes since Independence. Suffice it to say that the twentieth century was tumultuous, as the country struggled to create economic stability, a social support system, and a coherent culture while also navigating a War of Independence, civil war, and World War II (known in Ireland as the Emergency). Instead, let us begin by examining the social and economic changes that accelerated in Ireland as the twentieth century drew to a close, and their effect on the Irish relationship to religion. This is the period of change that is of most relevance for Irish Mormonism, as it is this period that, more than any other, has come to shape contemporary Irish identity. Since the 1990s, Ireland has undergone rapid and significant economic change that has reshaped the cultural landscape of the country. The Celtic Tiger period from the mid 1990s to 2008 saw unemployment and poverty levels plummet (Kuhling & Keohane, 2007, p. 1). Ireland became a globalized economy, reversed generations of emigration, and became a nation of mass immigration to Ireland for the first time (Riain, 2014). Following the Celtic Tiger's economic collapse in 2008, Ireland's success evaporated. Unemployment, which had dropped from 18 percent in the late 1980s to 4.2 percent in 2005, rose again to 15 percent in 2012 (Kuhling & Keohane, 2007, p. 1; O'Hearn, 2014, p. 38). Consistent poverty levels rose to a high of 9.1 percent of the population in 2013 (Central Statistics Office, 2020a). Ireland had gone from being a country of poverty and debt in the 1980s, to a country of extreme wealth in the 1990s and early 2000s, back to poverty and debt in just thirty years, demonstrating significant economic instability (O'Hearn, 2014, p. 40). By 2022, Ireland's economy had broadly recovered, and Ireland is attempting, often unsuccessfully, to avoid the unsustainable growth in some industries, which exacerbated the economic crash of 2008.

What are the social and cultural consequences of such economic instability coupled with demographic shifts? Analysis indicates that complex rearrangements of Irish culture have been under way. Kieran Keohane and Carmen Kuhling (2004) argue that the liminality of the early twenty-first century in Ireland represented a "collision culture" where old and new crash into each other, creating unexpected change; "the 'Celtic Tiger' is a striking example of an image in which are condensed elements of tradition and modernity, the global and the local, community and society, as they are in flux in the liminal contexts of collision culture" (Keohane & Kuhling, 2004, pp. 141–142). Sociologist Colin Coulter (2018, p. 14), citing the social psychologist Michael O'Connell, points out that these changes are most evident in younger generations, who are "less constrained by customary norms and practices than were their predecessors. The teachings of the Catholic Church have come to exercise relatively little moral influence. The younger generation in the Irish Republic conceive of themselves less as members of collectivities than as individuals. This sense of individuality is articulated principally through material possessions rather than spiritual dispositions." Coulter observes that the discourse around these changes has mistakenly assumed that "old" Ireland has been entirely replaced with "new" Ireland. For "old" and "new" Coulter (2018, p. 15) argues we should read "traditional" and "modern," as though overnight closely held beliefs and practices were supplanted "with a set more suitable to the rigours of modernity." Like

Keohane and Kuhling (2004), Coulter advocates for a more nuanced reading of Irish social change, however, that supports the notion of tradition continuing within a contemporary Irish society that appears at first glance to be the epitome of modernity:

> It is the experience of most developed societies that the onset of modernity allows for the persistence and even the revival of certain forms of tradition. . . . [I]n the course of their evolution, human societies tend to get both better and worse more or less at the same time. In the outlook of those who advocate a particular version of modernity there appears, however, to be little or no appreciation of the dialectics of social change. The present course of development is interpreted as singularly and uniformly progressive. The dislocations and casualties of the modernisation process are understated or even airbrushed out of the picture altogether. (2018, p. 17)

There have been many "dislocations" within Ireland's economic and social changes. In recent times there has been a rapid acceleration of a preexisting trend toward liberalization on family and sexual norms. Irish family life has transformed as Catholic teaching regarding family and sexuality became less influential in people's decisions. In the late twentieth century people began to marry later or to abstain from marriage altogether, in greater numbers than before. The average age at which heterosexual women marry increased from twenty-four in 1980 (Central Statistics Office, 2000), to thirty-six in 2020 (Central Statistics Office, 2021). Births outside of marriage increased from just 5 percent of all births in 1980, to 36 percent by 2016 (Central Statistics Office, 2016b). Until 1993 homosexual acts were criminalized but by 2011 Ireland had introduced civil partnership for gay men and women, and in a high-profile referendum in 2015, Ireland became the first country in the world to legalize same-sex civil marriage by popular vote (Gay and Lesbian Equality Network, 2013; O'Caollaí & Hilliard, 2015). These changes have resulted in a society that has been socially transformed since the 1980s.

However, despite a liberalization of family norms, Ireland is still more conservative than its European neighbors on many issues. The introduction of divorce in 1996 was seen to be a symbolic statement of Ireland's increasing liberalization; however, it passed in a referendum by a margin of just 1 percent of the electorate (James, 1997). Ireland maintains the lowest divorce rate in Europe at 0.6 percent per 100,000 people, significantly lower than the EU average of 2 percent (Central Statistics Office, 2016a). Ireland also has higher fertility rates than many of its European neighbors, while maintaining until recently an almost complete ban on abortion. Since 2018, abortion is legal up to twelve weeks and in exceptional cases thereafter, but Ireland remains one of the most restrictive systems in the EU.

Irish attitudes toward immigration reveal a mixed picture. There was a decline in the average perception of the positive impact of immigration on the economy, on culture, and on the quality of life between 2006 and 2010 during the Great Recession, but perceptions of the impact of immigration have become more positive with economic recovery. In 2018, three questions regarding the effect of immigration on economy, culture, and quality of life were asked of European Social Survey respondents, with an eleven-point scale for responses. Irish respondents returned an average score of over six for all three questions (O'Connell et al., 2019). However, other studies return more mixed results. Ireland, like most countries in Western Europe, is more likely to favor immigrants from Eastern Europe than from the Middle East or Africa, revealing a strongly racialized understanding of "good" immigration. Seventy-five percent of Irish people perceive immigrants from Eastern Europe to be "hard-working," in comparison to 53 percent for immigrants from the Middle East and 58 percent from Africa (Pew Research Center, 2018). This confirms other research that illustrates a strong racial hierarchy in Irish perceptions of immigration and work (Joseph, 2018).

Surveys on religion and religious identity find that levels of religious literacy are low in Ireland, and that a large minority of Irish people incorporate negative attitudes toward religious minorities alongside anti-immigrant sentiment and strong nationalism. For example, 67 percent of Irish people report that they know little or nothing about Islam or Judaism, and 30 percent of Irish people would not be willing to accept Muslims as part of their family (Pew Research Center, 2018). Twenty-one percent of Irish respondents agreed with the statement "due to the number of Muslims here, I feel like a stranger in my own country" (Pew Research Center, 2018), which is significant given that Muslims in Ireland make up just 1.3 percent of the population (Central Statistics Office, 2017a). The median response to this question across Western Europe was 23 percent; however, other Western European countries often have a much larger proportion of Muslims in their country in comparison to Ireland, such as France at 8 percent of the population. In France, 20 percent of respondents indicated they agreed with the statement. Recognizing that views on nationalism, immigration, and religious minorities are strongly associated, the Pew survey developed a ten-point scale to establish levels of nationalist, anti-immigrant, and anti-religious minority sentiment within individual countries of Western Europe. The survey found a median of 22 percent of people across Western Europe scored higher than five on this ten-point scale. In Ireland, 25 percent of Irish people scored higher than five. In France, a substantially more diverse and multicultural country than Ireland, 19 percent of people scored five or more. In summary, Ireland has rapidly modernized and liberalized, but remains more conservative and insular in its outlook than many European nations. In this respect it continues its history of having much in common with its European neighbors, while also diverging from European norms in significant ways.

The Dislocations of Irish Secularization

To understand Mormonism or any religion in Ireland, we must acknowledge the dominance of the Catholic Church for much of the Ireland's development alongside the contemporary moment, where Ireland's relationship to Catholicism has been rapidly transformed. The historical and contemporary place of Catholicism in Ireland continues to shape the experience of all religions in the country. In other words, we can never understand Irish Mormonism without a grounding in Irish Catholicism and its relationship to social change. What is the relationship between recent social change and Irish religion? It appears that the decline of Catholicism in Ireland has provided a space where small religions, previously crowded out of the religious market of Ireland (Ganiel 2016a), can grow. This could be seen as an unintended consequence of secularization, and a reminder of why an examination of religion in modernity must move beyond a narrative of religious decline to also examine how religion persists underneath those changes.

Secularization can be described as "a process by which religious institutions, actions, and consciousness lose their social significance" (Wilson, 1982, p. 142). Connected to the effects of modernization, it is often associated with aspects of social life that are deemed to be affected by the modernization of society, such as the decline of community and traditional family and growing urbanization and individualization. Given Ireland's rapid modernization we might expect a swift secularization to be under way, so it may be helpful to first offer an overview of how sociology has considered secularization.

Secularization has been debated and even rejected by some, such as Peter Berger, who broadly agreed that secularization was under way in 1967 only to reject that proposition in 2012, when he maintained that the secularization thesis "has been empirically falsified" and "most observers have come to the same conclusion" (2012, p. 313). Others adapted their assessments surrounding secularization, such as Grace Davie (1994, p. 94), who has moved away from the concept of "believing without belonging" toward "vicarious religion" (Davie, 2007) as an explanation of an active minority who perform religion on behalf of a majority who at least implicitly approve. Some of the difficulty around scholarly discussions of secularization have been the varying ways it can be defined, measured, and explained. For example, secularization can incorporate a decline in the importance of religion in the wider society, a decline in the social status of religious institutions and roles, and a decline in the extent to which people engage in religious practices, display religious beliefs, or are guided in their actions by religious beliefs (Bruce, 2002).

A core component of the secularization thesis, that as a society modernizes religiosity will decrease, has been problematized. For example, Steve Bruce (2002) has clarified that this may not always occur in cases where religion has come to play an instrumental role in the culture's identity, and Ireland was one such example offered by him to demonstrate this point. Ireland has long been recognized as an interesting case in the discussion of European secularization, given its strong ethno-national associations with religion and its high levels of religiosity even as its neighbors' declined. Ireland was, for almost all of the twentieth century, an extremely religious country where church and state where intimately intertwined. Tom Inglis notes that "the power of the Catholic Church in Irish society, its monopoly over morality, was founded on its influence in Irish social, political, and economic life. Such was the dominance of the Church in other social fields, besides the religious, that it was able to limit and control what people did and said when they met socially, engaged in politics, and dealt in the marketplace" (Inglis, 1998, p. 63). For much of the twentieth century, the Catholic Church controlled or had significant influence over the Irish healthcare and educational systems, the welfare system, and government itself. It structured and sustained local communities (de Cléir, 2017) and as Inglis (1998, p. 2) notes, it also controlled the "minds and hearts" of the Irish people. Such all-encompassing power has a long legacy, and we can still see its influence in Ireland today (Ganiel, 2016b).

However, in the twenty-first century the decline of Catholicism in Ireland has been astonishingly fast. Ireland's measures of religious decline are often now similar to other European countries (Turpin, 2019). Various analyses have observed a shift away from the institutional Catholic Church (Inglis, 2007; Breen & Reynolds, 2011; Anderson, 2012), and a move toward more privatized and individualized belief and practice (Breen & Reynolds, 2011). This leads some to argue that Ireland is undergoing a rapid secularization (Cragun, 2017) and others to argue that Catholicism's public discourses are under adaptation in Ireland (Conway, 2014). Numbers of people reporting as Catholic in Ireland have been declining since the 1960s, with significant declines from the 1980s onward. The 2016 census figures report the lowest number of Catholics thus far at 78.3 percent of the population, down from a high of 94.9 percent in 1961 (Central Statistics Office, 2017b). It is likely this figure will have decreased further upon the publication of the 2022 census. Vocations for the priesthood have been declining for many years including a 13 percent decline between 2002 and 2012 (Irish Catholic Bishops Conference, 2014). Attendance at Catholic religious services has similarly dropped precipitously. The archbishop of the Dublin Diocese of the Catholic Church has been open about his deep concern about what declining attendance represents (Martin, 2011, 2013): "It would appear that on any normal Sunday about 20 percent of the Catholic population of the Archdiocese of Dublin is present at Mass. . . . In more than one parish the Sunday practice rate is about 3 percent . . . these statistics are to say the least, a cause of great concern" (Martin, 2011).

As the number of Catholics has declined, the numbers of atheists, agnostics, and those of no religion has increased quickly, particularly in urban areas. Again, the changes have been dramatic and swift. Numbers of atheists, agnostics, and those with no religion increased 700 percent between 1991 and 2016. Taken together, they are 10 percent of the population and are the second largest "religious" grouping according to the national census (Central Statistics Office, 2017b). Ireland's last census was conducted in 2016 and given the rapid level of decline, it is likely that in the upcoming census of 2022 these figures will have grown further. In the interim, other surveys provide a glimpse into Ireland's current position. A 2018 European Social Survey found that the "religiously unaffiliated" in Ireland makes up 32 percent of the Irish population, while the Pew Research Center found this to be 15 percent of people in 2017 (Pew Research Center, 2018; O'Connell et al., 2019).

Ireland's religious change has been accelerated by processes of immigration (Kmec, 2014). It is estimated that in 2020 foreign nationals comprised 12.9 percent of the population compared to just 5.8 percent in 2002 (Central Statistics Office, 2012, 2020b). These migration patterns have brought changes to the religious experience in Ireland inside and outside of Catholicism. Increases are visible most notably in Pentecostalism (Ugba, 2009) and Islam (Scharbrodt & Sakaranaho, 2011), but most small religions are growing, demonstrating that the weakening of the links between Ireland and Catholicism has allowed for different experiences of Irish religion to emerge. While immigration has driven growth in these religions, it must be noted that given Ireland's historical religious homogeneity, religions other than Catholicism still constitute tiny minorities in Ireland. Adherents of Islam and Orthodox Christianity, two of the largest migrant religions, each make up just 1.3 percent of the population (Central Statistics Office, 2017b).

Despite the collapse of institutional Catholicism, a personal spirituality is persisting. In an analysis of the aftermath of the Catholic Church's sex abuse scandals of the 1990s and 2000s, which irreparably damaged the reputation and influence of the Catholic Church in Ireland, Susie Donnelly and Tom Inglis (2010) constructed an index of personal religiosity using data from the European Values Study and found that individuals' personal religiosity has remained relatively stable over that time. This is despite the decline of institutional Catholicism as described above (Donnelly & Inglis, 2010, p. 10). In 2018, 69 percent of Irish people reported they believed in God, the third highest level of belief in Western Europe, behind Portugal and Italy. In France, a country with a long-established division between church and state, 56 percent of people responded similarly. Across Western Europe, the median was 58 percent.

Despite transformative changes in the Irish religious landscape, the Irish are still more religious and attend services more frequently than people in most other European nations, particularly in comparison to tradition-ally Protestant nations (Breen & Reynolds, 2011). Twenty-four percent of Irish people continue to be "highly religious," one of the highest numbers reported across Western Europe (Pew Research Center, 2018). As the Cath-olic Church has declined New Age spirituality and new religious move-ments have grown in popularity (Cosgrove et al., 2011; Mulholland, 2019). Additionally, the separation of the Catholic Church and Irish state is not complete. Significant influence of the Catholic Church in state affairs is still evident in its control of the educational system where 90 percent of schools are run by the Catholic Church, with the ability to control school admissions and ethos (Malesevic, 2010; Department of Education, 2013). In a similar demonstration of continuing ideological influence, the Catholic call to prayer—the Angelus—continues to be broadcast on the main public service television channel twice a day prior to the lunchtime and evening news.

Despite wide variances within and between societies, a decline in reli-gion is still generally evident as each generation becomes more secular than the last. This is a trend that is unlikely to be reversed given the isolation of those who remain religious in modernity, and the "absence of positive social interaction between the religious and the religiously indifferent" (Bruce, 2016, p. 619). Bruce asserts that religion is now primarily carried by, and hence associated with, people who are "demographically, ethnically, and culturally distinctive ... it is concentrated in specific minority populations, which reinforces the sense that religion is what other people do" (Bruce, 2014, p. 17). This is illustrated in the Irish case, where growth in Ireland's minority religions is predominantly fueled by immigration, leading to small religions being associated with racialized Others who are, as a result of this marginalization, further removed from Ireland's mainstream.

Given that secularization is an "uneven process that is complicated by individual and country-level variables" (Conway, 2013, p. 61), however, I believe we should be careful in our discussion of it. I agree with Bruce that secularization is a reality, and it is also one of (if not the most) significant factors affecting our experience of religion in modernity. However, it is variously defined and analyzed, and quantitative measures of religious decline only tell us part of the story. I agree with Amy Erbe Healy and Michael Breen (2014, p. 24), who suggest that "religion, religious faith, and religiosity are not simple variables, representing something deeply complex within the human experience whose domain of meaning is difficult to capture in simple empirical measures." As the evidence above indicates, there can be many "dislocations" (Coulter, 2018) in the narrative of Irish modernization and secularization. Notably, in the course of overall decline, a mini-religious resurgence can materialize. For example, in Ireland the secularizing trend away from Catholicism has provided the space for small and/or new religions to grow. Thus, this book is not designed to reject or support the general secularization thesis. Rather, I emphasize the complexity of secularization and suggest that we work to understand the various (and sometimes unexpected) ways it is experienced within a broader story about the nature of belonging and exclusion the modern Irish religious experience.

Theorizing Irish Religious Change: Religious Memory and the Chain of Belief

The concept of collective memory in religion is a useful tool to understand how religion is experienced in Ireland. By viewing Irish religion as a form of collective memory that has sustained collective and individual identity and supports belonging and inclusion, we can examine how religion is maintained in the face of significant societal change. It can be particularly useful for understanding what is happening to Irish religion in the midst of secularizing trends. If Irish religion persists in unexpected ways despite secularizing processes, how is that achieved, and what are the challenges within this persistence?

One of the most useful analyses of Irish religion in recent times is Gladys Ganiel's *Transforming Post-Catholic Ireland* (2016), in which she analyzes the decline of the Catholic Church in Ireland to argue that "extra-institutional religion" has more salience in modern Ireland. This she describes as "how people's experiences and practices are so often described not only as outside or in addition to the Catholic Church (extra), but also in the Irish Catholic Church's own terms (institutional). Post-Catholic Ireland, then, is paradoxical: the role of the Catholic Church has changed so dramatically that it is possible to identify a new era. But at the same time, Catholicism retains a different, yet still important, influence in people's personal lives and in the public sphere" (2016b, p. 21).

Ganiel argues that Catholicism continues to shape Irish society, even as Irish society appears to reject it. She finds that Irish people use Catholicism as their religious frame, as the lens that they use to make sense of the place of religion in their lives. Even within an apparent decline, Catholicism continues to have relevance in modern Ireland as it continues to structure how people consider not just their own religious experiences, but religion as a category more generally. In this respect, Ireland's experiences with Catholicism could be said to be akin to a collective memory of religion that works to create and sustain belonging. This book will illustrate the phenomenon of Ganiel's post-Catholic Ireland in the context of Irish Mormonism where Catholicism continues to be used to orientate Irish Mormon identity, particularly after conversion from Catholicism to Mormonism.

In this characterization, the work of Maurice Halbwachs is useful. Halbwachs argues that collective memory cannot exist in any coherent way outside of groups; "there is [thus] no point in seeking where . . . [memories] are preserved . . . for they are recalled by me externally, and the groups of which I am a part at any time give me the means to reconstruct them" (Halbwachs 1992, p. 38). In other words, memory is inherently social, and is created and maintained through the group. Such a Durkheimian collectivist interpretation of memory has been debated, with a key criticism being that reducing memory to the collective overlooks the role of the individual (Fentress & Wickham, 1992). For this and other reasons, many scholars have used different terms than collective memory, such as James Fentress and Chris Wickham's (1992) "social memory" and Jan Assmann's distinctions between "communicative memory," which contains images of the past transmitted from older generations to younger and utilized in everyday communication, and "cultural memory," which is an accumulated knowledge of the distant past "that directs behaviour and experience in the interactive framework of a society and one that obtains through generations in repeated societal practice and initiation" (Assmann, 1995, cited in Olick, Vinitzky-Seroussi, & Levy, 2011, p. 212). For the purposes of this book, I use the catch-all and perhaps more familiar term of "collective memory," but this is not to infer that I reject the usefulness of later interventions.

There have until recently been few attempts to examine memory in the context of Irish identities, with notable exceptions being the work of Oona Frawley (2011b, 2021) and her contributors, and Emilie Pine (2011). Scholarly contributions tend to address the collective Irish sense of self more broadly rather than focusing on the concept of collective memory specifically. Work often focuses on themes of race where it is clear that collective understandings of Irishness have been equated with Whiteness (Loyal, 2003; Garner, 2005; Lentin, 2007). Commentators have also emphasized the role of colonialism in Irish collective memory, where Irishness is shaped in the shadow of the British occupier (Howe, 2000; Cleary, 2004; Moane, 2014; Scanlon & Satish Kumar, 2019). An analysis of Ireland's religious memory and how that has come to influence Irish people's contemporary identities has received less attention, with some notable exceptions discussed below.

Yet, the role of religion in collective understanding of what Ireland is has been fundamental to the development of Irish identity (Sen, 2011) and religious memory is well established as a field of study in many other contexts.[2] During times of social change "much of the structural scaffolding of 'traditional Ireland' remains stubbornly in place despite, and perhaps even because of, recent societal transformations. Community, class, gender, and nationality remain salient to how people define themselves and how they are defined by others" (Share and Corcoran, 2010, p. 16). From this viewpoint, Ireland's collective memory of tradition can be viewed as an attempt to sustain belonging in an era of flux.

It is notable that Perry Share and Mary P. Corcoran (2010) did not include religion in their list of identifiers the Irish still cling to. Perhaps this is because Irish nationality and religious identity as Catholic are deeply intertwined in Irish consciousness and difficult to separate (Halikiopoulou, 2008; Ruane & Todd, 2009). It has become clear that Irish people hold onto religion as part of their collective understanding of self, but that this conception and experience of religion is undergoing adaptation:

> What we are seeing here perhaps is the demise of the influence of grand, ascribed social identities in the way contemporary Irish people see and understand themselves. [Church and nation] are dependent on getting people to think of themselves as Catholic and Irish. This study would suggest that people still do think of themselves in these terms, but it is not part of their everyday image of themselves. It operates within specific contexts

such as encountering people from other religions, going to Mass, going abroad, or watching the national team in sports. It may well be that it is only when culture becomes unsettled, when the routine and ordinariness of everyday life is threatened, that ascribed social identities come to the fore. (Inglis, 2007, pp. 218–219)

It is when confronted with change that the social identity of Irish as Catholic emerges. It also persists through the continuance of complex intermingling's of national and religious identification. The continuing Irish identification with Catholicism despite much lower active participation in the religion indicates that such continuing identities are now important for maintaining the continuity of the category of "Irish." These Irish can reconcile their religious distance from the Catholic Church and their concurrent embrace of its cultural connotations, as to do so is to make a statement about what it is to be Irish in the twenty-first century. It is revered as a marker of belonging, of being the "true Irish" (Kuhling & Keohane, 2007, p. 67) in a changing country. Similar complex deployments of religious identities have been identified elsewhere, such as in the United Kingdom, where understandings of Britishness and Christianity show similar entanglements in the modern era (Storm 2011; 2013). Why is it that such forms of belonging matter in modernity? One answer that draws on the Irish milieu comes from Donal Murray:

> It is no coincidence that recent years have seen a great upsurge of interest in tracing one's roots. In a world which finds it hard to face questions like "Who am I? Why do I matter? Will it make any difference in a hundred years that I lived at all?" it becomes more pressing to know where one fits in to something greater than oneself. It becomes important to see oneself as belonging, not as a cog in some great impersonal, uncaring machine, but as a living, organic part of the wider human family. (Murray, 1996, p. 23)

For the Irish in a time of flux, to know to what and to whom one belongs offers reassurance and connection in fast-changing times. In discussing the resilience of similar interminglings of national and religious identifications in countries such as in Poland and Northern Ireland, the French sociologist of religion Danièle Hervieu-Léger suggests that this phenomenon represents a subversion of Grace Davie's concept of "believing without belonging" (1990, 1994), which refers to those people who describe themselves as spiritual but not religious or who have a personal relationship with God outside of any membership in an organized religion. Hervieu-Léger (2000, p. 162) describes this subversion as "belonging without believing," which is "believing only in the continuity of the group for which the signs preserved from the traditional religion now serve as emblems." Why, in a book about Irish Mormonism, should we concern ourselves with how Irish Catholics use collective memory to sustain their collective and individual identities in modern Ireland? Irish Mormonism is intimately connected to Irish Catholicism, and modern Irish society has been formed through its Catholic history, with a legacy that still persists. In this context it is important to know how Irish Catholic identity functions in the contemporary age to fully understand Irish Mormon identity. Particularly, I show that the Irish Mormon experience of (non) belonging directly connects to the place of Catholicism in contemporary Ireland.

If Irish Catholicism now persists predominantly as a cultural identity bound up with nationhood, what are the consequences of this, both for Catholicism and for other religions? There is now diversity within Irish Catholicism that reveals a fragmentation of Catholic identity. In addition to "strong Catholics" mainly found in older generations, there are also "cultural Catholics" who identify as Catholic to assert a shared cultural heritage (Inglis, 1998, 2004, 2007, 2010; Inglis & MacKeogh, 2012). "Creative Catholics" collect a bricolage of various beliefs and practices including Catholicism and exist alongside large numbers of "alienated Catholics"—those born into the Church who now identify as atheist or agnostic (Inglis, 2007, pp. 214–216). Additionally, a significant minority of Irish Catholics do not believe in the specific doctrines of the religion with which they self-identify. Ten percent of Catholics in the Republic of Ireland do not believe in God, 23 percent do not believe in heaven, almost half of Irish Catholics do not believe in hell, and almost one-quarter do not believe in sin (O'Mahony, 2010, pp. 11–12). Though the inverse of these figures indicate that a majority of Irish Catholics *do* believe in the basic doctrines of their faith, they also show that a significant minority of modern Irish Catholics do not believe in aspects of Catholicism that many would consider fundamental. For many, Catholicism has become a cultural habitus (Inglis, 2004), rather than an active religiosity.

Catholicism's changing relationship with Irishness also has consequences for those of other religions in Ireland, as this book will illustrate. For example, Irish research with converts from Catholicism to other religions illustrates that a continuity of Catholic identification persists even as religious belief in Catholicism wanes (Sakaranaho, 2003, 2015; Scharbrodt, 2015). Thus, there exists in Ireland a Catholic legacy that can be seen as a "kind of religious memory" (Sakaranaho, 2003, p. 75), which causes converts to non-Catholic religions to struggle to be accepted as fully Irish due to their religious identity. Conversion to another faith is perceived by the Irish as a rejection of Irishness itself, due to the overlap of understandings of Irishness and Catholicism in Irish society (Shanneik, 2015, p. 196). Similarly, Lorraine Ryan (2011, p. 217) suggests that despite rapid change, "Irish memory is not taking into account the pace of social evolution and the enormous richness of multicultural Ireland . . . the hour has come for our memory culture to undergo a concomitant transformation," suggesting that Ireland has been slow to reinvent its collective understanding of itself to better reflect its current shift toward religious and ethnic diversity and multiculturalism.

To explain religious change in contemporary France, Hervieu-Léger argues that modernity has caused a "break in the chain" of belief (Hervieu-Léger, 2000, p. 124). Hervieu-Léger observes that "changes to family and the decline of rural life, both fundamental to the sense of community and lineage within the French Catholic parish, have contributed to a fragmentation and disruption of the transmission of religion" as a consequence of aspects of modernity such as rationalization, individualization, and urbanization. As modernity eradicates the means through which beliefs are transmitted, the ability of religious institutions to control belief is also affected. This is not to say that these processes directly lead to the abandonment of religion, or that religion ceases to have influence. Even amid European secularization it is possible to speak of "Catholic Europe" or "Protestant Europe" (Hervieu-Léger, 2003, p. 4), and "Catholic atheists" and "Protestant atheists" (Davie, 2000, p. 135). Rather, Hervieu-Léger suggests that religion adapts when the foundations upon which it rests are challenged.

France and Ireland are not directly comparable, and this means that not all aspects of Hervieu-Léger's work make sense in an Irish context. Though both countries have a strong Catholic legacy, France is more secular than Ireland, particularly regarding the role of religion in public life and public institutions. Nonetheless, Hervieu-Léger does also apply her ideas to a wider European context, and her discussion of declining religious authority, adaptations in religious transmission, and the nature of "ethnic religions" (Hervieu-Léger, 2000) are useful in analyzing what is under way in Ireland, as Tuula Sakaranaho (2006) evidences in an analysis of the place of Islam in Finland and Ireland. Here, I briefly outline the aspects of Hervieu-Léger's work that may assist us in the analysis of modern Mormonism and Catholicism in Ireland.

For Halbwachs, collective memory is the "repository of tradition" (Halbwachs, 1992, p. 78) and for Hervieu-Léger modern religious belief rests upon tradition. Tradition, she says, is invoked by both religious adherents and institutional religion to sustain a collective memory in the context of modernity where common understandings are more difficult to sustain. In a modern world where "all symbols are interchangeable and capable of being combined and transposed" (Hervieu-Léger, 2000, p. 75), contemporary religion cannot be analyzed solely by numbers of baptisms, or adherence to doctrine, or by typical measures of religiosity such as church attendance. It must also be understood as a *way* of believing, a particular form of belief that, for Hervieu-Léger, rests upon the legitimization of tradition as a form of authorized collective memory. Tradition is "the body of representations, images, theoretical and practical intelligence, behaviour, attitudes and so on that a group or society accepts in the name of the *necessary* continuity between the past and the present" (Hervieu-Léger, 2000, p. 87 [emphasis in original]). This is used by adherents to sustain a "chain of belief" that binds the religious group to each other.

The content and meaning of the tradition are less important than what the tradition itself represents—the sense of belonging to something beyond our contemporaneous existence:

> In keeping with the individualization of modern societies, the individual can imagine the tradition which is being invoked in their own way and consequently, what is significant in defining religion is not the actual substance of belief but the ingenuity, the imaginative perception of the link which across time establishes the religious adhesion of members to the group they form and the convictions that bind them. . . . It is not the continuity in itself that matters but the fact of its being the visible expression of a lineage which the believer expressly lays claim to and which confers membership of spiritual community that gathers past, present, and future believers. (Hervieu-Léger, 2000, p. 81)

For example, a Mormon who arrives in church on Sunday to partake of the key weekly ritual of the Sacrament may find the meaning behind the tradition to be the sacred role of the priesthood holder who administers the Sacrament. This is a role given to male Church members, which is reinforced each Sunday in the Sacrament ritual. For another member of the congregation, what is significant in the tradition of the Sacrament might be the opportunity to formally reaffirm their covenant with God, as other members of the Church have also done since its founding. The individualized meaning of the tradition being invoked (in this case, the weekly Sacrament) is less important than how the tradition represents a continuance of a line of believers to which both members claim to belong. Sakaranaho (2011, p. 146) also notes that "what a religious community accepts as tradition comes from the past but carries authority in the present. Here it is less important how far back this past reaches, and whether it is historical or mythical, but rather that it is actively invoked by individuals and/or religious communities. We can thus speak of the Hindu tradition, which has lasted nearly five thousand years, or of the new pagan tradition, which is only some fifty years old but which in its own rhetoric aims at invoking the pre-Christian traditions of Europe."[3]

How might we make use of these ideas to better understand modern Ireland, Catholicism, Mormonism, and the relationship among the three? Both Catholicism and Mormonism rest upon reference to formal and informal traditions that legitimize the ongoing beliefs of their adherents. Both incorporate ideological standpoints that support the group, such as an association between Catholicism and Irish national identity, or a veneration of history and genealogy in the case of Mormonism. Both reference symbols that support the values of the religion and allow for individual and collective meanings of the same to be maintained. This is in evidence within Mormonism through the symbol of the beehive, representing Mormon values of hard work, perseverance, and working for the good of the group. Within Catholicism, the Lenten symbol of the cross marked in ashes on the forehead on Ash Wednesday symbolizes the importance of repentance. Both operate a system that maintains and develops a "chain of belief" among its adherents.

Theories explaining the fragmentation of collective memory and the chain of belief are useful to help illustrate that Irish Mormonism is now experiencing what Irish Catholicism has been experiencing for the past thirty years, and to explain why this is occurring. The breakdown of institutional control over belief and the fragmentation of experience accelerated by cultural change and international growth within the religion has caused the institutional Church to lose its grip on the reproduction of Mormon tradition. The effects of this are evident in Ireland, as this book illustrates. Recent high-profile debates within Mormonism such as those regarding the social and doctrinal position of LGBTQ+ people in the Church (Petrey, 2020; Riess, 2021), the Church's emphasis on using the official name for the Church (Riess, 2018), or the recent shift toward more Christ-centric imagery to promote the Church and its message, all reflect institutional adaptations under way as an attempt to retain and sustain a collective memory of Mormonism. Contemporary Mormonism has been placed in a peculiar position. To thrive, it has had to rely upon global expansion, but this has also threatened the collective memory of Mormonism and forced the Church to confront its own identity as never before. Jake Johnson (2019, p. 116) has noted the centrality of memory for Mormonism: "Mormons enter history as interlocuters and see historical landscape as malleable in their hands. Thus,

Mormons conceptually move in and out of time to recreate it in the manner most fitting to their needs all whilst being sanctioned implicitly, and sometimes explicitly, by leaders who likewise suggest that the chaos of the past can be made sensible through the prism of Mormonism." Perhaps the flexibility of temporality for Mormonism makes sense of not just the chaos of the past, but also the chaos of the present. This has particular resonance in an Irish context where Irish Mormons are simultaneously coping with the transformations within their own religion while also navigating a wider society that is undergoing significant changes.

Regarding Irish Catholicism, understanding the fragmentation of religious memory facilitates an analysis of the Irish religious landscape that involves both rapid religious change *and* continued Catholic influence. Within this milieu, identifying with another religion such as Mormonism represents a rupture of the Irish collective memory of Irishness, as well a divergence from traditional understandings of Irish religion. The variety of Catholicisms remaining in modern Ireland and the continued influence of Catholicism on converts to other religions demonstrates that collective memory, though fragmented and damaged, lingers within modernity to continue to sustain collective belonging. Through an examination of issues such as national identity, congregational cohesiveness, White supremacy, and family ideals, I explore the challenges in creating a coherent narrative of Irish Mormonism within contemporary Irish society where collective understandings of religion, Irish identity, and belonging are undergoing great change. In the following chapter, I illustrate how Irish society perceives Mormonism, how this perception is received by Irish members and Church missionaries, and the strategies used by Irish Mormons to navigate a society that has excluded them from belonging to collective understandings of Irishness.

The Challenges of Belonging in Modern Mormonism

Maintaining Continuity in a Global Religion

Though Ireland has its own specific historical and cultural reasons for its complicated relationship with religion, which were outlined in the previous chapter, the relationship is also shaped by wider European attitudes toward religion, which are often markedly different to those in the United States, where Mormonism is both symbolically and administratively centered. In this chapter, I illustrate a complex and dialectical relationship between the global Church and the local areas where it is lived by providing a European context in which to situate these ideas. I demonstrate that structural and cultural differences between European and US experiences of religion are at the core of the Church's struggles in Europe in contemporary times. My focus on Europe in this chapter is to provide a regional context for the Irish data discussed in the following chapters; however, the Church is facing challenges regarding the management of identity and belonging worldwide (Shepherd, Shepherd, & Cragun, 2020). Here, I examine the key debates regarding the Church's rapid growth outside of the United States and explore the challenges associated with creating and maintaining a presence in societies that are far removed from, and often resistant to, American Mormonism.

Mormonism has transformed rapidly in less than 200 years to become a church with a presence across the globe. Official global membership now stands at over 16 million members, with more members now living outside the United States than within it (Church of Jesus Christ of Latter-day

Saints, n.d.-d). Though recent indications show that this growth is slowing (Lawson & Cragun, 2012), the Church has nonetheless been transformed by these developments. A policy introduced in the 1960s known as "correlation" standardized the Mormon experience and facilitated a common understanding of Mormonism among its members (Phillips, 2008). Resources such as lesson plans and Church manuals for lessons and the architecture and internal layout of Church buildings were made uniform. Sunday services were consolidated into one long block, where once they had been spread throughout the day. Most decisions regarding when, what, and how to teach were made by the Church hierarchy in Utah, clearly placing Church headquarters in Utah as the center of power for the religion. Because of this, Utah as a geographical region maintained its role as a homeland for the religion internationally (Phillips & Cragun, 2013). Creating a sense of familiarity in Church buildings and teaching worldwide, supported belonging to an international religious group undefined by national borders. Correlation continued an idealization and mythologizing of Utah as a religious homeland for a diverse people, and broadly maintained a common understanding of Mormonism among members as the Church expanded. It was therefore useful in ensuring a smoother transition toward becoming a global religion (Allen, 1992).

Despite a growing international presence, Americanism persists throughout the religion through historical-geographical, ideological, and behavioral components of Church culture (Sherlock, 2018). The continuing spiritual significance of Utah specifically, and the United States more broadly, functions as a key aspect of this. Terryl Givens (2016) observes that the association between the United States and the *Book of Mormon* means that unavoidably, the United States remains a focus for Mormonism. He notes, "the Book of Mormon was physically connected as an actual artefact, in the minds and in the tactile experience of early Saints, with America. And the history in the Book of Mormon was explicated in terms of that very physical terrain over which the Saints themselves trekked and camped" (Givens, 2016, p. 430).

Those who study Mormonism from a variety of disciplines such as sociology, theology, and history maintain that Mormonism has within it a Church culture. For example, Givens (2007) refers to "Mormon culture," including in the title of his 2007 book *A People of Paradox: A History of Mormon Culture*. Douglas Davies refers to "the Mormon culture of salvation" (2000, p. 7) and "LDS culture" (2003, p. 251), while historian Patrick Mason refers to "LDS church doctrine and culture" (2016, p. 7). A Belgian scholar of Mormonism, Wilfried Decoo (2013b), has discussed the development of Mormonism within Europe. He summarizes the core components of Mormon culture as incorporating: "Religiosity (faith in the doctrines, daily prayer, scripture study, fasting, church and temple attendance), morality (chastity, modesty, honesty), family (monogamy, focus on marriage and children, togetherness, fidelity, family home evening, food storage), health (no alcohol, tobacco, coffee, and tea), dedication and involvement (serving, tithing, going on a mission, doing genealogy), education (schooling, degrees, and diplomas), work (work ethic, professional advancement, economic success), material objects (book of remembrance, Mormon pictures in the home, recognition medallions), and its own lexicon" (Decoo, 2013b, p. 7).Thus, we can conclude that although culture is variously constructed and interpreted and in a continual process of adaptation, nonetheless, we can speak to, and of, a Church culture that shapes the experiences of members across the globe.

Integrating the Local and the Global

The shift within Mormonism from small sect to global church has caused scholars of Mormonism to reflect on the future of the Church as it continues to transform. Jehu Hanciles argues that Christianity is the most globalized religion because it is "the ultimate local religion" (2015, p. 43), being capable of adaptations that allow the faith to expand to new locations that have not historically been associated with Christianity. This flexibility means that global Christianity is transforming traditional understandings of what Christianity is. It is becoming less White, and in terms of language, Spanish rather than English is now the most spoken language. But global Christianity incorporates more than just geography, race, or language: "The new global Christianity is also marked by an immense diversity of expressions, theological understanding, forms of worship, spiritual dynamism, biblical interpretation, and responses to critical issues of the day—all of which raise important questions about ecclesial identity, theological priorities, and power differentials within global Christian movements" (Hanciles, 2015, p. 39). Contemporary Mormonism appears to be increasingly moving to position itself as a global Christian movement. Recent changes to official Church imagery have emphasized the name and image of Jesus Christ, while an aggressive clampdown on use of the term "Mormon," despite the term's being embraced by many members as a key component of their identity, illustrates an attempt to reassert the Christian components of Mormonism while also drawing clearer boundaries between the CoJCoLDS and other Mormon sects. Contemporary Mormonism, then, has sought to be perceived as more Christian at precisely the time when Christianity itself is being transformed.

Hanciles (2015) suggests that localization (local adaptation of the religion to cultural specificities) and multidirectional transformation (where change travels not just hierarchically from the center to the periphery of the religion) are the markers of successful global Christianity. For Mormonism to be a truly global religion it must be comfortable with achieving both. Yet as this chapter evidences, Mormonism continues to exert tight control from Church headquarters, which does not appear generally receptive to local adaptations. It seems more comfortable issuing policy changes from the Mormon Culture Region that all are expected to adhere to than it does in accommodating changes that originate at grassroots level outside of the institutional Church. In 2003, Davies proposed that rather than becoming a world religion in the model of Buddhism, Christianity, or Islam, it is more likely that Mormonism would become a religion that "makes its presence felt within hundreds of societies yet retains its distinctive identity. . . . It will appeal to and attract people in need of a distinctive identity and who are prepared to be different from their neighbours" (Davies, 2003, p. 248). To examine this proposal, we can explore how Church culture is experienced away from the predominantly White American Mormon Culture Region. The remarkable adaption of Mormonism in a global context then becomes visible as we begin to see how reworking Mormon traditions becomes part of the process through which religious memory shifts and Mormons across the globe create belonging to the faith in ways that work for them.

For example, Taunalyn F. Rutherford (2016) discusses the experience of Indian converts to Mormonism from Hinduism. She notes "moments of intercultural adaption" such as the Mormon convert who no longer cleans her home every Friday in expectation of the goddess Durga, but "to create a better atmosphere for her family and because cleanliness is a gospel principle" (Rutherford, 2016, p. 52). The Church often has to adapt to existing structural social systems in particular countries, and in India, the caste system remains a key organizing principle of postcolonial society. Rutherford notes that although most participants said that "there is no caste in the church" (2016, p. 53), she believes this to be a partial truth. She observes: "Caste is never taught as a principle in Mormonism and is in fact clearly condemned. However, church members come from castes and live in a world with castes—for instance, marriage outside of one's caste is still frowned upon. . . . Caste-like identities develop in Indian Mormonism corresponding to those who are endowed in the temple, BYU-educated, returned missionaries, fluent English speakers, and so forth" (Rutherford,

2016, p. 53). It is apparent that the social structures of the majority society are feeding into the experience of members, despite the doctrine and culture of the Church officially rejecting those same systems.

Rutherford suggests that scholars of Mormonism have hitherto underestimated the capacity of local members to adapt their faith to the environment that surrounds them in ways that may ultimately influence the center of the faith itself. She argues that "Mormonism is lived at the local, not general, level . . . policies are interpreted and applied by local leaders who are products of their own culture. . . . The outcomes of this dynamic translation of the general to the local often surprise everyone" (Rutherford, 2016, pp. 57–58). Thus, we can see that Mormon faith and culture is not experienced as a simple one-way system from center to peripheral regions. Rather, it is a dialectic system of interactions, where each is shaped by the other. Rutherford's argument that a hybrid form of Mormonism and local culture creates significant adaptation of Mormon tradition may seem as though it sits in contrast to the comments of Davies (2003), who argues that Mormonism is likely to develop in the future by keeping its identity distinct from the majority society wherever it grows. Certainly there is no doubt that the Church prefers to present a coherent and clear image of itself as set apart from society which belies Rutherford's claims.

However, this book illustrates that Davies and Rutherford are both correct, and that the two positions can be reconciled in the everyday experiences of Mormons in peripheral regions such as Ireland. Although their experiences of stereotyping and stigmatization leaves no doubt as to their Otherness, Mormons in Ireland are also re-creating Mormonism for an Irish milieu, reshaping it in ways that assist in a reconciliation of Irish and Mormon identities. This is a Mormon remaking of tradition at a local level and "just how that renegotiation takes place is, itself, of prime importance" (Davies, 2007, p. 59). While the official Church continues to resist localization and multidirectional transformation, these processes are nonetheless occurring in the lived experiences of local members across the globe.

This renegotiation of Mormonism is evident in Britain, where Matthew Lyman Rasmussen has demonstrated how British Mormons created a form of Mormonism fit to survive the ebbs and flows of religious revival and decline across the nineteenth and twentieth centuries. Rasmussen (2016, p. 47) illustrates how a "gradual adaptation" of the Church's nineteenth-century doctrine of "gathering" in Utah[1] "guaranteed the successful perpetuation and maturation of Mormonism in the British Isles." Of particular interest for this book is Rasmussen's (2016, p. 102) observations of how British Mormonism's reliance on American missionaries for direction in the latter half of the nineteenth century "reduced membership involvement in missionary work, increased congregational vulnerability, and cost the Church its Britishness." Rasmussen's work also highlights the interrelationships between the stability of the Church's congregations in local areas and the perceptions of the Church among the wider society. Noting that anti-Mormon agitation and general suspicion in the wider British community caused local membership to lose confidence in the nineteenth and early twentieth centuries, he suggests that these challenges also had the effect of creating tight-knit Mormon communities that were then well placed to grow in the period after World War II.

Rasmussen's historical findings regarding the effect of an American missionary program on British congregations is also confirmed in contemporary analysis. Alison Halford suggests that a dilution of the Americanism of the Church's current missionary program would be useful in a British context to facilitate the Church to "adapt its approach to accommodate different forms of secularization occurring in different nations" (Halford & O'Brien, 2020, p. 485). In fact, in a recent article Halford and I suggest that the Mormon missionary program be transformed to "empower local units" to create proselytizing efforts that understand and celebrate regional difference (Halford & O'Brien, 2020, p. 490). The Church's continuing adherence to its American-infused missionary program is just one example of how the Church is not as receptive to multidirectional transformation as it needs to be to truly become a global religion, and this topic is discussed further in an Irish context in later chapters of this book.

So, we know that when the Church is transplanted to social and cultural contexts quite different to that of its origins, complicated relationships with the host society will emerge. Rasmussen (2016) observed how British society's rejection of Mormonism came to shape British Mormonism at a local level, but we also have evidence of the reverse—where Mormonism reshaped the cultural identity of the host society, which is perhaps a different form of multidirectional transformation. Such evidence comes from the work of Julie Allen (2017) whose *Danish but Not Lutheran* outlines how Danish Mormonism challenged the homogeneity of Danish cultural identity, which was intimately bound up with the Lutheran faith. As with Ireland and its relationship to Catholicism, it was difficult to conceive that one could be Danish and not an adherent of the country's dominant religion. As in Ireland, rapid social change in Denmark caused religious minorities to be targeted as Other, and to be excluded from collective understandings of belonging. Yet, over time Mormonism and other minority religions came to be accepted under a renegotiated understanding of who Danes were.

Under this new multicultural model, Danish identity adapted. Allen (2017, p. 246) points out that contemporary conflicts caused by immigration and multiculturalism need not be "grounds for decrying the degenerate state of modern society." The historical evidence of Mormonism's engagement with Danish society illustrates that such conflicts can diminish over time if one chooses to take a "longer view" (Allen, 2017, p. 247). This is an interesting observation in relation to contemporary Ireland where rapid modernization and associated increases in immigration are transforming Irish society and culture.

Melissa Inouye suggests that rather than seeing the global expansion of the Church as an oak tree, with one central root spreading up and out into smaller branches that stem from the center, we should interpret global Mormonism as similar to the banyan tree common in Asia. The banyan tree goes up and out, much like the oak, but its branches also reach down to the earth to form new roots. Inouye posits that "the future of global Mormon studies will describe a Mormon reality that is more like a banyan than an oak: a bit chaotic, growing wherever it can find a foothold, each branch with many of its own sturdy trunks and roots, yet all forming a single living organism" (Inouye, 2014, p. 79). This perspective argues for a redefinition of the meaning of center and periphery within Mormonism, with an urgent need to recognize multiple centers and peripheries (Inouye, 2014, p. 73). Certainly, the evidence from Denmark and Britain illustrates that identity can be renegotiated, resulting in interconnected relationships between the Church, local congregations, and the majority society they sit within.

Although Inouye (2014) is right to advocate for a wider interpretation of center and periphery as it relates to Mormonism, there nonetheless remains a culturally powerful spiritual and administrative center to which most Mormons orientate themselves. The close association with the Utah mountain region and Mormonism has been well documented (Yorgason & Robertson, 2006; Yorgason & Chen, 2008; Reeve, 2015; Patterson, 2016). Historical connections, strong Mormon demographics, and key familial ties to the religion in the Mormon Culture Region, coupled with identifiable cultural indicators such as unique architecture, food, and music, are proof that Mormonism has embraced cultural as well as religious components in the region (Upton, 2005; Starrs, 2010).

With such a powerful orientation toward the Mormon Culture Region within Mormon culture we might question if, and how, Mormonism would be able to move away from its strong regional origins (Mauss, 1996a; Gedicks, 2011; Mason & Turner, 2016). Perhaps most famously on this theme was the pronouncement of Rodney Stark in 1984 that the growth rates of the Church at the end of the twentieth century indicated that we might be witnessing the emergence of a new world religion (Stark, 1984). This dramatic prediction was greeted with pleasure by the Church hierarchy (Haight, 1990; Haroldsen, 1995), and was much discussed throughout the 1990s by those attempting to make sense of growth within the Church. They questioned whether these expansive growth trends could be sustained in the long term and what it might mean for the Church and the religion (Bennion & Young, 1996; Mauss, 1996b; Duke, 1998). It seems clear as we move further into the twenty-first century that Stark's prediction was overly optimistic. Growth internationally has slowed from 4–6 percent per year in the 1980s to 1–2 percent in the 2010s (Martinich, 2020). Baptisms are in decline in many regions, including in Eastern European mission areas such as Warsaw and Kyiv (Stewart, 2020b), and between 2008 and 2018 the European region experienced a net decrease of 7.8 percent in the number of congregations (Martinich, 2020). This does not negate the fact that according to Church figures 10 million of Mormonism's 16.5 million members now live outside of the United States (Church of Jesus Christ of Latter-day Saints, n.d.-c),[2] leading to a fundamental shift in the geographical balance of religious membership. Where once problems outside of the United States could be ignored or downplayed as incidental to the general experience of Mormonism, this no longer holds true.

Where has the Church grown in recent decades? Latin America has been identified as a region of considerable success for the Church (Knowlton, 1996; Grover, 2015). It is interesting in light of this project to note that in explaining the reasons why this is so, "problems in the internal structures of Catholicism" have been posited for the Church's success in this region (Knowlton, 1996, p. 161). The Catholic Church in Latin America is losing followers to Mormonism and to other Protestant churches as part of a global shift in the experience of Christianity, as established churches decline in favor of charismatic evangelicalism (Decoo, 2013a; Grover, 2015). However, Mormonism has not gained as many converts in Latin America as the other churches have (Knowlton, 1996), and retention of Mormon converts in the region is a significant challenge for the Church (Grover, 2015). As Ireland is a majority Catholic country, the shift in the experience of Christianity in Latin America from Catholic to Protestant, and the positioning of Mormonism within that, is of interest. Protestant religions have also been key beneficiaries of Ireland's increased religious diversity in recent years (Jackson Noble, 2011), partly due to increased numbers of recent immigrants (Nuttall, 2015). Therefore, in Ireland, as in Latin America, it appears that the decline in the influence of the Catholic Church has allowed for a

Protestant resurgence, to which the Church of Jesus Christ of Latter-day Saints potentially stands to benefit.

Understanding Belonging in European Mormonism

Efforts to retain converts as active members have been less successful in Europe than in other regions for quite some time (Mauss, 2008; Beek, 2009; Decoo, 2015; Stewart, 2020a, 2020b). True active membership figures across Europe could be as much as three-quarters less than the official figures provided by the Church (Decoo, 1996; Mauss, 2008). Comparative examination of the international growth of Mormonism alongside that of other growing religions such as the Jehovah's Witnesses and Seventh-day Adventists shows that increases for proselytizing religions such as these slow within a country once a particular level of socioeconomic development has been reached. Whether this is due to the development of stronger social safety nets or modernization more broadly is unclear (Cragun & Lawson, 2010; Lawson & Cragun, 2012). However, this does help to explain why growth in Europe has stalled, while growth in the Global South is still increasing. In addition to socioeconomic explanations, there are also cultural reasons for the Church's struggles across Europe, as outlined further below.

We should be mindful, however, that as a region incorporating 748 million people across forty-four countries (Worldometer, 2021), with a diversity of religious histories and contemporary experiences, it is not possible to speak simply about Mormonism "in Europe." Contrary to some Mormon perceptions in the United States, European Mormonism is neither representative of the blessed "blood of Israel" nor is it a homogenous hedonistic socialist bloc, "neither fairy-tale nor dystopia" as Allen (2019) describes it. Significant differences across European countries ideally necessitate "individual treatment" and the term "European Mormonism" is by its nature too generalizing (Properzi, 2010, p. 42). Walter E. A. van Beek, Ellen Decoo, and Wilfried Decoo acknowledge this in a discussion of secularization in the Low Countries and its effects on Mormonism, where they note that "even adjacent countries can have different pathways" (Beek, Decoo, & Decoo, 2020, p. 507). Ireland and the United Kingdom are an excellent example of this, having vastly different experiences of religion and secularization despite their proximity to each other and cultural connections. Additionally, political and cultural circumstances in many Eastern European countries diverge significantly in religious experience from Western Europe, and this must also be acknowledged in any analysis of Mormonism in Europe (Stewart, 2020b).

Homogenizing perceptions of Europe are not helped by Church organization, which often neglects to offer national representation for the Church in each European country. Beek, Decoo, and Decoo (2020) outline the serious and complex difficulties this causes for Flanders and the Netherlands, and indeed this is also noted by Irish Mormons as a source of ire for them because they are administratively coupled with the United Kingdom, from which Irish independence was only achieved 100 years ago. So, we must be wary when generalizing and mindful of the nuance that can be lost therein. Yet, Mauro Properzi (2010) and other observers of Mormonism in Europe argue that some commonalities *can* be identified across countries, which reveal why it is that Mormonism appears to particularly struggle in Europe (Decoo, 1981, 1996, 2013b, 2015; Beek, 2005, 2009, 2010). To provide a general sense of how Irish Mormonism fits within European Mormonism, an articulation of some of these common themes is useful.

Cultural and Structural Isolation among European Mormons

It is difficult for US members, and therefore Church leadership, to appreciate the ways in which being Mormon in Europe is manifestly different to being Mormon in the United States (Decoo, 1996). There is often little support within the wider culture in Europe for the Church and its cultural differences. This is partly due to differences in how Europeans experience religion (Davie, 2005). However, it also relates to how joining a minority church in Europe often excludes you from the shared customs and traditions that your family, friends, and the wider culture take for granted. For instance, in Belgium long church services for Mormons on Sundays often clash with other community events traditionally held on that day (Decoo, 1996). In Sweden, Norway, Finland, Denmark, and Iceland, the social isolation from both the Church's US center and the majority society in those countries has offered challenges and opportunities. While Mormons in these countries have been stigmatized and cut off from the norms and values of their societies to some degree, they have also had the chance to create tight-knit communities made up of multigenerational families who are strong enough to face such challenges. The complexity of their experience on the margins of their Church and their society has also allowed them to create a "distinctive hybrid culture informed by both the Church's American roots and each congregation's local context" (Allen & Östman, 2020, p. 546).

Nonetheless, the Church has a low level of religious respectability in many European countries such as Finland, Belgium, and the Netherlands (Beek, 1996; Decoo, 1996; Östman, 2002; Mauss, 2008), often being associated with other outsider sects such as Scientology, the Unification Church (Moonies), and others who are "marginalized and stigmatized" (Mauss, 2008, p. 6). Carter Charles (2018, p. 186), writing in a French context, describes this as a "cult/not cult" discourse when speaking of a new or minority religion. Though he writes specifically about France, this could be said to be a common discursive framework across much of Europe in discussions of religion. Mormonism has undergone a period of rehabilitation in the broader American consciousness, particularly in the latter half of the twentieth century (Haws, 2013), something that might exacerbate a lack of understanding in the Mormon Culture Region about life as a stigmatized religious minority in other parts of the world. This stigmatization may explain why European families belonging to established churches such as Catholicism react so strongly to the conversion of their relatives (Decoo, 1996). These instances confirm the complexity of the position of new religious movements (NRMs)[3] in Europe where small religions are often seen to be a threat to the established religious traditions (Davie, 2000). Additionally, there is a strong sense in many European countries of "being a 'cultural Catholic' or 'cultural Calvinist'; raised in that tradition, defining identity in terms of the tradition . . . but one does no longer go to church" (Beek, 2009). Citing the example of Belgium, Beek notes that "becoming a Mormon is not done, not so much because one is a Catholic, but one is a Belgian, and Belgium is a Catholic country!" (Beek, 2009), echoing similar interconnections of Catholicism and Irishness shown in chapter 3 of this book.

While there is a strong ethno-national association with religion in countries such as Greece (Halikiopoulou, 2008; Martinich, 2020) (this being a point of commonality with Ireland), public expressions of religiosity do not have the same cultural acceptability in many parts of Europe as they do in many parts of the United States (Davie, 2006). Globalization is "transforming the nature of religion" (Hanciles, 2015, p. 37) and migration from the Global South to Europe has caused adaptations in the public expression of European religiosity. Tensions have arisen regarding how visible religion in twenty-first-century Europe is, or should be (Hjelm, 2015). On one hand there is an expectation of cultural religiosity as part of one's national or ethnic identity, and this is achieved through maintaining the same religion as one's ancestors (Inglis, 2007). On the other hand, expression of this religiosity should ideally be in the form of cultural nationalism rather than a traditionally religious expression. Additionally, in Europe the legitimization of minority religions in the public sphere is even weaker than that of majority religions. This limits their ability to participate as meaningfully in public debate as established religions continue to do some degree (Axner,

2015). Given that the incorporation of religion into nonreligious encounters is generally frowned upon and that recent resurgence of visible religion in Europe has become a cause of tension, rather than celebration, it appears that this environment is not conducive to developing a supportive culture for European Mormons to practice their minority faith. This is particularly the case given the nature of Mormon religiosity, which is recognized as a religion of activity and made visible through proselytization and lifestyle differences.

The Effects of Distinction versus Assimilation

The Church often constructs membership in exclusionary terms with strong boundaries between members and nonmembers, which has led to the Church developing as "a global counter-church, not a world religion" (Beek, 2009). Church discourse "supports and ratifies processes of identity formation that are characterised by oppositional definitions of self, polarised constructions of identity that do not fit in with the notion of a global church. Instead, it defines itself as a global counter-church, set against the world" (Beek, 2009). The Church maintains conservative positions on many aspects of social and family life that are in opposition to mainstream European attitudes toward such matters, and even within the United States, it seems that younger generations of Church membership are rejecting these positions (Riess, 2019). Nowhere is this more evident than in relation to the Church's position on LGBTQ+ members and same-sex marriage. Elder Jeffrey R. Holland, during a speech to BYU's faculty, urged them to engage in more "musket fire" to defend the Church's policy opposing gay relationships (Riess, 2021; Church of Jesus Christ of Latter-day Saints, 2021); this comes after other high-profile incidents that illustrate that the Church is using debates surrounding LGBTQ+ people to enhance its difference from mainstream society. In Europe where same-sex marriage is widely supported and legal in many countries including Ireland, such aggressive comments from senior Church representatives are jarring.

Similarly, research finds that female European Mormons often differ dramatically from US Mormons in their opinions on marriage and dating, education and employment, gender equality, modesty, and sex education (Decoo-Vanwelkenhuysen, 2016). US Mormonism is known in Europe for its "Molly Mormon" stereotypes of Mormon women, associated with the domestic sphere, childrearing, and striving for perfection. In England, Halford (2020) finds that such stereotypes are seen to represent a nineteenth-century pioneer woman, in other words someone quite removed from contemporary English Mormon women. The women of Halford's research confirm Carine Decoo-Vanwelkenhuysen's (2016) findings by distancing themselves from simplistic definitions of womanhood and narrow Molly Mormon ideals, even as they continue to value motherhood and marriage. It seems that as the Church rejects progressive ideals, it commits itself to the slow death of the Church in many parts of Europe, where a rejection of these values inevitably isolates the Church to the fringes of society.

As the sociologist Armand Mauss observed, there is a utility to maintaining strong boundaries between the Church and the rest of society, including from other religions. This ensures its message is clear and memorable, and attracts those seeking something different from the values espoused in the majority society. Ironically, however, the Church in Europe tends to focus on more generic Christian messages such as the atonement of Jesus Christ in Church lessons and publications at the expense of elements of Mormon doctrine that make it unique, such as the Plan of Salvation (Decoo, 1996).[4] This strategy is an eradication of "all the characteristics that could be perceived as too weird or too American" (Rigal-Cellard, 2018, p. 207). I believe that in Europe this strategy is counterproductive. Most converts are familiar with Christian morality already and join the Church seeking something different—seeking doctrines and practices that set the Church apart from other religions that have structured the European experience for centuries.

Why go to such efforts to create a counterculture, only to then present the religion as a generic Christian faith? It appears that the Church is caught between exceptionalism and universalism (Mauss, 1994a, 1994b, 1996a, 2011), which is causing particular difficulties within the European context. Like all social movements, Mormonism needs to sit somewhere between the extremes of assimilation and distinction that might otherwise destroy the movement. This is the joint predicament of "disrepute and respectability" (Mauss, 1989, p. 32). We can view this as a process in which the Church's level of assimilation with the majority society swings forward and back like a pendulum; "the growth and strength of the Church depend on periodic 'course corrections' to maintain an optimum level of cultural tension with the surrounding society, which itself is constantly changing" (Mauss, 2011, p. 21). The Church is caught between these two tendencies but neither appears to be a successful strategy in the European context. By highlighting difference and maintaining strong boundaries, the Church and its members are a target for stigmatization, suspicion, and misunderstanding in a region that has a long and well-developed relationship with key religions that even now dominate social and economic life in many

European countries. Yet, by emphasizing Mormonism's Christianity and doubling down on its self-presentation as the quintessential Christlike church, it offers nothing new to Europe and becomes just another Christian church. Ryan Cragun (2020, p. 838) argues that holding an "'optimum' level of conflict with prevailing social norms may be in the best interest of the Church's survival, if not its possibility to flourish, as a twenty-first-century global religion." Norms vary widely from region to region, however, and it seems that in the European region, the Church is failing at maintaining this "optimum" level of conflict.

The All-American Church in a Global Milieu

There is one aspect of Mormonism that might be particularly attractive to potential US converts in an environment where that society appears increasingly influenced by Christian Nationalism (Whitehead, Perry, & Baker, 2018), and that is the Church's strong doctrinal and cultural ties to the United States itself. Likewise, in parts of the world that admire a US way of life and aspire to US forms of economic success, Mormonism's Americanness can be a significant incentive for conversion. However, in a European context, the all-American nature of the Church becomes one more barrier to acceptability. Correlation centralized control within the United States, and while the Church claims "gospel culture" to be separate from personal, familial, national, or other traditions (Oaks, 2010), it is undoubtedly influenced by the US milieu that created and sustains it. This causes some unintended consequences in the experience of Mormonism internationally. Primarily, this manifests itself in the perception that Mormonism remains a US religion, hindering growth and integration into non-American cultures worldwide (Lobb, 2000; Östman, 2002; Hansen, Noot, & Mema, 2016). The continued US influence has meant that Church publications, doctrines, customs, and even missionaries often hold an inherent US bias. "When the original Salt Lake City product itself is exported to each locale, it does not arrive as a culturally neutral orthodoxy, all ready to be interwoven harmoniously with the local colors" (Mauss, 1996a, p. 15).

Rather, the "gospel of Americanism" (Newton, 1991, p. 10) as the Church goes about "reproducing American colonial dynamics" (Colvin & Brooks, 2018b) often causes "bemusement," "frustration,'" and "spiritual confusion" among members in Europe (Hansen, Noot, & Mema, 2016, p. 315). The Americanism of the Church also alienates nonmembers in Europe who perceive too much difference between Mormonism and the majority culture. An example of this comes from Kim B. Östman's (2002) descriptions of the Finnish media's coverage of an open house for Finland's first Mormon temple. Mormon temples are sacred, associated with specific rituals, and only "worthy" Mormons are eligible for entry. No nonmembers are allowed inside once the temple has been officially opened. Alleviating concerns by nonmembers about secrecy in the temple and its rituals, the Church holds an open house for a short period after the construction of any new temple, to give non-Mormons an opportunity to visit the building.

Östman (2002) analyzed the media coverage of this event to establish the views of the Finnish majority, as represented by the media, toward the Mormon minority. The Finnish reaction to the new Mormon temple predominantly emphasized its US nature. He says, "Some reporters thought the temple felt American due to its architecture and its furnishings" and "the totality was, in one writer's opinion, 'undeniably' American" (Östman, 2002, p. 82). The standardization of almost all aspects of Church life through correlation therefore becomes a kind of "cultural imperialism" (Allen, 1992, p. 14). Östman (2002) notes that "the Mormon Church in Finland has never shaken off its foreign image. . . . The foreign image is, of course, not unique to Mormonism in Finland. Mormonism fights an identity of otherness and foreignness in all new host cultures into which it spreads" (Östman, 2002, p. 75). The other Nordic countries share similar perceptions of the Americanism of Mormonism, "due at least in part to the visibility of its (often American) missionaries and the non-visibility of its local members, who bear no outward signs of being Mormon" (Allen & Östman, 2020, p. 547). I found the difficulties of visibility for local members to be an interesting aspect of my work. As noted by Allen and Östman, if local members are not visible then the religion is presumed to be "foreign." If local members are visibly Mormon, they become an object of curiosity and ridicule. Yet increased visibility for local membership is the only way to challenge assumptions that Mormonism is a foreign faith.

The Church's policy of correlation has raised questions about whether the Church is capable of dealing with the diversity of cultures it encounters internationally, and whether the Church should be willing to adapt itself locally to the particular culture it is attempting to establish itself within (Gedicks, 2011). The inability to adapt to local cultures, the lack of awareness of, or consideration given to, cultural differences in the experience of religion, and the imposition of standardized materials and regulations are part of the explanation for the poor growth and retention of Mormonism in Europe. The tensions between Mormonism and the majority society in Europe as outlined above have led Mauss (2008) to state that "for today's European converts . . . the cost of Church membership is likely to exceed the benefits" (Mauss, 2008, p. 9) and the contemporary experience appears to bear this out.

Using Race to Sustain Commonality in Church Culture

Notably absent from Decoo's (2013b) summary of Mormon culture as incorporating religiosity, morality, family, health, dedication and involvement, education, work, material objects, and lexicon is any mention of race and ethnicity. Yet, Mormonism has had a notoriously troubled relationship with race (Bushman, 2006; Brooks, 2018; Bush, 2018). The *Book of Mormon* and the Mormon temple liturgy explain race by "defining whiteness as evidence of personal righteous-ness and Blackness as evidence of individual selfishness" (Hendrix-Komoto & Stuart, 2020, p. 26), while the Church also infamously maintained a ban on Black men serving the priesthood and on Black men and women entering the temple until 1978. Pressure from increasing numbers of Church members of color in Africa and South America, coupled with growing civil rights discourse within the United States, have been cited as among the reasons for the decision to eradicate these bans (Bowman, 2012). Thus, although the Church has reported the relief felt by Church leadership upon receiving the revelation from God to reverse the ban, it could be suggested that the reversal was also driven by Mormonism's relentless twentieth-century drive for international growth. If global expansion did not require it, would change have arrived when it did? Mormonism's relationship to race, so typically representative of the United States in many ways, is also intimately tied to its internationalization.

The legacy of Mormonism's racial discrimination works with the majority-White influence of its Utah origins, and the effects of this can still be seen today. This history has shaped the development of Mormonism, with Whiteness coming to form part of dominant expressions of Mormon culture (Reeve, 2015; Benally, 2017; Brooks, 2018; Colvin & Brooks, 2018a). The Church also retains fewer African American converts than any other ethnicity within the United States (Young & Gray, 2015, p. 381). In this book, I suggest that the role of Whiteness in Mormon culture is complex, but that it serves to provide a continuity for the Church and its culture during a period of wide-ranging transformation and instability. Like family norms, the use of Whiteness as a cultural tool works to present a coherent and cohesive sense of belonging for contemporary members. The continually constructed history of Mormonism and Whiteness, like many histories, obscures the true complexity of Mormonism's past, which reveals opportunities for Mormonism to have taken a different path away from "the negro doctrine" that ultimately came to so forcefully shape both doctrine and culture (Young & Gray, 2015, p. 363). Nonetheless, the White narrative of Mormonism does function as a significant framework that works to support Mormonism's collective memory and to sustain and stabilize the religion within a broader context of widespread social and economic change.

It is important to note that the role of Whiteness in Mormon collective memory is not something that is only sustained by White people, nor is it something that only White Mormons use to make sense of their Mormon identities, though it is clear that White members approach this culture from a position of privilege that is not accorded to others (Rutter Strickling, 2018). It is also important to emphasize that the place of Whiteness in Mormonism is not historical. Although focused on the experiences of undocumented Mormon Latinas in the United States, Brittany Romanello (2020, p. 14) argues that "racialized hierarchy and differentiated levels of inclusion by race maintain their historical grip in the modern Church as they continue to influence organization, policy, and gendered social relations between Anglo-American members on the one hand and communities of color and migrants on the other," an argument that also applies beyond US borders. As this book will demonstrate, Mormons of all backgrounds continue to move through this culture of Whiteness and use it as a framework within which they can maintain a coherent understanding of what Mormonism is, and who they are in relation to Mormonism.

In Europe, Whiteness is inevitably shaped by colonial understandings of race that makes White privilege invisible at the same time as it exoticizes and undermines those who are not White. Within the Church, Europe has historically held a special meaning that is informed by theological understandings that "Europeans, especially northern Europeans, are literal descendants of the House of Israel and hence heirs to the Kingdom. It is surprising to discover that this 'Blood of Israel' theology, relating to the Lost Ten Tribes, is being taken seriously again as it pertains to the indigenous populations of Europe" (Lobb, 2000, p. 55). Gary Lobb's examination of the future prospects for people of color in the LDS Church in Europe notes that such attitudes have been referenced by Church leaders as late as 1995. Yet, as Lobb (2000, p. 63) observes, Church growth among White Europeans has stalled in many European countries, and baptisms that do occur in Europe are often migrants of color from Africa and Asia: "During interviews with missionaries and mission presidents in all five of the study sample cities, much greater acceptance of the gospel message by minority immigrant groups was reported. Almost all agreed that African immigrants were by far the most accepting of visits, church attendance, and conversion. Tracting is difficult or even futile among indigenous Europeans." The divergence between the construction of Europe as White, and the European trends of baptism among people of color, results in a situation where the Church has defined Europe and European Church membership in ways that bear little relation to actual reality.

Are migrants and people of color living in Europe considered to be "European" in the eyes of the Church? The race and ethnicity of members is not recorded by the Church, but we can look at other sources of data to establish that the European membership is increasingly populated by migrants and by people of color. Irish census data provides evidence of this: 57 percent of Mormons in Ireland reported to be White Irish in 2016 (Central Statistics Office, 2017b). Given that Ireland's latest census is overdue due to COVID-19 constraints and that there have been rapid increases in immigration to Ireland, it is likely that current census figures will come closer to a fifty-fifty split between those in the LDS Church in Ireland who are White Irish and those who are not. This is not uncommon in an era of globalization, and scholars have long emphasized the important role migrants play in the development of their local congregations and in the wider society (Yang & Ebaugh, 2001; Kmec, 2017; Ritter & Kmec, 2017). Gerrie Haar (1998), for example, observes that minority immigrants can make use of religion in their new countries to create upward mobility and foster new connections of belonging, while Phillip Connor (2014) notes how immigrants' faith comes to shape not just their own lives or their congregations, but also the wider society. These experiences seem to be less reflected in Church discourse. When Church leaders speak of the special role for Europe in the Church, are migrants and people of color the people they envisage?

Narratives from church members illuminate more specifically how Whiteness operates within Mormon culture. Moana Uluave-Hafoka (2017) powerfully describes the complexity of life in the United States as a young Mormon from Tonga, an island with a high number of Mormon adherents, which has led to a strong Mormon Tongan community in Utah. She says, "As a child, I learned to be proper, obedient, and submissive to the paintings of the White Jesus that hung in our home" (Uluave-Hafoka, 2017, p. 102). She maintains that Tongan Mormons, both in Tonga and the United States, are pressured in the Church to do as she herself had done. "I was asked to make the same sacrifice as my foremothers had once done: Forget my familial ties. Forsake my ancestral lands and my ancestral tongue. And I did so. Because all the promises of heaven were tied to this" (Uluave-Hafoka, 2017, p. 102). Uluave-Hafoka argues that this forgetting, or perhaps denial, of heritage has consequences. For Mormon Tongans it is to "live on the margins of Mormondom" (Uluave-Hafoka, 2017, p. 104) as a result of "racial, socio economic, and gender discrimination" (Uluave-Hafoka, 2017, p. 103). Uluave-Hafoka experienced a complex interaction of religious, cultural, and national identifications as exemplified by her example of Tongan "tribal tattoos under a white shirt and tie" (Uluave-Hafoka, 2017, p. 103).

As a Latino Mormon, Ignacio García argues that a "cultural Whiteness" remains in the Church in the present day. He says it "remains entrenched in our institutional memory, in our manuals, sometimes in our conference talks, and too often in the deep chambers of our minds and hearts" (García, 2017, p. 4). García's suggestion that Whiteness forms part of the "institutional memory" (2017, p. 4) of Mormonism is reflective of Uluave-Hafoka (2017), who maintains that being Mormon as a Tongan involves a certain "forgetting" of Tongan heritage. Their experiences appear to suggest that within Mormonism, collective memory is constructed to be perhaps simpler than it is in reality. Uluave-Hafoka (2017) found forgetting her Tongan heritage difficult to achieve, yet still expected by the Church in order to put the collective memory of Mormonism in its place.

In many European countries, too, Mormonism continues to be constructed as White (Lobb, 2000) in spite of the diversity of lived experience at a local level that disputes this. In Ireland, as elsewhere, the Church forms a diverse community whose lived reality sits in stark contrast to dominant understandings of the Church as a White, US-focused faith. In Ireland, a nation of little racial and ethnic diversity, the Mormon community shows greater levels of diversity than the majority society it resides within, but nonetheless it remains a majority-White faith in a majority-White country. The following chapters will illumine that like Uluave-Hafoka (2017) and García (2017, 2018), Mormons in Ireland who are not White experience multiplicity and complexity in the management of their Mormon identities, and use Whiteness as defined through Mormon culture as something against which they can position their own racial and religious identities. These experiences must be understood as forming part of Mormonism's challenges in transitioning toward a truly diverse church. There is a strong and critical body of scholarship examining the role of race in global Mormonism, and some of this best work illuminates the experiences of people of color whose voices have until recently been written out of dominant Mormon narratives. However, there is much less scholarship exploring how race is experienced and considered by White Mormons outside of the United States. In this book, I hope to begin to add to this knowledge, by describing how White Mormons feel about Mormonism's relationship to race, far from the Mormon heartland of the Mormon Culture Region.

This chapter has illustrated the relationship between the local and the global within Mormonism in the modern era, with a specific focus on Europe. Outlining Mormonism's challenges in the transition to becoming a global religion emphasizes continuity and discontinuity from US Mormonism, which frames the position of the Church in a European context. This leaves modern Mormonism facing a difficult paradox: how can there be a continuity of faith in the global era without marginalizing those whose backgrounds and experiences differ significantly from the religious traditions the Church is attempting to uphold? The evidence presented here demonstrates that there is no easy answer to that question. The religion may be forced to make more effort to adapt to local cultures to survive in the long term while remaining conscious that much adaptation could cause the religion to lose what makes it unique.

3

They All Seem Very Nice
but It's a Bit Weird Isn't It?

From the Outside Looking In

How do those in Ireland outside of Irish Mormonism view the Church and its members, and how do these perceptions shape Irish Mormon identities?

On a chilly January morning in the Appleby branch after that Sunday's meetings had concluded, I helped to pack up the chairs and put away the hymnbooks. On my way out of the chapel, I had the usual casual conversations with members as we walked along the corridor toward the foyer. On this particular occasion I chatted with David about his project for college and offered to review some of his rough drafts for him to make sure he was on the right track. I made my way out into the foyer, where many people were gathered having conversations before heading home. I was quickly approached by a curious investigator who had met the missionaries earlier that week in town, and at their invitation had attended church for the first time. He asked me if I was doing research at the branch. I knew he already knew that I was, because I had overheard Elder McGuire tell him as much earlier in the day. Nonetheless I tell him that yes, I'm a researcher, and as part of that I am attending church here for six months.

He eagerly asks me what I think of the group, and goes on to ask me a series of questions. There seems to be urgency to his questioning as he furtively looks around us, and it occurred to me that he was trying to gain as much information from me as he could before our private conversation was interrupted. "Do they really not drink or have sex outside of marriage?" he asked me. "Where do the missionaries get the money to go on missions, does the Church pay them?" "Where does the Church get its money from?" and "They all seem very nice but it's a bit weird isn't it?" were just some of the questions I was presented with.

In answering his questions about the funding of the Church, I told him about tithing.[1] He seemed shocked by this, but I have come to know that most Irish people are. Typically, it is not a system they are familiar with and there are not strong traditions for tithing in Ireland or across Western Europe (Pew Research Center, 2018). He asked me what sorts of jobs Church members had; perhaps he was trying to gauge the social class of the average member, or perhaps he was simply wondering how they could afford to give the Church a percentage of their income. I responded that I had encountered people with a wide variety of occupations, everything from cleaners, to teachers, to drivers, to business consultants. Our conversation moved on to what is expected of members in the Church. I tell him that Mormons read the scriptures and pray every day. He nods slowly, telling me that it seems like a very active religion particularly in comparison to Catholicism, "where the priest stands at the top and nobody speaks." He notes that "you would want to be a confident person" to be a member, as you can be called upon to give a prayer at any time. I agree that participation is expected, and tell him that many members develop good public speaking skills because of this.

I sensed that he seemed taken aback by his visit to church, and so I confided in him that I felt very overwhelmed at my own first visit. He was relieved; "yes, me too," he admitted. Those born into the Church, or those whose conversion was many years ago, may not understand this emotional response to something as ordinary as attending a new church. But I understood how this man felt that morning. Many Irish people do not even know someone of another religion, and many may not ever have entered the religious space of another denomination. Such is the ubiquity of Irish Catholicism. I recall so many small aspects of Mormon worship being very alien to me on my own first visit; their clothes, the handshaking, the tiny Sacrament cups of water, the corporate-style architecture of the chapel space, the use of hymnbooks, and, as my co-conversationalist observed, the level of member participation in the service. Cumulatively, to an outsider, the experience can be overwhelming.

It was clear to me that this man approached me due to my status as a nonmember. He saw me as an outsider, like him. He seemed unwilling to ask these questions of the missionaries who accompanied him to church on this morning, but my outsider status made him comfortable asking these things of me—someone who knows the Church but is not a part of the

Church. I was surprised by his very direct and urgent line of questioning, as I had never met him before that moment. However, I was not surprised by his questions, many of which I had fielded before from others outside of church who heard of my research. I learned quickly that many Irish people seem to be intensely curious about the Church. During my fieldwork this manifested itself in questions about missionary life; I found that an encounter with a missionary is often the only form of engagement nonmembers ever have with the Church and they remain curious about missionary life long after their brief interactions on the street have concluded. I was also often asked about polygamy; it appears the Church is unsuccessful in shaking off the reputation of its polygamous past, at least in Ireland. Due to these frequent questions about Mormonism in my everyday life, I was not overly surprised by the man's persistent questioning of me that day. It did serve however, to remind me of my complicated insider/outsider position with regards to Mormonism.

I recount this story of my encounter with the Appleby investigator to illustrate how the Church and its members are viewed from the outside in contemporary Ireland. Though members often like to talk about how theirs is the one true church, or about the values and ideas of Mormonism that frame their worldview, outsiders are often mostly curious about the mundane practicalities of money, family life, and dietary habits. Nonmembers often offer to me something similar to the Appleby investigator's crushing evaluation—"It's a bit weird isn't it?" Understanding how Mormons process the majority Irish Catholic population view of their faith and culture is fundamental to comprehending the experience of life as a religious minority in Ireland. The narratives that follow in this chapter emphasize that Mormons in Ireland of all backgrounds are stigmatized and marginalized from Irish narratives of belonging. As the majority of Mormons in Ireland are White Irish, as is the majority population, they view themselves, and are viewed by others, as *both* insiders and outsiders within their own country. This chapter identifies the Mormon experience with the majority society as one of tension. I illustrate that stereotyping and stigmatization shape the Irish Mormon experience in the everyday and identify the key strategies employed by Mormons in Ireland to manage this fraught minority status.

Proselytizing Mormonism

The missionaries of Appleby and Sweetwater during my time there were all White North Americans, except for one White British woman for a time. Of the missionaries mentioned here, Elder Prince and Sister Ross had been born into the Church, while Sister Fisher had been a convert of just one year before deciding to go out on her mission. They were well placed to provide a unique insight into the religious lives of the majority in Ireland as they were on the streets proselytizing and teaching interested individuals about the Church all day, six days a week. Being North American, they also brought a different perspective to discussions of how the Irish engage with religion. They encountered a wide variety of people from all walks of life. Their stories paint a picture of a majority population that is uninterested in other religions, fearful of change, with a generational gap made up of older active Catholics and younger "cultural Catholics" (Inglis, 2007, p. 215) who are nonpracticing.

Elder Prince was based in Sweetwater during my fieldwork. He spent his days trying to make connections with locals in the Sweetwater area. He noted the patterns he observed: "The ones that are least likely to do anything with what we teach is the older people. Because the Irish Catholic culture is just so ingrained in who they are, I feel they just wouldn't know what to do." During an interview with Sisters Ross and Fisher of Appleby, Sister Fisher told me of her struggles to convert the Irish: "Older people are stuck in their ways, younger people aren't so religious." Identifying that younger people are more likely to display cultural Catholicism, Sister Fisher says, "A lot of people are like 'I'm Catholic' and then you are like 'Oh cool' and ask them the question 'What church do you go to? and they say, 'Oh I don't go' so you always ask them are they practicing or not." Elder Prince commented that "the overall, average conclusion would be that people are ignorant toward spiritual things in general, even Catholic, but even kind of nervous about the Church of Jesus Christ of Latter-day Saints, due to a lack of understanding. I feel that most are just unwilling to listen because they fear change, they fear what others will think, so they make fun of it because of a lack of understanding."

The missionaries are clear that their engagements with the majority are challenging for two opposing reasons. Older active Catholics are happy with their beliefs and hold a strong sense of religious tradition, which precludes them from considering another faith and which buffers them from a "fear of change." The younger generations are nonpracticing or often nonreligious and they have no interest in religion other than identifying with Catholicism as a cultural, rather than a religious, tradition. Both scenarios make the work of conversion difficult for the missionaries:

> SISTER ROSS: Irish people seem just very set in their ways. Very comfortable with their life and they don't really want to step out of their comfort

zone. . . . The most receptive people I think, actually, are people from Nigeria, somewhere like that. Where they are foreigners, they are in a new place, their church might not be here. They are looking for something to believe in, a church to go to, so it's kind of fun to talk with people who are foreigners, I guess.

HAZEL: So do you think it is a cultural thing too?

SISTER ROSS: Yes, it's a cultural thing too. Correct me if I'm wrong but I think with you guys in Ireland, it's not just your religion, but it's your country background, it's your, it's your history, it's a place. I can see how it would be so hard to grow up here, to have that history. . . .

SISTER FISHER: It's a way of life.

Sister Ross demonstrates her own understanding of culture as being the "country background," "history," and sense of "place," showing a clarity that this means something different from religious beliefs and practices. As Americans, the missionaries are perhaps able to observe the Irish from a different perspective. This sense of difference is present in Sister Ross's comments; she uses the phrase "you guys" when speaking to me about the Irish, thereby revealing an awareness of the national differences, which provides her with an outsider perspective on religion and culture in Ireland, as well as demonstrating a conscious awareness of my own Irishness.

Despite the missionaries' struggles to convert the Irish, Catholicism and Mormonism do share many key elements of faith, such as a focus on tradition, family, community, and Jesus Christ, which could make conversion from one to the other an easier process. These commonalities are important to assist in identifying the points of connection and disconnection between Mormonism and Catholicism. In fact, in speaking to missionaries, I came to understand that a key problem they face daily is that some Irish struggle to understand the unique nature of Mormonism. The specifics of doctrine that make Mormonism different, such as sacred temple rituals and the central Mormon doctrine of the Plan of Salvation, are not usually taught to an interested person until they have established a grounding in the religion. This makes it difficult to pique the interest of potential converts at the early stages with any engaging points of difference from Catholicism.

I once sat in on a lesson with Sisters Ross and Fisher while they were teaching an African woman about the Church.[2] Sitting in a less-than-ideal location for a religious lesson—a busy and loud Bagel Factory cafe—I ate lunch with the missionaries and their investigator. The missionaries had intended to conduct their meeting at the local library, but upon arrival we had to change venues due to a water leak that forced the library to close. In addition, the investigator was a half an hour late for the meeting, which left the missionaries under pressure for time to eat before their next appointment, which was a bus ride away.

While we were standing at the counter chatting and waiting for our orders to be taken, I could feel someone staring at me. When I turned to see who it was, I saw a woman in front of us in the queue, who was staring intently at Sister Fisher's missionary badge[3] and looking at her clothes. She caught my eye and gave me a long look before she turned away. I also felt that the two women working behind the cafe counter were very curious about why the Black African investigator (who happened to be wearing bright blue mascara), the two White American sister missionaries (in their missionary garb), and myself (dressed in typical business attire as it was a workday) would all be coming to have lunch together. This feeling of being watched didn't leave me throughout our meeting. Later, when we were praying and talking about Jesus Christ at the table, I felt quite self-conscious about the people seated at the table directly behind me. I was sure they could hear all that we were saying, but I couldn't see them or their reactions. Why did I care? Afterward I came to realize that I am one of those younger cultural Catholics who are deeply uncomfortable with religion being discussed in public places. Our lunch forced me to confront my own assumptions about the place of religion in everyday life.

After the false starts of the library closure, the delayed arrival of the investigator, and the curious stares of onlookers, we eventually sat down to eat. So, surrounded by the lunchtime rush, I observed as the missionaries attempted to introduce the woman to the basics of the religion. We started with a prayer over our food and then the missionaries began talking. Their lesson was on the origins of the Church, establishing what is a prophet, and who Joseph Smith was. Upon leaving, the missionaries gave our new friend a copy of the *Book of Mormon* and a pamphlet of the Plan of Salvation, and they arranged to meet with her later in the week. She seemed to be quite eager to go to church, so they arranged for her to go on Sunday, though when Sunday came I noticed that the missionaries were alone. Just a few weeks after that I was surprised to hear that the investigator had decided to be baptized.

Through observing this lesson, having conversations with the missionaries, being taught a lesson by the missionaries myself (not by Sisters Ross and Fisher, but by their predecessors), and through information gleaned from conversations in Gospel Principles classes, I came to understand how the first few encounters an interested person will have with the missionaries are relatively generic. They are taught about Jesus Christ and told a little about the central messages of the Bible. They will be asked if they accept that Jesus Christ is our savior, and if the interested person agrees with this, then this becomes the building block upon which the specifics of Mormon faith will be slowly introduced over several further lessons. Therefore, an interested person could have had several lessons with missionaries focused upon general Christian teachings, which are not dissimilar from Catholicism.

The effect of this was evident when Sister Fisher tells me about the mainly Catholic people she meets during her proselytizing on the street. She says, "They don't understand, like what the difference is [between Catholicism and Mormonism]. Which is so funny! Because I'm thinking how can you not see a difference?" She recounts the feelings of an older Irish man who is considering joining the Church from Catholicism. He struggles to differentiate Mormonism from the one religion he has lifelong experience of, Catholicism. Sister Fisher tells me that "he sees the churches as all being similar. So, he says, 'Yeah, but as long as I've a good life and I'm a good person, right, God is not gonna be like oh you are a part of this faith or this faith.'" For this gentleman, the denomination of the church he is affiliated with is less important than the need to have a connection to God and live life in the "right" way. In this case, he is following a tradition of belief, where the specific content of that belief is of less value to him than the tradition itself. Here, the traditions of "Irish Catholic culture" (Elder Prince, Sweetwater) are too entrenched for the young missionaries to be able to make much progress with their proselytizing.

A North American I refer to as Mandy who attended the Sweetwater congregation had been in Ireland for about a year when I first met her. She told me that she feels that an awareness of other religions aside from Catholicism is not something she feels even younger Irish people display:

> I think people are almost surprised when someone is not Catholic. . . . I was just getting my hair done a couple of weeks ago, and the girl was washing my hair and she was asking me how old my kids were, and I told her about my son and she said, "Oh, he's doing his First Communion,"[4] and I said, "No, I'm not Catholic" and she said, "Oh! [surprised tone]." Like, it didn't even dawn on her that there might be other religions.

Mandy's anecdote about the hairdresser and the insights from the North American missionaries reveal just how assumed Catholicism is in Ireland, even among the younger generation. It illustrates how the rituals of Catholicism permeate everyday Irish life. It is this context that allows Elder Prince and others to argue that if Mormons are misunderstood, it is through a lack of knowledge, rather than a lack of acceptance of diversity. However, it seems that missionaries face a quadruple challenge when proselytizing in Ireland. First, many people they meet know no other religion than Catholicism, and whether they are practicing or not, they have no desire to find out more about another. Second, some practicing Catholics may be interested in religion more generally, but cannot see the distinction nor the benefits of Mormonism and so are reluctant to move away from the religious traditions that support their entire lives. Third, the Irish are in keeping with those in many European countries in their reluctance to speak about, or practice religion, publicly. For missionaries to proselytize publicly is a significant breach of European cultural norms. Lastly, and as I articulate below, Mormonism is often stigmatized in Ireland. This fact coupled with the existence of those who are antireligious ensures that Mormonism in Ireland is not always met with neutral indifference, but sometimes with violent opposition and strong suspicion.[5]

The Visibility of Difference

Stigma, abuse, or at best indifference from the majority is a regular part of life as a Mormon in Ireland. As the visible face of the Church, the missionaries are often a target for those who don't respect religious difference. Sister Fisher and Sister Ross told me of their negative encounters with the majority. Sister Ross says:

> As soon as they see the badge they say, "Oh no, don't talk to me." And you're trying to skirt around it—I'm wondering, do I have the plague? I'm just trying to give a card to someone once, and I just said, "Hi, how are you?"' and he just looked at me like what the heck? And then I was like, "Oh, I was just going to give you this card," so I took a step, just a tiny bit of a step toward him, and he like, full on like ran away from me and started screaming "GET AWAY."

James in Appleby served a mission abroad when he was younger. He confirms that life as a missionary brings with it a higher level of religious visibility, which might explain the levels of hostility that missionaries, particularly, endure. He says, "When you have badge on and you are dressed up in a suit, that's our identity and people expect that of you."

However, these stories of stigmatization and even abuse were also echoed by many who were not missionaries, and therefore not as visible to the majority. Most had encountered stigma and stereotyping, with some encountering physical violence such as bottle throwing (James, Appleby), being spat at on the street (James, Appleby), and threatening behavior

(Andrei, Sweetwater). Anna, in Sweetwater, tells me of the stereotyping she has experienced:

> I was at a funeral one night, and I was standing in the kitchen. There was one particular woman . . . she said, "So I can't believe you're actually Mormon. I can't believe it." And I just thought, okay, keep your voice down. And she's like "Just, wow! I watched this documentary." . . . She is just like "Oh my gosh you know they're just so weird." And I'm going "No, actually I'm not. I don't think I'm weird." And then I go and I turn around to Louise and I'm like, "Am I? Am I weird?" I don't like doing that to people, but I had to make her feel a little bit uncomfortable because she was coming out with some crazy stuff. "Yeah, they get married really early and they get married when they're like, fifteen" and I just was like, "Well, I don't know that person" and you know, "Actually we don't believe that, so sorry if you think that." You know, it was dreadful.

For her faith to be discussed so publicly and inaccurately without her consent was troubling to Anna. In her telling of the incident above, it is clear she felt objectified, like a curiosity to be stared at. Her pointed question to her friend, "Am I weird?" was designed to make the other person aware of how inappropriate she was, but also reveals how Anna herself was feeling in that moment of the exchange. Anna is a private person who is generally uncomfortable with publicly discussing her faith. In this moment, her faith is made visible. Her narrative also demonstrates the frustration she felt when her attempts to educate the woman about her faith fell on deaf ears.

Stephanie in Appleby is in her twenties and enjoys socializing, but she struggles with her sobriety as a Mormon in a society in which alcohol is often central to social events. She has also had experience of being publicly humiliated due to her faith. She tells me of a night out with friends where her religion was made unexpectedly visible by an acquaintance:

> I remember there was one night we went out for the Twelve Pubs at Christmas [a pub crawl] and I was standing there chatting away, wasn't talking to anyone, nothing had come up about religion at all. And this guy pulled my arm up like this [she raises her arm high in the air] and said, "This is the one with the weird religion," and I was like, "What are you doing?" I was like, "That's so mean." I was so drop-kicked by it that I actually left. I just thought, Why? Why? It's not like I had a *Book of Mormon*. I was just out for a normal night, and that's what I get.

Often, these negative encounters are normal incidents, almost a taken-for-granted part of being a minority religion in a homogenous country. Maura, an elderly woman from Appleby, casually mentioned to me as we walked along a corridor one morning on our way to a Sacrament meeting in the chapel, "People think we are like a cult, you know, but we aren't, we are like a family. We have our ups and downs and get over them. We are just ordinary people." I was struck by the casual way in which the revealing comment was inserted into an otherwise mundane conversation, but for Maura, these experiences form part of her everyday life and are reflected in her everyday discourse.

Maura, Jason, Anna, Stephanie, Elder Prince, and Sisters Fisher and Ross all told me that the Irish were mostly "ignorant" (Elder Prince, Sweetwater) about Mormonism. Most participants were reluctant to outwardly accuse the majority of deliberate discrimination against them, choosing instead to frame negative encounters in a discourse that emphasized the majority's lack of knowledge of Mormonism. Yet, it is also clear that the participants perceive that the majority in Ireland identify them as a minority group that is different. This is despite the reality of life as a Mormon in Ireland, which is often lived as a member of the minority on the basis of religious identity, yet also as a member of the majority on the basis of other characteristics such as Irishness or Whiteness.

It was a sunny spring morning in Sweetwater and about thirty-five people were gathered for a Fast and Testimony Sacrament meeting when David got up to give his testimony. He noted that "many times people who are not religious mock us a lot, especially the media. It is a fashionable thing to mock us, to say that we are so stupid." I found that Church members were painfully aware of how those on the outside perceived them. Suzanne commented during a Sweetwater Relief Society meeting that "when you tell people you are a member of the Church, they might treat you differently. You might lose some people, or they might ridicule you." On another occasion, I was astonished during an evening interview with an Irish woman called Marilyn in her small apartment. I always asked interviewees if they had anything else they wanted to discuss with me that they thought was important to them, or that perhaps I had overlooked. When I asked Marilyn this toward the end of our evening together, she immediately responded:

MARILYN: I know it's difficult because you never read scriptures or anything,[6] but would you kind of think, like would you ever think that I was brainwashed or anything?

HAZEL: No, no definitely not.

MARILYN: No, definitely not? Because you know I came back voluntarily to it.[7]

HAZEL: Like, you make your own decisions. I can see that.

MARILYN: Yeah, and I do know this for a fact. How could they honestly think that two seventeen-, eighteen, or nineteen-year-old young boys could brainwash you? Especially me, at my age and what I've been through. I know the score, I've been around.

HAZEL: Are you afraid that people *think* that your brainwashed?

MARILYN: Well, they've said it to me! Even that girl . . . [she refers to a girl she knows whom she mentioned earlier in our interview]. She says things now and again like "I hate religions." It's a bit ignorant, because she also says she believes in the spirit world and she's seen her [deceased] father. Now if there was nothing afterward, even that statement . . . but she swears she seen her father.

It struck me as poignant that this was what Marilyn felt the need to raise with me when given the opportunity to speak about anything she might like. The exchange speaks to a need for reassurance; an outsider being able to confirm something she already feels in herself, that her belief is authentic and not created through the manipulation of others. She is clearly affected by the negative reputation of the Church, and of how those around her are disdainful about religion.

Jason in Appleby expanded further on why life as a Mormon becomes a form of separation from the majority population: "The changes that are expected—when you come from a society where premarital sex is completely acceptable, there is no question about it, alcohol is completely acceptable, smoking tobacco is maybe less acceptable but still it's okay, and being a Catholic now is no big deal to anyone. So, I think it's just a difficulty of living the standards that makes it difficult. There is a lot expected of Mormons; we have this constant need to be better. To improve, to challenge yourselves, to push forward."

Jason connects conversion to Mormonism with a break with Irish societal values more generally. He told me, "We have a member list in Appleby of, I think it's 203, and we had 70 in church this Sunday. So, the other 130 don't come. And probably will never come again." The answer as to why this is lies in the particularities of the high cost of Mormon membership in a European and/or Irish context. European members must aspire to the same high standards as American membership, but with no social status, minimal societal acceptance, and little community support. I often heard participants express the general idea that "it's hard being a Mormon" (Jason, Appleby), or spoke unprompted of the challenges of being Mormon in Ireland. These comments occurred during interviews, in my conversations with members, or during talks and lessons in church. This indicates that although Irish society may still be Catholic, it is also moving away from traditional Catholic values. Conversion to a high-activity religion such as Mormonism in this context is viewed as a breach of Irish social norms and values.

It should be noted that not everyone felt that they regularly experienced negative responses from the majority population. Although everyone I spoke with who had current or past missionary experience noted that the visibility of missionary life makes them a target, some felt that there was nothing unusual about the responses they received in Ireland, as opposed to elsewhere. Elder and Sister McGuire were a senior missionary couple from North America who were spending a year doing missionary work in Ireland.[8] They noted that they had experienced some negative reactions such as being yelled at, but they observed that they had also experienced some negative reactions at home, too, so this was not something specific to Ireland. Elder McGuire told me, "The bad stories may only be a couple, out of the thousands of good. So it's, we've already decided we like Ireland and we like the people here, and it's different but it's acceptable; it's not bad, it's different."

However, the McGuires appeared to agree with the other missionaries on the issue of the Irish, their complicated relationship with Catholicism, and how that shapes their engagement with all religions, including Mormonism:

ELDER MCGUIRE: From our little view we see people who are, uuummm, not trusting religion anymore. That's kind of the way we, our little diagnosis—they're not trusting religion. Consequently, they don't attend, but many of them we talk to say they believe in God, they still profess to be Catholic or whatever religion they are, but they don't attend and they even say "We're not happy with it." And yet they're not interested in hearing about something else. So they're such a, they're very steeped in the tradition of Catholicism or whatever, they're very steeped in that, and they're dissatisfied but they still cling to that as their religion. As far as living with their religion, we've talked about that a little bit with them and we feel like from the small conversations that we get, that they still pray—some of them—but not a lot. They still have a belief in God, as I mentioned, and it's interesting to watch, to see that there's this distancing from *church*. [Elder McGuire uses the air quotes gesture as he says the word "church."]

HAZEL: I was wondering is the answer to that—the distancing from religion yet unwillingness to give it up—related to the fact that Catholicism is interacting with national identity, that it has become a thing that to be Irish you must be Catholic?

SISTER MCGUIRE: Mmm hmmm [nods in agreement].

ELDER MCGUIRE: I think you hit the nail on the head. I think that's a big thing.

Despite this marginalization, Mormons in Ireland are also expected by the majority to "perform" an active religiosity, and are defined by their faith by others in Irish society. As Stephanie's experience in the pub shows, a Mormon identity becomes a master status that obscures other pertinent aspects of that individual's identity. In informal conversations in church and during social events, participants told me how others in Irish society police their behavior; they are scolded for cursing or questioned about why they aren't at church. Jason has experienced chastisement for both of these breaches of behavior. He expresses his frustration by saying, "If they expect me to be a Mormon all the time, and they class me as a Mormon and their view of me is as a Mormon, then that's all I am. I'm also Irish, I'm also doing research, I'm also obsessed with computer games, you know? So, Mormonism is just one part of who I am."

Maureen in Appleby told me during our interview about how her work colleagues police her actions based on their perception of her as a Mormon: "He [a colleague] was after bringing us in a box of sweets, and they were liqueurs and they were beside the photocopier . . . and I picked up a liqueur and ate it and he says, 'You'll have to tell them on Sunday about that,' and I said, 'Huh?' and he said, 'You're not supposed to be eating them, there's drink [alcohol] in them, you'll have to tell that on Sunday,' and I started laughing because I had never spoken to him about the Church, you know?" Although Maureen told me this anecdote to exemplify how her religious identity is policed by Irish society, it occurred to me that it was also a good example of how Catholicism is the lens through which Irish people view all religions. By mentioning twice that Maureen would "have to tell" her church about eating something containing alcohol, her colleague obliquely referenced the Catholic sacrament of penance; someone confesses their sins to the priest in order to be absolved. Later, she tells me another anecdote about her work colleagues that referenced the common Mormon abstention from tea, coffee, and alcohol in obedience to the Church's health code called the Word of Wisdom (Doctrine and Covenants, 89, 1–21). "I brought back in a cup of hot chocolate but the paper cup it was in said 'coffee' and I put it down on the desk and Sheila comes over and she looks at it and she says, 'Maureen Murphy, are you drinking coffee?' and I said, 'No, it's hot chocolate' and she says, 'Oh, that's all right.'"

Maureen's husband, John, also tells me that he has been chastised for eating meat, as some mistakenly believe Mormons are vegetarians and are concerned that he has breached his religious obligations. The Word of Wisdom does specify that meat should be eaten "sparingly," which could explain where this misconception springs from, though I very much doubt most Irish people are familiar with the precise wording of the Word of Wisdom, or in fact with the document at all. Given the lack of general knowledge of

Mormonism by the public in Ireland, it is more likely that this misconception actually springs from confusing Mormonism with some other small religious minority. The participants and I often swapped stories of how our explanations of Mormonism had often caused confusion when others imagined we were speaking of religious groups such as the Jehovah's Witnesses or Mennonites, both of whom had a presence in Appleby, while the Jehovah's Witnesses were also well established in Sweetwater. In fact, I once had an amusing exchange with two Jehovah's Witnesses missionaries on my doorstep, when I happened to mention that I was researching Irish Mormonism. "Why didn't you choose us?!" the more senior-looking gentleman exclaimed with genuine resentment.

Maureen's, John's, and Jason's experiences show that being a Mormon is viewed as a master identity by the majority society. They demonstrate that there is an expectation among the majority in Ireland regarding the behavior of religious minorities, and that when those expectations are breached, Mormons experience judgment from the majority for not performing their religious role correctly. Given the growing number of cultural Catholics in Ireland, this policing of the religious behavior of other religions is interesting. It illustrates that although increasing numbers of Irish are less religious than in previous generations, they are still very familiar with the active adherence that normally accompanies religious belief and are quick to enforce it on others whom they consider more religious than themselves. From the comments of Suzanne and David and the experiences of John and Maureen, it is apparent that members are conscious of their break with Irish religious tradition, and they experience life as Mormon converts in Ireland as one of difference from the majority. This is despite of a continuity from Catholicism to Mormonism based upon family and Jesus Christ, which might be thought to ease such disruptions.

Strategies to Live By

Given the challenges of life as a religious minority, we can expect that adherents will create strategies to manage their complex position. Olivia Cosgrove (2013) identified that strategies used by Irish religious minorities for coping with the perceptions of the majority are mostly centered around concealment. This is evident in my research through participants' discussions of religion within the educational system. Most participants who spoke to me about their own or their children's education told me that given the religious nature of Irish education they will invariably be pushed into a public disclosure of their faith, or encounter circumstances where they feel it becomes a relevant point of discussion. This is the case even where those individuals feel generally that they would prefer to be quiet about their religion.

For Anna in Sweetwater, her dealings with her children's schools reflect her position generally on managing her religious identity. She tries at all costs to avoid discussing her religion for a fear of negative reactions. She tells me, "I don't go out of my way to talk about it. Because then it's kind of like, 'she rams her religion down people's throats.' You are always, even when you're trying to be nice about it, and they are the ones asking the questions. I'll just give yes or no answers if I'm asked usually." Anna's quiet strategy in navigating her own religious identity is reflected in her management of her children's religious identities within their Catholic schools: "I didn't tell them what we were, to be honest with you. Because I just didn't want the, you know, 'they have more than one wife, they're from Utah,' you know, the usual. So, I just said, 'No, we are just a different religion, we're just not Catholic.' I left it like that for ages and ages. I don't go out of my way to tell people. If they ask I will tell them, but I don't go out of my way." Anna's position reflects many of the themes that recur when Mormons in Ireland discuss how their identity is managed in public spaces. Fear of others' reactions, anticipating negative stereotyping, and a desire to stay quiet unless it is directly addressed are almost universal experiences in the management of a Mormon identity in Ireland. Many Mormons in Ireland such as Anna are Irish of many generations, and many have converted from Catholicism. Therefore, they have a preexisting natural familiarity with the subtle indicators of belonging, which perhaps allows them to pass more easily than non-Irish Mormons.

Another key social space in which members confront their own identities is within the workplace. Many who spoke with me about the intersections of religion and employment were clear that they did not see the workplace as an appropriate space to begin a conversation about religion. For example, Maureen joked with me, "We don't really go around asking people what they think." Work can become a site where religious identities are hidden, both consciously and unconsciously. In contrast to Irish schools, the workplace tends to be seen by the participants of this research as a secular space. Many, such as North American Chase, told me that they felt they were more easily able to hide or downplay their religious beliefs should they want to. Chase is a successful business consultant in his forties who was born into the Church. His employment causes him to relocate with his family across the globe every few years. During my time in Sweetwater, he and his wife Abbey were living a few miles away, although they have since moved abroad once more. In church every Sunday, Chase epitomized the clean-cut image of a confident, successful Mormon, and was very popular within the congregation due to his cheerfulness and outgoing nature. During our interview, held in his large sprawling home in one of the wealthiest parts of Dublin, a more cautious and less confident Chase emerged during discussions of how he managed his Mormon identity outside of church:

> If I'm somewhere on business and I don't want religion to come into things, and they'd ask me if I want something to drink, sometimes I don't make a big deal, I don't drink but I won't say it's about religion I'll say, "I just don't drink for health reasons" or whatever. But I don't always have to bring it up—"No, because I'm Mormon," which probably I should do all the time. But I weigh it, I don't know. It depends. If I want to make it an issue, I can. If I don't want to make an issue, I don't.

For many Mormons, then, the workplace is not constructed as a religious space. Their religiosity becomes mainly privatized, and the decision to make it public is very much dependent on context. Like Anna, Chase is careful about how he addresses his religion and, depending on the context, he will hide his religious identity, particularly when on business. This privatization of religious identity causes a paradox to emerge. The hegemony of Catholicism in Irish everyday life continues unchallenged, as alternative expressions of religiosity that could challenge such dominance are hidden.

As Cosgrove's (2013) research has identified, members of minority religions will sometimes choose to explicitly reveal their religious identity, though this is less common than strategies of concealment. Jason in Appleby is one such example of how revealing strategies operate. Jason is quiet about his faith in most circumstances. He says, "I wouldn't be starting a conversation [about religion] because I pretty much know people's opinions and I know the difference so I wouldn't be starting a conversation to voice my own opinions."

However, Jason decided to take a more open approach in his relationship with the educational system, precipitated by the way in which he felt his child's faith was not being accommodated appropriately by the Catholic school that his son attended:

> JASON: We had our oldest son in a Catholic school, a local small rural school and we had a lot of difficulties. . . . In primary school religion goes throughout the day, prayers, and preparations for the sacraments, holidays and celebrations . . . it's everywhere. When his class were preparing for Easter, the whole class had to go over to the local chapel and decorate the place and learn the hymns and all that. So, we would try to

get them to disengage, to not be teaching our son, and they just could not let him. It just wasn't physically possible.

HAZEL: Were they used to dealing with children of different religions?

JASON: They really were, they really were. I think there were, there was a couple of Muslims in the class with dark skin, so they were treated much differently because they were seen as an ethnic minority, so they [the school authorities] went out of their way. Because we were White Irish from a different background, they just . . . it would be ignored. . . . If you want to be anonymous, it's easy. If you want to be different and not make a fuss about it, it's okay. But if you want to make a fuss about it, there is resistance because you are not that different.

HAZEL: And is it important to make a fuss about it? Is it important that he is able to have an active identity as a Latter-Day Saint and not have that minimized?

JASON: Well, for us in the school, it was. Because our concern is that we are teaching him what we believe at home, and he is being taught separate beliefs in school and he's being confused.

Jason and his wife, Catherine, were so upset by their experiences that Jason's wife became heavily involved with the establishment of a new multidenominational school in their local area, and their second child attended primary school in that new school.

Jason's experience is reflective of the complexity of managing religious pluralism in modernity as described by Grace Davie (2000, 2014). In noting tendencies within Europe to welcome ethnic diversity while rejecting religious diversity, Davie (2014, p. 616) reminds us that "the management of ethnic pluralism overlaps with the management of religious pluralism but is not coterminous with it." In Jason's case, he maintains that his son's White Irish identity prevented an understanding of his religious difference in a way that his classmates who were also of a minority faith, but were not White, did not experience. Yet, the ability of the White Irish participants of this research to choose when and how to reveal or conceal their religious identity illustrates a White privilege that other religious minorities in Ireland may not experience.

Despite the generally invisible nature of religious identity within the workplace and other spaces, there are cases where this is revealed by choice or by necessity. This can be seen in the case of Sue, a second-generation Mormon who is one of the only Mormon schoolteachers in the country. Sue teaches in a Catholic school, and must provide Catholic religious teaching as a necessary part of her employment. Her employers and some of the inspectors who evaluate her teaching are aware of her religious status. Sue deliberately ensures that her teaching of religion is exemplary, because she feels vulnerable due to her religious difference: "It's just when I know I'm different I don't want anyone to come back and say, "You never taught religion because you are . . ." You know what I mean? I always, that box is always ticked for me. And I'm one of the first ones to go to the principal and say, "Look we are coming into Lent, we should be going to Mass at least once a week now here."" Wendy Cadge and Emily Sigalow (2013) have observed two strategies used by healthcare chaplains when working in US hospitals with patients and families of a different faith to themselves. They identify "neutralizing" (2013, p. 151) as a way to speak of spirituality in broad terms, and to focus on the commonalities of the different faiths. They identify "code-switching" (2013, p. 151) as switching between the religious language, rituals, and practices of the people whom they work with. Sue utilizes both strategies in her work: neutralizing, by focusing on what Mormonism and Catholicism have in common with each other, and code switching, by familiarizing herself with the language and practices of Catholicism through an explicit embrace of the majority religion that surrounds her.

Sue tries to adapt her own positive experiences of her Mormon faith into her Catholic teaching practice. In one example, she created "Pope-Watch," a teaching tool designed to pique the children's interest in the election of a new pope:

> I was recording at home [on the TV] what was going on, because the different color smoke for when the pope was elected. And this is back in the days of videos, and we'd watch ten minutes of the video of the wrong-color smoke coming up, and then they'd see the change and they were all excited. Like, my religion would be important for me, and I do what I can to make religion important for them, regardless of what that religion is. Because there is going to be times in their lives they are going to need it.

For Sue, the contours of her religious difference are made visible through her work, and she manages this through an embrace of the majority religion that surrounds her. Sue describes this approach, including the management of her own children's education within Catholic schools, as "pragmatic."

Whereas Sue's strategy of engagement with a Catholic educational system has been to embrace the elements she feels she can adopt, Jason's strategy has been more combative, arising from a sense of exclusion and inequality that he struggles to ignore. Sue is a second-generation Mormon, who has experienced being the outsider all her life. Her sister mentioned to me in church one day that they "know no different" than being Mormon in a Catholic majority country. Jason converted to Mormonism as a teenager and so has not had such experiences all his life. His son's very different experiences of religion in school are a source of frustration to him, and may explain why he has chosen to engage with the Catholic school system in such a different way than Sue has.

Religion is always experienced in conversation with the wider cultural landscape within which it sits. The narratives of this chapter have demonstrated that Irish Mormonism is molded by its relationship to Irish Catholic society, and even more specifically, it is shaped by Irish society's changing relationship to Catholicism. The missionaries who generously allowed me to accompany them around town and to interview them about their experiences, and who taught me general introductory lessons about Mormonism, see four ways in which Catholicism continues to shape Irish understandings of all religions:

1. Some Irish people, predominantly the elderly, are comfortable in their Catholic faith and have no interest in, or are even suspicious of, other religions.
2. Some Irish people, predominantly younger people, have negative opinions about all religions due to their relationship with Catholicism.
3. Some Irish people are curious about other religions but see no major differences between Catholicism and Mormonism and prefer to stay within the safety of what is known, rather than convert to the unknown.
4. Recruitment to Mormonism in Ireland is often most successful within immigrant communities, as they are already marginalized in Irish society and are not influenced by the Irish Catholic cultural milieu to the same degree as the Irish.

The Mormon experience with the majority society is one of tension, and attitudes toward Mormonism in Ireland could be best described as cool. Mormons in Ireland engage in a complex and nuanced system of strategic revealing and concealing of their religious identities, in direct response to the fear they have developed of the response of others toward their religion. To me, a typical cultural Catholic who was never exposed to strict patterns of religious practice as a child and who now identifies as an atheist, this seems exhausting. Being Mormon in Ireland involves a constant evaluation of context and circumstance in order to decide how much or how little to reveal of oneself, and in what way this should be achieved.

My time in Appleby and Sweetwater has shown me that I share the experience of the majority in Ireland: those for whom religion doesn't come up in everyday conversation because there is no need for it to. I have learned from the Mormons I spoke with that they do not see the world this way, however. For them, there will often be circumstances where their religious identity *must* be revealed, whether because of their child's schooling, or their sobriety, or their inexplicable unavailability on all Sunday mornings. Additionally, some Mormons *want* to bring up their religion in everyday conversation because it is a part of who they are; it matters to them. Both scenarios are fraught with the difficulties and delicacies of being a minority religion in a homogenous country that has become suspicious of religiosity.

4

Their Ancestors Are Watching Them

A Family Tragedy

"In the European setting, whether or not a family is 'religious' it is almost always seen as a tragedy for a family member to join the LDS church" (Decoo, 1996, p. 102). Why is it that conversion to Mormonism has become a modern family tragedy? How could conversion to a famously family-orientated religion be considered as a threat to family? Why do these experiences seem particularly pronounced in a European setting? The answer, it seems, is based upon competing interpretations of family tradition and ancestry. In Ireland, families often position themselves within a lineage of an Irish Catholicism so intertwined that to leave Catholicism is to leave a part of Ireland behind also. The emotive responses toward Mormon conversion in Ireland reflect contested understandings within family groups regarding the "chain of belief" of that family.

The continuance of a chain of belief transmitted through and shaped by the family is strong within Mormonism. This is achieved through marrying a fellow Mormon, raising children within the Church, and conducting religious family rituals, which ensure the continuance of a Mormon family in the afterlife. At the heart of this framework are ideas of connectedness and community. Through a continuity of religious traditions transmitted through the family, Mormons maintain connections to each other and to relatives both past and future. Mormon families, therefore, work to maintain community and tradition across temporal boundaries. Mormon identity itself is underpinned through idioms of kinship and descent, particularly Mormon interconnections among time, space, and family. In an argument reminiscent of Danièle Hervieu-Léger (2000), Fenella Cannell (2013b, p. 12) says that "time and space re-arrange themselves in the experience of the person," which culminates in an "endlessly linked sequence of human generations." This outlook on temporality, kinship, and identity demonstrate how Mormonism succeeds in maintaining tradition in the chaos of modernity. Hervieu-Léger (2000) argues that given the fragmented conditions of modernity, continuity of this kind becomes more difficult to achieve. Yet modern Mormonism is broadly successful in maintaining core traditions that have supported a common understanding of the collective. This common understanding incorporates a sense of connection across time from past to future, and simultaneously across spiritual and temporal worlds, between the living and the dead. This worldview is central to the maintenance of a strong collective Mormon identity, particularly in regions such as Europe where the Church does not have a wider cultural acceptance to support new members in their conversion. Such strong distinctions from the majority, however, inevitably lead to exclusion. The centrality of Mormon doctrine on family also reinforces a sense that a convert must choose which interpretation of family they align themselves with—their tightly defined Irish Catholic family or a Mormon family whose boundaries are more wide-ranging and complex.

In this chapter I interrogate the experience of such conceptions of family and community within an Irish context. This is with a view to illuminating why families who are culturally and geographically distant from the Mormon heartland might react so viciously to conversion. The LDS Church in Ireland is small yet multinational and diverse, as in many European countries. This means that many Mormons in Ireland struggle to marry and raise children with a fellow Irish Mormon. Mormons in Ireland, as elsewhere in Europe, often must negotiate a family life that is divided along religious lines, as "part-member" families. At the same time, converts from Catholicism are often thought to have breached family and national loyalties through their conversion, and some cope with ongoing guilt about such perceptions. In this environment, it becomes apparent that Mormons in Ireland have particular challenges to overcome in their attempts to maintain a continuity of Mormon tradition of family.

Competing Ancestries

Doctrine plays a foundational role in the formation of Mormon beliefs regarding the role of kinship in salvation. During fieldwork, I learned this worldview through a process of trial and error, making assumptions about what phrases like "the eternal family" might mean from a Mormon perspective, and checking my assumptions with others through interviews and conversations with friends from church. Over time, I came to have a strong understanding about how Mormon doctrine on the afterlife and Mormon ideals of family here on earth are intertwined. Within the Plan of Salvation, all people are brothers and sisters to each other, even those outside the Church. It is for this reason that in church members often refer to each other as "Brother" or "Sister," particularly in more formal contexts. So strong is this belief of a family connection to God and to all others that during fieldwork I rarely heard members of the congregations use the word "God" in church or outside of it. Instead, Mormons refer to their God as "Heavenly Father" and to Jesus Christ as their "brother," as this reflects their true familial relationship to them. "He is Heavenly Father; he wants his family to be back with him. Otherwise we would just call him God" (Jeremiah, Appleby). This worldview has been described as a "doctrinal kinship" (Davies, 2010, p. 175), a form of family supported by Church doctrine that is essential for salvation according to Mormon belief. Members frequently remind themselves of the significance of doctrinal kinship (Davies, 2010, p. 175) as can be seen in this comment from a young European convert I have named Stella during a talk she gave during a Sacrament meeting in Sweetwater. She said: "When you realize you are a child of God—do you *really* know it? Is it something we really integrate within our personality and identity? A lot of things identify us—birth, ethnicity, nationality, hobbies— but true and steadfastness is being a child of God. It is essential that our permanent self is as a child of God." The message Stella offers here illustrates an attitude often presented to me during my time with the two congregations. Being Heavenly Father's spirit child is the key to who we are, and that knowledge should shape our entire selves, and go beyond any other differences between us.

Sacrament talks each Sunday serve as an important public declaration of faith. Giving talks is a central part of the ordinary Mormon experience (Shipps, 2006; Cannell, 2013a). For new members, their first talk can be a watershed moment, the point at which they realize that they have been recognized as a true member. In Appleby, a new convert I have named Ruby was open in expressing her nerves when she got up to give her first talk on the topic of "Following Christ" during a Sacrament meeting early in my fieldwork. Ruby said, "I was having a panic attack during the week thinking about speaking and wanted to make up some excuse that I was sick so that I wouldn't have to do it, but I realize that this is what I have to do, that there is a reason that I was asked to do it." For many, listening to and giving talks is a way to support each other in their faith. John Murphy observed that "what the speakers do is uplift us and send us home with a better spirit." Typical talks by members would be on topics such as the temple, eternal families, developing a testimony, or the atonement. Many members use the opportunity of giving a talk to make connections between Church doctrine on family and their lived experiences of family in their personal lives. I found that it was often through giving and listening to talks that members made sense of their family lives and created a narrative that helped them to support their faith.

Ron is an Irish convert in his fifties. I came to understand his perspectives on God and family through a Sacrament talk which he gave on an otherwise dreary, dark, and damp winter morning in Appleby. After we had all shuffled into the chapel, greeted each other, and settled down, he first told the congregation of the importance of maintaining active relationships with his three adult children. He tells us that when his children were small,

> Every Saturday . . . I would make breakfast. We used to make pancakes and it was messy. Egg, flour everywhere. We would sit and eat until we were about to burst. To this day it is still one of the best things I remember from when the kids were small. Pancake Saturday. Daddy Day. Even now I still am conscious to make time for my daughter and sons. If a new restaurant gets recommended to us, we will go together, for instance. It gives me a comprehension of them as adults I wouldn't have otherwise.

He continues by using his good relationship with his children as a model for his own relationship with his Heavenly Father:

> I do pray, don't get me wrong; when I'm driving, I speak to Heavenly Father in heaven but I can't say that I've ever prayed all day and all night. Sometimes I have to work away from home. I text and phone the kids and my wife but come Friday I just want to be at home and spend time with my family. Heavenly Father understands that sometimes our prayers are like a text message, but we have to make sure we get to spend some time together too. So, remember to keep holy the Sabbath day. It is our Daddy-Daughter/Son Day. It is our date with Dad.

Ron's words helped me to understand how Mormon family relationships move beyond the physical world to incorporate an ongoing relationship with the spirit world, which includes an active familial relationship with God as "Heavenly Father." Stella, Ron, and Jeremiah all testified to a personal relationship with God. Jeremiah's comment above, which was thrown into an otherwise mundane discussion during a Sunday School meeting, shows that he feels as though he understands what Heavenly Father is thinking: "He wants his family to be back with him." Ron's Sacrament talk shows how he engages in running conversations with Heavenly Father. This notion of a real fatherly figure, with whom one has a true understanding and a personal relationship, is at the core of Mormon understanding of the spiritual family, and God's place in it.

In Stella's same talk in Sacrament meeting in Sweetwater she continued to explain her perspective: "I know that I am a child of God. I know we are here for development and improvement. I know that the Plan of Salvation was created for us, and we can now better understand our potential. The Church gives me power, hope, and strength. It gives me comfort—no matter what I am an eternal being. I want my future children to know that too." Stella argues that the Plan of Salvation assists her in her understanding of her eternal existence. Her reference to her future children despite being childfree and single at the time of her talk demonstrates how assumed a lineage of belief is within Mormonism, even for converts who have no previous generations of Mormonism within their families. Stella, a convert to Mormonism, does not doubt that her future generations will share the same worldview as herself, and in doing so, she places herself within a complex web of kinship connections based on faith, which stretches toward an imagined future.

Within Mormonism, achieving heterosexual marriage and children is built into Mormon doctrine as essential for earning the highest rewards in the Mormon afterlife: "For Mormons, heaven comprises three degrees of glory; the highest of these, the celestial kingdom, comprises three heavens, the highest of which is exaltation. While all others will be single, those who are exalted will live with their families, while husbands and wives continue to increase their posterity. The reward of living in an eternal family is not simply a hope but rather is embedded in Mormon theology and temple ordinances Mormons believe are essential for exaltation" (Daynes, 2015, p. 334). Genealogy work, facilitated by the Church's Family History database, is an important part of what Church members describe as "family history work." This is work necessary to be completed before a deceased person's name can be brought to temple to be baptized by proxy in a temple ritual called "baptism for the dead." Through genealogy work, members identify ancestors and work to take those names to the temple to be baptized into the Church vicariously. The purpose of this is to ensure that all family, living and deceased, have the opportunity of full salvation and will be connected to each other through the faith for eternity (Davies, 2000). The Church has been accused of baptizing people posthumously against their will through baptisms for the dead. The Church's explanation of its intentions in this regard is as follows: "Each individual has agency, or the right to choose. The validity of a baptism for the dead depends on the deceased person accepting it and choosing to accept and follow the Savior while residing in the spirit world. The names of deceased persons are not added to the membership records of the Church" (Church of Jesus Christ of Latter-day Saints, n.d.-a). Nonetheless, baptism for the dead is often perceived by nonmembers as an unusual and controversial practice, especially in countries with little knowledge of Mormonism. This serves as a clear boundary marker between Mormonism and the majority society, and between Mormonism and other religions, as the ritual is unique to Mormonism.

Members spend much time tracing family trees, recording ancestral history that might otherwise be lost, and sourcing ancestral names for baptism, described as being "rites of salvation for kinsfolk" (Davies, 2010, p. 180). Family history therefore becomes a spiritual practice in which active connections with deceased family are maintained. Genealogical research can be seen as providing an "opportunity enough for a sense of the other world to impinge upon this one" (Davies, 2003, p. 103). Anna, a convert from Catholicism, explained to me why baptism for the dead and its associated genealogical work is so important. She says of its purpose:

> Nobody will be lost. It's that chain. That's why family history is so important, because it's the idea that nobody will be left out. So, everybody will be linked. There are people in the Church who can go back to emperors and stuff in their families. It's so that nobody will be lost, everyone will be together. I don't have the family history bug, I don't have that, you know, people go off to find their ancestors. Like my mother-in-law, she's a genealogist, that's what she does. From morning till night. That's what she does, finding people for people. But yeah, it is that idea that nobody will be lost, the human race will all be together regardless of where they are or what they're doing.

Despite admitting that she doesn't have the family history "bug," genealogy work is clearly still an important part of faith and life for Anna. For her, family history provides an assurance that the "chain" to which everyone is connected is sustained. Each generation must be gathered through research and ritual so that they can be linked to all the generations that came before them, and who will come after them. Anna's frequent description of ancestors being "lost" unless this work is completed for them illustrates the importance for Mormons of ancestral remembrance. By researching and conducting rituals on their behalf, previous generations are recalled and cease to be past, but present. Anna tells me: "The spirit world is right here. I mean that I do have a surety of. Definitely. They are right here. They are here everywhere . . . people don't think about it at all which really bothers me sometimes. I mean we're not just here [gestures in front of her], and the spirit world is not just here [gestures across the room], and heaven is not just here [gestures elsewhere again]. Like, it is *all* here. That's why people feel that their ancestors are watching them." This description illustrates a worldview in which the spheres of the living and the dead are not delineated and are actively engaged with one another. These understandings of family illustrate that for Mormonism, "baptism for the dead operates with an eye to an afterlife realm in which the deceased are conscious and aware of what is being done or not being done for them on earth" (Davies, 2003, p. 96).

Meredith is a middle-aged woman originally from South America but now based in Ireland for some years with her husband, David. During a talk on the topic of family history work in a Sacrament meeting in Sweetwater, she emphasized that genealogy work will have temporal benefits for the living as well as spiritual benefits for the dead. She says of doing family history, "If we start that work, we will get the strength to do more. Finding families is work for us here. Family history is a way to fortify our family here on earth. Parents can involve the kids. If we struggle with computers, we can involve the kids, making it a family thing." From this perspective, family history work benefits the living who have an opportunity to strengthen existing familial relationships through such work.

In Appleby, Jeremiah echoed Meredith's perspective during a Sunday School lesson, when he emphasized the mutual dependency between the living and dead that sits at the heart of Mormon doctrine of salvation. He mused, "In relation to ordinances for the dead, we can't be saved without them [the dead] and they can't be saved without us." Per Mormon beliefs, only baptized Mormons can reach the highest levels of heaven, and Jeremiah illustrates his understandings of this in his observation that the dead are reliant on the living for salvation through the ritual of baptisms for the dead. Furthermore, conducting family history work and baptisms for the dead is a key part of achieving the Plan of Salvation, and so Jeremiah's observation that the living are dependent on the dead for their own salvation also shows his understanding of the complexity of the interconnections between living and dead. Jeremiah, like Meredith, understands the interdependency at the heart of these relationships. Like Anna, Jeremiah and Meredith do not envision the dead as separated from their own existence. In completing family history work, they bring the dead back into the temporal world and ignite a personal relationship with them. Thus, we can see a "dynamic interplay between the living and the dead in a theology that pervades several aspects of everyday LDS life" (Davies, 2003, p. 96).

Anna's description of Mormon genealogy as being a "chain" and the understandings expressed by Meredith and Jeremiah are useful for illustrating the relevancy of the theoretical analysis of this book. By valuing genealogy and associated temple rituals, Mormon families in Ireland deliberately support a familial chain of belief that disrupts conventional concepts of time. Formalizing this chain through baptisms for the dead both increases the numbers of family who are spiritually connected and enhances those connections. Mormon genealogy therefore represents a continuity of religious Mormon tradition, which is maintained through the family. Additionally, converts from Catholicism to Mormonism such as Anna baptize their *Catholic* ancestors into Mormonism through the work of family history and baptisms for the dead. They are symbolically rupturing an Irish Catholic continuity through time in order to create a new Mormon continuity in its place.

Anna originally comes from a traditional Irish Catholic family. Her large family lived in a rural part of Ireland with a strong farming heritage, and her parents are lifelong and devout active Catholics who are immersed in their local parish. Yet, she also tells me that many family members now exhibit a passive form of Catholicism that she struggles to understand. Many of her siblings do not attend Mass yet they baptize their children into Catholicism and have them participate in the Catholic sacrament of First Communion. She says this behavior "drives me demented. Sorry, but it drives me crazy." Of Mormonism, she tells me, "Family is crucial, the traditional family, that is what the Church is based on. That's what I love about it, to be honest." The frustration with her Catholic family's lack of active participation and her preference for a traditional family focus within faith might explain why it is that Mormonism became so attractive for Anna. In modern Ireland, the Mormon version of family has in some ways become what the traditional Catholic family used to be, with an emphasis on traditional gender roles and conservative attitudes toward sexuality incorporating no sex outside of marriage and a rejection of same-sex marriage. In this way, family can be said to be a key commonality between modern Irish Mormonism and traditional Irish Catholicism.

Anna's experiences of her own baptism into Mormonism further demonstrates this perspective. She articulates how conscious she was about betraying her Irish Catholic ancestors through her conversion to Mormonism:

> On my baptism day, I was crying outside the church because I thought they are all going to turn in their graves, all the ancestors who died for

Ireland and all that kind of stuff. They are all gonna think because I was turning my back, and then I thought, I'm not turning my back on being Irish, you know I can be Irish, and I can be Mormon. It can be done. But it was very hard for me. That part of it was. I found that part really hard.

In Anna's mind at that time, she was leaving one family to begin another. It took her some time to reconcile her membership of the wider Mormon family with her ongoing relationship with her Irish Catholic heritage. Her narrative speaks of her trying to convince herself that such a reconciliation "can be done," and that her Mormonism does not represent a rejection of her Irishness.

Yet, there is no doubt that the differences between the faiths also serve as a point of separation. Jason in Appleby says of Irish Mormons, "When you think about it every person who was baptized, unless they grew up in the Church, they are pioneers. They are moral pioneers. They are doing something that no one else has done in their family." Jason's mention of pioneers is not accidental. Here, he invokes the Mormon lineage of the original pioneers who trekked to Utah to avoid persecution and to create Zion in the nineteenth century (Eliason, 2002; Shipps, 2006; Bowman, 2012; Patterson, 2016). Although his use of the term within the context of Irish converts from Catholicism to Mormonism implies a rupture, a group who are breaking away from old traditions to create something new, his use of that specific phrase also draws connections to a Mormon founding narrative. Thus, through his use of language Jason is simultaneously emphasizing the rupture and the continuity that lies at the heart of every Mormon conversion. Jason and Anna both imply there is a disconnection with Irish heritage upon conversion, which is centered upon the place of family in both Irish society and the Mormon faith. For many Irish Catholics, conceptions of Irishness are carried through the generations through family, and conversion to Mormonism can be interpreted as a rejection of Irishness itself. As Jason articulates, "They are doing something that no one else has done." Irish part-member families and first-member individuals must navigate this challenge as they attempt to bridge the divide between Irishness and Mormonism.

Tradition and the Temple

For Mormons, completing genealogical research and keeping family records are only part of their spiritual obligations. The names gathered in this research must then be brought to the temple so that ancestors can be baptized into the Church. Baptisms for the dead and other key rituals such as "sealing" take place in the temple. Mormon belief emphasizes that a family who have been sealed in a temple marriage ceremony is the core foundation for a collective understanding of what family is. Sealing is a form of "temple marriage" through which Mormon couples, and any children born to them, are sealed to each other for all time and all eternity. It is designed to strengthen familial relationships here on earth and after death for eternity (Holman, 1996; Davies, 2003; Otterstrom, 2008; Faulconer, 2015). It is for this reason that Davies has referred to exaltation—the highest level of glory in the Mormon afterlife—as "family-destiny" (2010, p. 175).

The significance of baptisms for the dead and sealing, both family rituals that can only be undertaken in the temple, illuminate the sacred significance of the temple for Mormonism. It sits in juxtaposition to regular church buildings where Mormons attend meetings and other events throughout the week. This distinction is perhaps most notable in the different styles of temples compared to church buildings. Anna tells me that the reason why church buildings are so architecturally mundane and simple in decoration is because "church is just church. You can have church anywhere; you have church in the middle of the garden [as she speaks, she points out the window to her own back garden]. That's why it wouldn't have to be ornate. It's not that nothing ever really important happens there—I know we partake of the Sacrament, but again, you can do that anywhere." In contrast, Mormon temples are well known for their distinctive architecture and ornate furnishings. This reflects their elevated position within Mormonism as the most sacred spaces; "The role of the physical temple, and its separation from civil society, is notable in the Mormon faith" (Starrs, 2010). The importance of the temple and its family-centered rituals also provides an insight into how central family is for the Mormon worldview and proves the essential purpose of the temple building in playing a mediating role in the development of that worldview. Though sealing and baptisms for the dead are rituals that emphasize the communal nature of Mormonism, it should be noted that the central ritual of the temple is, in fact, individual. Through the "endowment ceremony" members make personal covenants with God, a process many experience as deeply powerful and sacred (Buerger, 2001).

Like Mormon conceptions of genealogy, the temple and its rituals serve as a unifying and conforming force for Mormonism (Powell, 2016). Yet, it also excludes those who do not meet various criteria necessary to enter the temple in the first place. Unlike chapels, which are used for Sunday worship and are open to all members and nonmembers, temples are reserved for the carrying out of sacred and secret salvation ordinances that are essential for exaltation after death, and entrance to them is restricted to members who meet clear entry requirements (Mitchell, 2001, p. 11). Thus, the temple and its rituals highlight distinctions within Mormonism between "temple Mormons" and "chapel Mormons" (Davies, 2007, p. 65), *and* between members and nonmembers. Restrictions on who can enter the temple, and what can be discussed about it with nonmembers, draw obvious boundaries around its sacred rites. The restriction on nonmembers demonstrates a clear boundary, but notably, not all Mormons are eligible to enter. Members must have an interview with their branch president and be approved for a "Temple Recommend" before they are allowed visit the temple. Seán in Appleby proudly pulled his Temple Recommend card from his pocket to show me during our first meeting. Looking much like an ID card in appearance, it is shown at the temple to secure entry and is proof that a member is "worthy" (Seán, Appleby) to enter. To be considered worthy, members must be adhering to the Word of Wisdom, contributing their tithes, regularly attending church, and otherwise living the doctrine of the faith in their everyday lives.

For those considered worthy, the temple rituals become an embodiment of kinship, and a way to take part in faith traditions that make individuals part of something bigger than themselves. During a Priesthood Meeting in Sweetwater one Sunday, the temple was the afternoon's topic of discussion, based on a lesson entitled "The Temple: The Great Symbol of Our Membership." On that day, there were seven men present, an average number for the Priesthood meetings in Sweetwater. As they sat in the tiny room with their chairs lined up neatly against the walls, David told the group about his long journey to the temple to be sealed to his wife, Meredith, when he was still living in South America:

> In the eighties, the closest temple to me was São Paolo; this was a forty-eight-hour journey. In the seventies, the closest temple was in Arizona. By the time you get to temple you don't remember what you are there for.... The temple president was very handsome; he had perfect white hair. He looked like a perfect person to lead the temple. The kids would come in and they would say "Are you God?!" People were coming from Colombia; this is for five days [of a journey] to get there. So, people would have parties there after the wedding, because they were not going to go home. The day of my sealing, afterward I was asked to do baptisms [for the dead]. So, I did about 150 baptisms that day and finished at ten o'clock at night. It was an interesting wedding night!

For David and Meredith, the long journey was worthwhile, as both the sealing ritual and the sacred temple building represent Mormon conceptions of eternal kinship, and both ensure the continuance of a chain of belief. It is for this reason that, for David and others who traveled from all over South America to visit the temple, the pilgrimage to the temple ends with a party atmosphere. Those asked to participate in additional kinship rituals of baptism for the dead are assisting in the smooth operation of the temple, but in return receive an opportunity to further Heavenly Father's Plan of Salvation, where baptizing deceased non-Mormons into the Church is a key element of achieving salvation. By acting in proxy for deceased family members to complete their baptisms, members assist multiple generations of their family. Thus, by conducting the baptisms that night, David was ensuring the expansion of Mormon kinship and making himself of part of a wider community of Mormons through his own role in the process.

As a non-Mormon, I am not allowed to enter the temple. For this reason, I built up a picture in my mind of the atmosphere of the temple based on comments from conversations throughout the fieldwork and across the field sites. All the Mormons I spoke to about the temple agreed it was a special and sacred place. They described the space as "peaceful" (Anna, Sweetwater), "clean" (Sue, Appleby), "quiet" (Mary, Appleby), or "silent" (James, Appleby). It was described to me as a space to pray (Donal, Appleby), to think (Abbey, Sweetwater), and to reaffirm your faith (Anna, Sweetwater). Anna described to me why the temple is so important: "You know you're getting sealed for time and all eternity; you're doing the baptisms, the baptismal fonts are amazing, you've got the twelve oxen underneath holding the actual font, it's just magnificent. Because it's such a huge thing to be baptized for the dead, you know what I mean? So important, you can't overstate how important it is. And it feels so lovely. And so sacred, it's so sacred and so precious. That's the word, it's so, so, precious." Her description of the sacredness of the temple reveals an awareness of the importance of time—she specifically mentions the importance of sealing as a form of marriage that lasts for time and all eternity. Similarly, she emphasizes how important the baptismal work in the temple is, perhaps because the ritual itself becomes a way to defeat time; for the deceased, their baptism into the Church will allow them to progress into the next world and for their family lives to continue. For the living, the dead are remembered, brought into the present.

Anna's description of the temple and its family rituals invoke anamnesis (Hervieu-Léger, 2000, p. 125), a recalling of the past. Others such as Meredith from Sweetwater similarly expressed a desire to bring the past into the present. In her family history talk during Sacrament meeting, Meredith explained her personal motivations for completing baptisms for the dead:

> When I think of genealogy, I think of the privilege that I have to have access to the temple and to bring names to the temple. All of my ancestors except my mum were born in a time when the Church wasn't in [her home country], or even on earth. I remember having a conversation with my sister about how come they [their ancestors] were so willing to come to earth when they knew they would have no gospel. But still they came, so they were good people. And it is a privilege to do this work for them.

Like Anna, who sees the spirit world as being watchful of the living, Meredith envisions her ancestors in their premortal lives, actively choosing to come to earth. Both Meredith and Anna imagine their ancestors, both before life and after life, as conscious individuals capable of agency. Their ancestors are not distant individuals from long ago, but people whom they have richly imagined, and for whom they have a current obligation to assist.

In acting by proxy for others, temple rituals such as baptism for the dead become a form of embodied spiritual practice, as does the wearing of "temple garments," which serve as a constant reminder of the sacredness of the temple building and what it represents. After a member is endowed in the temple for the first time, they are from then on required to wear sacred underclothing. Temple garments serve a purpose in ensuring conformity *within* the community (Powell, 2016). Temple rituals such as these are therefore a demonstration of the functions of tradition for the religious group, per Hervieu-Léger (2000). She identifies that such tradition serves a purpose in identification "ad intra (through incorporating into a believing community) and ad extra (through differentiation from those not of this lineage)" (Hervieu-Léger, 2000, pp. 81–82).

Only three participants (Sisters Fisher and Ross, and Michael of Sweetwater) mentioned temple garments to me, and I did not directly question anyone about them unless they raised the topic with me first. I understood that temple garments, like the temple itself, are sacred and personal, and did not want to intrude too forcefully upon such a sensitive topic. I did manage to ascertain that the garments are much like thermal underwear in appearance, with special symbols pertaining to the temple sewn into the fabric, and that temple garments are a symbolic reminder of the temple and its family-focused rituals.

However, given that the temple and its rituals allow Mormon conceptions of eternal kinship to be realized, the garments also become a lived everyday reminder of the doctrine of kinship that underpins the Mormon belief system. Temple garments are worn at all times, not just inside the temple, and therefore ensure that the experience of the temple as a fulfilment of family is always concrete through the feel of the garment fabric on the skin and through the consequent restrictions on behavior (Mitchell & Mitchell, 2008, p. 90). For instance, Sister Ross and Sister Fisher, the two young missionaries from Appleby, told me a little about how the wearing of "garments" (Sister Fisher, Appleby) changed behavior one afternoon while I drove them to a nearby town so that they could meet with an interested investigator. Sister Fisher mentioned that once she had been through the temple and received her garments, she was no longer able to wear "short-shorts" in summertime. The undergarments were too long to be covered by the shorts, and the Church instructs that they must not be visible. Temple garments therefore encourage more conservative dress among both women and men, perhaps particularly women. More significantly, they provide a direct connection between the family rituals of the temple and lived faith in everyday life. In this way, temple garments become part of the repertoire of embodied memory that Mormons utilize to reinforce their relationships with spiritual kin through time but also in the everyday.

Temple garments have been a point of mockery for those who wish to denigrate the Church's unique practices, and for some Mormons that is a sensitive issue when they feel that their religious beliefs and practices are not respected. Michael was insulted by the behavior of one member who had not "been through the temple" and so was not required to wear temple garments. In joking about the clothes, she gravely offended him:

> She was trying to mock our endowments—our special clothes that we wear, our garments. Who knows the reason, but she was mocking them. Because she was laughing, so I said, "I don't find it funny what you're saying" because our clothes are special for Suzanne and myself, we put our clothes not even with the other dirty clothes, we put them separate, we don't let them mix with anything. And she got real serious after that, said "sorry," and I said, "There is no secret about this, it is sacred. Because if you fulfil your requirements in the Church, you will have the same as what I have, you will have the same experiences. You don't have to be a special people; you just have to fulfil the requirements."

Michael's description of just how seriously he and his wife, Suzanne, look after their temple garments, by separating them from other dirty laundry, is proof of the sacred nature of the clothing and the importance of the rituals they symbolize. In responding to the woman who laughed at him, Michael emphasized that the rituals of temple are open to all those who meet the necessary requirements to enter the temple. In this way, he downplays the uniqueness and special nature of temple rituals and those who are allowed to participate in them. Yet, simultaneously, the continuance of distinction through the wearing of special garments every day, and the Church's instruction to keep the clothing hidden from view, denotes a distinction that is not obvious but always present—those who have "been through the temple" and those who have not.

The Church states in its manuals and in speeches from Church leadership that all types of families and single individuals are welcomed in the Church and that Heavenly Father understands that the ideal family may not be possible for everyone in this life. Teachers are advised during lessons in church to "be sensitive to the feelings of those who do not have ideal situations at home" (Church of Jesus Christ of Latter-day Saints, 2009, p. 207). Nonetheless, the close association between Mormon family ideology and the Plan of Salvation means that those who follow the preferred family path will also be those who are deemed to be adhering correctly to Heavenly Father's wishes. They are, in a way, closer to salvation. This brings with it a social status, an ability to "tick all the boxes" (Anna, Sweetwater) and to be viewed by others as more adherent, "a better Mormon" (Maria, Sweetwater), or a "good Mormon" (Jason, Appleby).

Jason is married to Catherine, and they have two children. He neatly summarizes what is involved in the expectations of the ideal Mormon family, and the challenge associated with achieving it:

> A lot of the members they, when they get married, they have this eternal view of the family. It somewhat idealized, rose-tinted glasses and all that, where they want to fulfil their role as set forth in the Church. And you have to kind of decide what you're going to do in your family. [What] your family is going to be, to set the tone for your family. Like, myself and Catherine got married, we had all these notions of getting the kids educated and sent off on missions, and then they would come home and get sealed in the temple, and then they would grow up in the Church, and it's all going to be great. And then you have a fourteen-year-old who says, "I am not going to church!" And you don't, you haven't planned for that.

Jason lists a series of criteria above that are necessary to fulfil the preferred Mormon family, including being sealed in the temple, having children who enjoy their faith, and missionary work. His reference to how to "set the tone" for your family implies his own eternal outlook. Jason therefore understands that this is just the beginning of his future eternal family.

Sue showed me how Mormon beliefs regarding eternal families shape how she raises her children, and how it guides her responses in times of tragedy. With a busy and bustling family home of four young children, Sue asked if we could hold our interview in her parents' house, so we could have a quiet place to chat without interruptions. Her parents weren't home at the time of our visit, and so we sat in her parents' living room in a still and peaceful house. Holding back tears, Sue told me that in addition to her four children, she had lost two babies as stillbirths. She told me that she took comfort in the idea of eternal families and could pass this comfort onto a non-Mormon friend who later went through the same experience.

SUE: We went through the most horrible things that can happen to you as a new parent, but it was a very spiritual experience at the same time.

HAZEL: That's just an incredible example of what that really means, eternally, taking comfort in the eternal. Are there ever moments where you doubt that feeling of the eternal, the forever?

SUE: No. No. It might sound crazy probably. . . . You have to deal with what shit life throws at you and for us to have gone through what we did and then go back again, and again, and have more [children]. Like, every time you get pregnant you open yourself up to the possibility of that, but it definitely gave us a different outlook. And a different outlook on our children and how we want to raise them. And they [the children] have a different outlook. Eva will tell you that she's the only person who has two sisters in heaven, and when they count the people in our family, they count them too. It's important for them to know that that's there, and that because me and James were sealed in the temple, that they have that family forever, the same as them. So, that probably has the most influence on how I would think.

Sue exhibits an awareness of her life that goes beyond an individual, temporal existence. For her, the eternal family is not simply a theological concept but a lived reality. It is underpinned by the actions she takes here in the temporal world such as being sealed in the temple, something she particularly mentions as central to the eternal family, as it is through these actions that spiritual family will continue and grow in the next life. Sue's mention of how her young daughter Eva has also absorbed this perspective on family is further evidence of the centrality of the family as source of transmission for religious tradition. Jason's articulations of his own family life illustrate a similar understanding of eternal family, demonstrating a common worldview pertaining to family, death, and eternity. Jason's and Sue's experiences confirm that Mormon faith creates and sustains a worldview in which "kinship, kinship networks, and extended families that include past, present, and future generations are all part of their collective culture" (Black, 2016, p. 286).

The Pressure to Achieve Mormon Family Outside the Mormon Heartland

Due to the very small number of Mormons in Ireland coupled with a high number of first-generation converts, many Mormons in Ireland find themselves as the only member of their family who is Mormon. Additionally, a common experience is what is referred to as "part-member families" where some family members are Church members and others are not, such as Maureen and John Murphy. Some of their adult children are members, and some are not. I have also encountered several families where the husband or wife is a member of the Church while their partner is not. These experiences lead to diverse negotiations regarding how to manage the faith of the children of these families. Given the nature of Mormon belief regarding eternal families and salvation as outlined above, these experiences mean that such families are not simply negotiating family life across multiple religions in wider environment of religious hegemony. They are also navigating their way through a faith in which a key aspect is the need to bring non-Mormon family members, both living and dead, into the Church. Achieving these ideals of Mormon family can often be difficult. Kristeen Lee Black (2016, p. 99) argues that "throughout the entire history of the LDS Church, conversion to Mormonism often means being separated from friends and family" who remain unconverted. A response to this experience has been to "create and legitimize new familial ties" through an embrace of Mormon family rituals (Black, 2016, p. 99). However, part of the legitimization of these new familial bonds means working to ensure that nonmember family, both living and dead, are brought inside the Mormon ties of family. Within this context, being a "first member" (Margaret, Appleby)—the first in a family to join the Church—is a daunting experience that continues to affect the member long after conversion.

On the first Sunday of each month, the usual Sacrament meeting with three speakers is set aside in favor of a Fast and Testimony Sacrament meeting. I came to understand that these testimony meetings served an important purpose as a form of conversation between members, allowing those who spoke to connect with the testimony of previous speakers. Identifiable themes would often occur within and across testimonies. One such meeting of the Appleby congregation illustrated to me how significant it is to be a first member. It was within this context that several members in the Appleby congregation shared their experiences of being the first and/or only Mormon in their respective families.

It began with the testimony of Emilio, a married European man with three children. Although his wife and children are active members, his parents, siblings, and wider family are not members of the Church. In the giving of his testimony he mentioned, "I am the first in my family to join the Church, and because of that I have a responsibility to bring the gospel to my family. I don't know if I am good enough for that, but I will share the gospel with my friends and family." Emilio's understanding of the Plan of Salvation means that he is aware of the need to ensure all his family members have an opportunity to join him in an eternal family in the afterlife, which can only be achieved by bringing his family into the Church, either through conversion in the present, or through baptism for the dead once they are deceased.

Others too, were motivated to speak about family that day. After Emilio's comments, Matthew, who is from East Africa, got up to speak. His wife and children are members, but his other family members in Africa are not. He told us:

> I am also the first to join this Church in my family. In this time, I have gained a lot of testimony—of my family, of this Church, of knowing that Jesus Christ loves us. I plan to go home to [his home country] next Friday. It is the first time to go home in a long time. Some of my daughters have never been there at all. We have planned it for a long time, but we are going back. I am going to share my testimony with those back home.

Some weeks after his return from Africa, I had an opportunity to ask Matthew how his attempts to spread the gospel with his family members had gone. He reminded me that Mormonism lives within families. "I encouraged the family that this is what they have to do; it is not just a Church, but it is the family. Because in Mormonism we believe we work together on the family. It's not a matter of practicing the Church outside, but we bring the Church inside of our families. So, the love which we show in the Church, it starts from our family." For Matthew, the heart of Mormonism as a faith lives within the family. For his family members to remain outside the Church therefore presents a tension between his beliefs and his experiences. Emilio's words in church that day had clearly influenced Matthew to speak about this, identifying with Emilio based on their similar family circumstances.

Margaret, an Irish convert from Catholicism to Mormonism in her fifties, was also inspired to speak about this issue after Emilio had finished. She directly acknowledged that Emilio's words had inspired her to speak about this topic. "I felt the Spirit when listening to Emilio say he was the first member in his family and so I wanted to get up. It can be hard to see why we are here [at church] when other people aren't. But I know the *Book of Mormon* can change lives. It changes how you feel, think, and who you want to be." She becomes emotional and starts crying. She tells the group that she was the first member of her family to join the Church, that only one sibling is now still active, and that her children are not members. I understood how isolating this experience was for Margaret when a few weeks later in a Relief Society meeting that was discussing the importance of Christmas, the teacher of the lesson asked the group to share their experiences of Christmas. Margaret volunteered, and explained that although Christmas is an important time for devout Mormons, she feels like she can't talk about the importance of it to her family who she feels don't and can't understand.

She told the group that on Christmas Eve the previous year she was at home upstairs by herself, feeling quite sad about experiencing Christmas as the only Mormon in the house, when her son came into the room. As during the Fast and Testimony Sacrament meeting, she became emotional, and through tears she told us:

> I was upset and wasn't in the humor to talk to anyone when he came up. He saw that I was a bit upset. Then, I couldn't believe it, but he started playing me some Mormon hymns. He sat with me and we listened to the hymns, and he told me, "Oh, I like this one." I wondered to myself how did he even know that song, but I was so touched that he did that for me. He recognized that it was important to me and that I needed someone to share it with. I'm so glad I got to spend that time with him.

Margaret's Christmas story emotionally affected everyone in the room; many were tearful; the atmosphere was somber and sympathetic. Those who also had part-member family or convert experiences empathized with her story. In this regard, a convert I have named Molly mentioned how good it was for her to hear that others in part-member families also feel lonely at Christmas. Margaret's story in the Relief Society meeting helped me to understand more deeply why she felt such a strong urge to speak after hearing Emilio's words in the Fast and Testimony Sacrament meeting. Like Matthew, she understood the interrelationships between Mormonism and family. In the telling of her story about her son, she offered a glimpse of a moment when family and faith aligned in her life. For one brief moment, Margaret felt as though there was no incompatibility between her position as a mother and her position as a Mormon. Her gratitude for that moment, and her emotion in the retelling of it, reveals just how meaningful this brief experience was for her.

There was one more person who chose to speak of his similar experiences after hearing Emilio's words in church. Significantly, it was the district president whom I have called Spencer, who was visiting the Appleby congregation for the day. As a key Church leader in Ireland, his affirmation of the others' experiences by telling his own family story was an important recognition by a Church leader of this difficult part of Mormon family life in Ireland. He said:

> Hearing so many of you talk about being the first member in your families has made me think about my own first member. That is my uncle Simon in [his home country]. He and my dad were part of the Catholic Church when he joined; my dad was the one who gave him a hard time about it. But Simon was patient and invited my dad to volleyball and soccer with the Church, and eventually he went to church. My parents met there and got married. My mum was getting ready to go to temple, my dad didn't want to go; he wasn't so into the Church then. One morning a man got in the car with my dad, and he had a gun. He said, "Drive or I'll kill you." At the next light, my dad jumped out of the car and ran as the guy was shooting at him. As he was running, he thought, "I have to go to temple with my wife," and from then on, he was involved with the Church.

In reflecting upon Spencer's story, it occurred to me that given the significance of the interconnections between death and family within Mormon kinship it is unsurprising that it was when Spencer's father was confronted with his own mortality that he decided to ensure his eternal family through the temple. Spencer's narrative about his family's experiences also shows that like Emilio and Matthew, Spencer's uncle was actively trying to bring family members into the Church. Due to his uncle's efforts, Spencer's family, and his wife's, are now well established in the Church in both Ireland and in Africa and when I met his wife, she proudly told me that she was a fourth-generation Mormon. In his role as district president, Spencer traveled to different branches each Sunday for church. As such, his attendance at Appleby was sporadic, and I saw him on just one other occasion after this particular meeting. This meant that I never had an opportunity to talk with Spencer about his testimony, and what might have motivated his intervention that day. However, given the pride shown by him and his wife regarding their families' membership of the Church, it appeared to me that Spencer's testimony was intended to comfort those struggling within part-member families.

The testimonies of Emilio, Matthew, and Margaret highlight the role of emotion within Mormon understandings of authenticity and meaning (Davies, 2011). Founder Joseph Smith's First Vision, in which he experienced powerful emotions while praying for wisdom from God as to the one true church, has continued to shape Mormon spirituality ever since. I have often observed that crying regularly accompanies a person's testimony or the telling of a story. Above, we can see that those who spoke of their first-member experiences used emotion to express meaning. Through their embodied feelings, these Mormons publicly signaled to others in the congregation the power and the authenticity of their faith. Margaret's telling of her experiences at Christmas as a lone Mormon family member serves the same purpose. By signaling the authenticity of their spirituality through emotion, these Mormons reassert the Mormon chain of memory, which goes back to the First Vision of Joseph Smith in 1820. It was due to the power of great emotion that Smith understood the authenticity of his experiences that day. Modern Mormons utilize tears and heightened feelings in the same way, to confirm to themselves and others the truth of their experiences. Thus, Mormons such as Emilio, Matthew, Spencer, and Margaret who speak of "feeling the spirit," "love," being "upset," and who cry in the telling of their testimony, are reaffirming the Mormon collective memory of meaning, which has so shaped Mormon understandings of truth and meaning.

Part of achieving an eternal family means being sealed within the temple so that any children born into that relationship will be automatically sealed to their parents in the hereafter for eternity. For this reason, marrying within the Church is about more than just the reproduction of faith through the generations, but is necessary to ensure that families remain together after death. Claire is in her forties with young children. Although she is a second-generation Mormon, her husband is a nonpracticing Catholic. Due to this, they have not been sealed in the temple. For our interview, she invited me to her small home on a quiet road. It was mid-morning when I arrived, and her older child was in preschool. She apologized that a younger toddler was awake and demanding attention; she had hoped to time our interview with mid-morning naptime. Instead, we sat in her living room to chat with *Peppa Pig* on the TV in the background. Her toddler's interruptions meant that our conversation was disjointed in parts; at one point, the interview paused so that Claire could get a banana for her child, on another occasion, a drink. Yet, Claire showed remarkable focus in her conversations with me, and she was careful to answer my questions as fully as she could. She had conducted qualitative interviews herself as part of her postgraduate studies and I felt that this gave a sense of understanding between us.

I asked her whether she is planning on raising her children in the Church. She told me:

> This is a very hot topic for me. . . . I made a decision . . . that I wasn't going to be dating anyone that wasn't a member of the Church because, just prioritizing what was important to me, a value system for how I would want to raise a family, and not just those things, but the connection, the shared goals and perspectives. . . .

Later, she met her husband, and despite not being Mormon she says about him:

> I really just felt that he was a family for me, not knowing him very well. . . . I just had a real sense of us having a connection without really knowing each other, and it being a family connection. And I really prayed about it, even before we started going out and all throughout, we went out for two years before we got married. And even though it didn't make a lot of sense to me about how we were going to go about it, it really felt right.

However, she told me that her husband has become very opposed to the Church in recent years:

> He would have very big problems with the Church in his experience of it, and it's very complicated, despite our marriage. But that's a challenge at the moment and I foresee for a long time that that's something for us to negotiate. The way he feels about the Church now is that it's not a positive influence at all really. . . . So, that's kind of that's difficult, and then we have to work those things out. It doesn't change anything about what I felt, the inspiration around my decisions for us to get married and have a family. But it is definitely a huge challenge.

It is clear that this issue is a source of pain for Claire. I was honored that she shared with me such personal and honest details with me. Claire's struggles reveal the challenges of managing a part-member family, particularly where the faith of children is at the center of a dispute. For Claire, raising her children within the faith means not just the provision of "shared values and perspectives," but securing a relationship with her children that will continue after death. For Claire's husband, although he has a familiarity with aspects of Mormonism through his own loosely similar experiences of Catholicism, Mormon beliefs regarding death and time are unique, and heavily family-focused. In the event of a divergence of opinion regarding faith, concepts of family are therefore at the center of the dispute in a way that is unavoidable for all concerned.

Claire's family life has also caused her to feel judged by some members of her congregation, whom she thinks disapprove of her decision to marry and start a family with a non-Mormon. She tells me, however, that despite being the focus of their disapproval, she can also see their standpoint:

> I can really understand the perspective when you view what's most important. I had been to the temple, and there are ordinances in the temple. And obviously, marriage in the temple is one of those ordinances . . . and so I think just with that perspective, I would be more understanding of how important it would be for me, or anybody, to have that kind of foundation of a family unit, with that shared eternal perspective of what the family means, and what the Savior means in the center of all of that. And I think for some people it's like I abandoned that priority. Because what I did [marrying outside the Church] would have looked like that, as though it wasn't important to me, when it *is* important to me.

Claire's sympathy for those who judge her decisions shows just how deeply family life goes to the heart of the Mormon faith. Within Mormonism, the family is not as private an affair as it might be outside the Church. Mormon theology sees all human life as connected, before, during, and after life on earth. Within this perspective, Claire is seen to have rejected the principle of Mormon family despite understanding its importance. This decision is interpreted as having affected the Mormon family as a whole, rather than being a private matter unconnected to the wider congregation.

Her experiences also point to the divergence that often exists between the rhetoric of the official Church and lived experience. The Church explicitly states that it accepts *all* types of families, and part-member families are to be welcomed and respected. Despite this, it is clear that their messaging in the specific case of same-sex-parented families has certainly been contradictory and often homophobic. Additionally, claims from leadership of all being welcome has not stopped a sense of disapproval at the local level from Claire's fellow congregants toward her and her decisions about family.

This disapproval is interesting considering the specific context of Ireland, where the small numbers of Church members means that in practical terms, it is often difficult to marry within the Church and begin an eternal family. In Appleby, for instance, in an active congregation of seventy, there was just one young single man regularly attending church during my time there, Mary Daly's son Andrew who was in his early twenties. Mary told me that fulfilling the Mormon family within these circumstances was on her son's mind; "We talked about this; I feel that Andrew will marry in the Church. I feel most likely he will marry an English girl or an American girl

... because there isn't a big pool of people." Such choices by young Irish Mormons are felt to be "pragmatic" (Stephanie, Appleby) based on the circumstances in which they find themselves.

Stephanie questioned how or where young Mormons in Ireland are supposed to meet their future partners: "I think that's for me anyway, the thing I find most difficult about being a member. It's that there are not enough men." She told me at the time of our interview that she was considering attending BYU to undertake postgraduate study but also because "There's loads of single people, loads of people that are members because of the Church school [BYU]. Of course, I'd do that. I think the hardest thing for me is, you know, you want to get married, you want to do all those things, but the options just aren't here for it [in Ireland]. So, you see, you have to just look somewhere else, or bring someone over [to Ireland]." Stephanie soon did move to the United States to study at BYU, and not long after that, she was engaged to be married. She now lives in the United States with her husband, and so although Stephanie has achieved her dream of marrying within the Church, she had to leave the country of her birth, and her Irish family, to achieve it.

In contrast, Andrew decided he wanted to "stay to build the Church in Ireland" (Mary, Appleby). As his mother speculated, he married a British member of the Church, perhaps inadvertently reinforcing existing perceptions in Ireland among the majority that Mormonism is not a faith to which Irish people belong. This perception is exacerbated by the national diversity that exists within Mormon congregations in Ireland. Sweetwater is very diverse, where Irish Mormons are a minority; however, even Appleby has as many as nine different nationalities attending church each week. In Appleby's Fast and Testimony Sacrament meeting described above in which four first-members shared their experiences, Margaret was the only Irish member of the four. Emilio, Spencer, and Matthew represent the reality of the national diversity in existence within Mormonism in Ireland. Therefore, by marrying non-Irish Mormons to fulfil Mormon ideals of family, Irish Mormons such as Stephanie and Andrew inadvertently continue a trend that aids perceptions of Mormonism in Ireland as a "foreign" religion.

The reality of Irish Mormonism is that all these diverse experiences, Irish and non-Irish, part-member families and families with all active members, represent the true lived experience of Mormonism in modern Ireland. This diversity of experience reflects the wider society of which it belongs, which is also becoming increasingly diverse. However, there does appear to be a perception of homogeneity in terms of how Mormon culture conceives of family. Therefore, despite the reality of lived Irish Mormonism, members such as Stephanie, Andrew, or Claire feel themselves to be placed in a difficult position when it comes to family formation in Ireland as Mormons.

The narratives throughout this chapter have illustrated that Mormon genealogy and its associated temple rituals symbolically reflect notions of time and tradition and recall family as the foundational component of Mormon doctrine and culture. The temple and its rituals of sealing and baptisms for the dead become a way to recall the past, and to reinforce the role of each individual family member in the chain of memory. Through an expansive conception of kinship that sees all humans as interconnected through space and time, Mormons maintain relationships with ancestors and future generations, while also imagining fluid boundaries between the spiritual and temporal worlds. Though these intergenerational connections are in many ways an act of imagination, claims of lineage need not be verifiable to support a sense of continuity. "It may be purely imaginary, so long as its recall is strong enough to allow identification to build and preserve the social bond in question" (Hervieu-Léger, 2000, p. 96). This chapter has demonstrated how Mormons in Ireland construct ideas of ancestry, imagining what life might have been like for those family members during their time on earth. Family, both real and imagined, becomes a central component in the transmission and maintenance of Mormon religious identity.

By conducting baptisms for the dead for non-Mormon family, by inviting family members to church and encouraging their conversion, and by marrying and raising children in the Church, Mormons can fulfil the expectations of a faith-centered kinship. However, in Ireland, a strongly established Catholic Church has resulted in a society in which changes of religious affiliation are uncommon, and stigmatized. This makes the legitimization of these new family bonds more difficult in an Irish context; young Mormons in Ireland may have to emigrate to find a partner, and Irish Mormons may marry a fellow Mormon of another nationality due to small numbers of young Irish Mormons in Ireland. Mormons in Ireland also often find themselves as the only member of the Church in their family, and experience this as lonely and isolating. Thus, in Ireland as elsewhere in Europe maintaining these Mormon threads of connectivity may present specific challenges that point to the importance of understanding Mormonism within the particular environment in which it exists. The struggles of younger generations of Irish Mormons to create a family that is both Irish and Mormon show the practical difficulties inherent in reconciling Irish family and Mormon family. There are significant barriers to overcome to be able to achieve the ideals of Mormon kinship within an Irish context. The adaptations to conventional Mormon patterns of kinship described here—marrying a non-Mormon, emigrating in search of a Mormon partner, marrying a Mormon from abroad—all demonstrate how conventional Mormon tradition must be molded into something new to uphold that same tradition.

Irish-Irish and Mormon-Irish

Summer Flowers

On a warm and pleasant midweek evening in June, I walked around the corner from my house to the Sweetwater branch building, clutching a yellow plastic window box. I was on my way to attend a Summer Flowers activity with the Sweetwater Relief Society. It was organized by the Relief Society president at that time, Jessica. This event was one of a number of social events offered by the Sweetwater Relief Society. Other events offered included arts and crafts activities, clothing swaps, and food storage classes. Jessica had told me that she expected about ten women for the activity, based on feedback from members who had told her they hoped to come. When I arrived that evening, Jessica was alone, and I asked her if she was concerned about the numbers who might attend. She admitted that she was, but soon after collecting some bags of compost from her car, she was relieved to see some other women had arrived. In total, there were six of us at this event. I learned quickly during my time attending church, however, that low numbers of attendees for events outside of Sunday's meetings were not unusual, as Andrei's mention of the Same Ten People from the introduction illustrates.

I was intrigued to notice that I was the only Irish person present at Jessica's Summer Flowers activity. The others, like Sweetwater's members more broadly, were a diverse group. Irena was originally from elsewhere in Europe but had been living in Ireland for many years. Marita and Vanessa had also made Ireland their home with their husbands and children, though they came from Southeast Asia. Meredith, originally from South America, had lived in the United States and in Europe before living in Ireland for a number of years, while it seemed that North American Jessica was now settling into Irish life with her family. After an opening prayer was offered while we were sitting on plastic folding chairs we had dragged outside, we started planting the window boxes and pots we had brought with us. That task was completed fairly quickly, and I was just beginning to wonder what else we might do to fill our time when Jessica suggested that we use our leftover flowers to replant the long-abandoned flowerbeds that edged the side of the pathway to the front door. This task was trickier; stones and clay littered the beds, but once completed, the exterior of the building was transformed into a bright palette of beautiful colors. With our work complete, Jessica brought out some watermelon and we relaxed.

Quickly, the conversation turned to the topic of life as an immigrant in another country. It began with Meredith and Irena joking about the good and the bad of Irish culture, and the necessity to have a sense of humor and the ability to adapt to the culture in which you find yourself as a migrant. Meredith mentioned that she believed that to be accepted as an immigrant in any country, you must work hard and prove yourself to the majority. Soon, the conversation drifted toward languages, being bilingual as a migrant, and their difficulties in managing this. Meredith told us that when her children were teenagers and living in the United States, they didn't want to speak Spanish because to do so led to assumptions that they were Mexican. The stigma surrounding Mexicans led them to abandon Spanish. Vanessa and Marita noted that since moving to Ireland, their children had become used to their classmates speaking one language in school and another at home. Both are aware that this is relatively new for a traditionally homogenous country like Ireland, but in their experience, bilingualism is celebrated in Irish schools and nothing to be ashamed of.

I found it interesting how quickly, and easily, the women's conversation that evening came to be dominated by this discussion of life as a migrant. As the only Irishwoman present, I felt that I had been given a glimpse into how such experiences must dominate the everyday lives of migrants in Ireland. Always identified as different, they must work to gain acceptance, to navigate cultural differences and stigmatization, and to overcome the challenges of language and culture. The women's conversations on this evening also revealed to me that in a small group of six with five different nationalities, what united the women in sociability was their common experience of life on the margins of Irish life. This contradiction, that migration both disrupts and assists belonging, came to be a theme of my time spent in Sweetwater. The diverse branch was majority non-Irish, and it seemed to be engaged in a struggle to forge a common identity during my time there. Its diversity was at once the experience that caused conflict and discord but also moments such as this, of commonality and unity.

The Complexity of Mormon Identities in Ireland

As outlined in chapter 1, Irishness and Catholicism are still unavoidably intertwined. Within this context, Mormonism is not associated with being Irish, and so Irish converts from Catholicism are thought by others to have in some way lost a part of their national identity. Mormonism is often considered as a small, strange, and foreign religion in Ireland. For adherents of Mormonism in Ireland, this framing of Mormonism has significant consequences for their sense of identity in the everyday. Viewed as "traitorous" (Seán, Appleby) to Irish nation and culture, both Irish-born Mormons and Mormons of other nationalities living in Ireland attempt to assert belonging to Ireland in various ways. Though their very presence constitutes a break with Ireland's Catholic past, their attempts to belong signify that they recognize the importance of the continuance of traditional conceptions of Irishness and are active in their maintenance of such understandings.

To illustrate some of these ideas, I'd like to tell you a little more about Seán, Ron, Suzanne, and Matthew. Seán was the very first Mormon I made contact with in connection with my research. In fact, he was the first Mormon I ever (knowingly) met. As I made my way to the hotel he had suggested for our meeting, I had no idea of the journey I was about to embark upon, and of how Seán's experiences as a member would reveal so much to me about the nature of life as a religious minority in contemporary Ireland. I was clueless back then, or so it appears to me in hindsight. I often feel that a whole new arena of my life opened up in front of me that day, and for that reason I look on my time that day spent speaking with Seán as a line in the sand: life before Mormonism, and after.

Seán is a retired Irish convert to Mormonism in his seventies who had previously served in various leadership roles. When I first met him, I was struck by his impeccable manners and his sharp attire. While I had arrived to our meeting wearing jeans and a blouse, Seán was wearing a three-piece suit and tie. He was careful to shake my hand, to open the door for me, to offer to pay for my coffee. He brought me a variety of Church pamphlets and a *Book of Mormon*, which is still one of my most treasured possessions as a memento of my time in the field. Every aspect of Seán's personality seemed to me to be taken up with doing the "right" thing. He confided in me that he had suggested we meet at the hotel because it was a public space;

he worried perhaps his home might be too intimate, and therefore inappropriate. Yet, seated in the hotel restaurant of his local town, he also worried that we might be spotted by someone he knew; he, a married man, meeting a much younger women at a hotel! Perhaps the nature of our meeting might be misinterpreted. I know now that to be polite and helpful, well-dressed, and concerned with propriety might be considered to be standard Mormon characteristics, but I didn't know that back then.

Seán was earnest and principled, and this made him a compelling conversationalist. He told me about his Irish Catholic upbringing, and the Irish Republican ideals that his father instilled within him. Upon conversion to Mormonism, Seán was faced with a terrible reality; while within himself he felt as Irish as he ever had, others suddenly perceived him differently. He says:

> I served in the army reserve for thirty-seven years. When I became a member [of the Church], I went to my company commander at the time and said I want to change my army record [on religion], and the immediate reaction was "Oh, I will organize for you to meet a Jesuit friend of mine." And I said, "Hold on a second, I'm second-in-command of the company of soldiers, do you not think that I have the ability to decide, you know, who or what it is that I want to follow?"
>
> "Oh yeah, yeah, but I mean they are brainwashed" [commented his company commander].
>
> I said, "Hang on a minute!" I said, "Look, I want the record changed." He then for me [sic], unknown to me at the time, I arrived in one evening and he said, "The battalion commander wants to talk to you." So, I went up to the battalion commander and he bared his teeth at me like a dog. When I told him I wanted the record changed, he goes "ARRRRGGGHHH" . . . [Seán mimics someone lunging across a table, growling aggressively].

Seán believes he understands where these attitudes stem from. The army, as an agent of the Irish State, upholds "Irish" values, and his conversion to Mormonism meant he was less than Irish. "With the army, the distinct impression I got was that it was a traitorous act. I mean to be Mormon, and then Protestant as well, you know? I mean anything that was, anything at all that would smack of Protestantism was to be avoided." It is clear, then, that Seán's conversion to Mormonism was constructed by his superiors in the army as a rejection of Catholicism, and due to its connection to Protestantism, a rejection of Irishness itself.

While Seán's Mormonism caused problems for him within the Irish army, conversely, his Irish patriotism became a source of tension within the Church. He found himself embroiled in conflict with higher levels of

Church leadership in Ireland and in Europe, as he strived to raise the Irish profile of the Church in Ireland. Resentful that the LDS Church in Ireland had its administrative center in the United Kingdom, he tells me:

> I believe that people in Salt Lake need to be educated properly with regards to what I've been pushing lately, and to be honest it's that this is a sovereign republic. You either give us due recognition or continue to insult us by telling us we have to do what England tells us to do. And they say, "Oh no it's not like that," then I say, "Well, the facts prove otherwise." . . . My father was very much involved in the War of Independence [from the British], I'm a Republican to the core. . . . I refuse to be told by anyone in England how we should behave, or where we should go, or when, and that includes the Church.

Seán tells me of the small ways in which he actively attempts to emphasize Irish Mormonism's unique nature in church:

> As an Irish man I'm looking at things Irish, you know? And about the Church in Ireland—let's celebrate that. . . . I would hope that eventually the message will get across that these [Irish people] are a separate nation, they speak another language. I keep emphasizing that, that we use our own language. I use it on a regular basis all the time in church; if I am asked to do a prayer I do it in Irish to let them know that we are a separate nation, we are different culture and it's high time I think that the Church recognizes that. They don't, as far as I'm aware anyway. Like, I've attended church in Nigeria and the Nigerians are not expected to behave as anything other than Nigerians.

Seán's experiences show that an Irish Mormon identity can disrupt belonging both within and outside of the Church. He deliberately inserts Irishness into Mormonism. He is aware that this sometimes causes conflict, but feels strongly nonetheless that Irish Mormonism should be celebrated. His narrative also highlights the struggles of Irish Mormons to be recognized, and to recognize themselves, as truly Irish.

Ron seemed a little suspicious of me when I first arrived at his branch. However, one afternoon after church we had a long and interesting conversation where he seemed more relaxed with me, and we enjoyed getting to know each other. We talked about many things that day, but I noticed that he seemed to be interested in Ireland's demographic changes. He told me, "In Ireland, we were closed for so long and now new religions and races have come flooding in." He then quoted a line from the William Butler Yeats poem "September 1913." "Romantic Ireland is dead and gone," he said, which led me to finish the sentence of the poem, one I learned in school.

"It's with O'Leary in the grave," I quoted back to him. He laughed, enjoying the moment of understanding between us, and left me to reflect on the significance of his recitation of this particular poem, and my own familiarity with it. "September 1913" is a famous poem in Ireland, referencing figures and themes from Irish history while also speaking to the changed nature of Ireland as the twentieth century progressed. Ron seems to link the loss of "Romantic Ireland" to the growing diversity of Irish society. He reflects the idea that through change, Ireland is losing something of itself. On one hand, we can view this as an Irishman mourning the way things used to be. But it also seems that despite his melancholy about Ireland's changes, he cannot recognize his own role in it, as a convert to Mormonism.

Suzanne in Sweetwater shares Seán's and Ron's strong sense of patriotism. I spent the Easter of 2016 conducting fieldwork within the Sweetwater branch and that Easter Sunday helped me to better understand Suzanne's Irishness. Easter 2016 was the 100th anniversary of the Irish Easter Rising, a 1916 Dublin rebellion against British occupation. After the unsuccessful rebellion was quashed, key rebel leaders were executed, creating martyrs whose deaths subsequently fueled a popular backlash against the British occupation in Ireland. The Rising therefore became a key event in Ireland's eventual independence from the British just a few years later. The anniversary was not referred to at the lectern by branch leadership that day. I initially assumed this to be due to the institutional Church's tendency to avoid engaging in political discussion even though on another occasion the branch president made reference to the anniversary of a day of independence celebrated in his home country. Despite the lack of "official" recognition in church, the Easter Rising commemoration was discussed by the congregation in casual conversations among themselves, usually by asking each other if they were planning on attending a commemoration ceremony being held in Dublin city center later that afternoon.

In Sacrament meeting that day I noticed that Suzanne and her mother, Mavis, were wearing shades of pastel green and yellow; Easter colors, I thought to myself. Fastened to their chests were small Irish flag pins, which I assumed to be a visible commemoration of the Rising's anniversary. I felt that their physical commemoration of the event through their clothing was a significant statement of identity. Suzanne and Mavis had converted to Mormonism from the Church of Ireland, a form of Anglicanism. Suzanne's motivation for conversion was the sense of exclusion she felt in her old faith community, based on social class differences. Suzanne's conversion to Mormonism did not resolve her feelings of difference, however, but rather created a new framework of distinctions, which she utilized to position herself both within the Church and outside of it. During a conversation with me in between church meetings one Sunday, Suzanne told me that "Irish people in the Church are different to Irish-Irish people." Her description of Irish non-Mormons as "Irish-Irish" implies that Irish Mormons such as herself are less Irish than others. She shows understanding, as Seán does also, of the difficulties involved in reconciling Mormon and Irish identities. As Suzanne was born into the Church of Ireland, she intimately understands how non-Catholic experiences are marginalized within the national narrative. It was within this context that I understood that Suzanne's clothing and Irish flag pin worn on Easter Sunday served to reassert her Irishness within a religious space that is deemed by the majority culture to be outside the Irish boundaries of belonging.

As I spent more time with Suzanne and her mainly Irish friends in church, I came to understand that Suzanne was somewhat resentful of other nationalities within the congregation, particularly the large number of North Americans. Her friend Marilyn told me "she thinks they take over" church. In conversation with me, Suzanne referred to her Irish friends from the branch as "regular people", her language constructing others in the branch as unusual in some way. Already feeling marginalized by the majority Catholic society due to her Mormonism, it seemed that Suzanne now also felt excluded within the congregation as one of the few regularly attending Irish people in a diverse congregation.

Most people in Sweetwater acknowledged that its cultural diversity exacerbated interpersonal conflicts and was a barrier to congregational unity. One of those with whom Suzanne sometimes clashed was Abbey, a wealthy North American. Abbey told me how she viewed these sorts of difficult dynamics in multicultural Sweetwater:

> The fact that we don't have a lot of White Irish [in the branch] is kind of a strange thing. I definitely notice that it's very different in our branch than it is in the other wards . . . which are much more Irish than we are. . . . There's no question that cultural behaviors are different between Polish and Irish and American and Filipino and South American, and it's easier perhaps for feelings to be hurt and misunderstandings to happen because your default mode is so different than someone else's. There is a tremendous amount of working together and opportunities for interaction that can forge friendships, that also can be very divisive and hurt feelings. "You didn't understand me," or "I did this, and this was your response." I have seen that.

Like Seán, Suzanne's complex experiences of her Irish Mormon identity caused conflict in church as she tried to incorporate her interpretation of Irishness into her congregation's dynamics.

Non-Irish Mormons also navigate a complex relationship between religion and national identity in Ireland. They are often also part of Ireland's fast-growing minority groups, and are often racialized as people of color within a majority White society. Matthew attends church with his wife and children. He is an African man in his forties who has been in Ireland since 2008. He converted to Mormonism in 2013 after some time spent attending a local Black Pentecostal church. As one of the only Black families in his branch and the only Black participant of this research, he told me of his sense of responsibility to grow the Black Mormon community:

> MATTHEW: I think my presence in the Church, it makes a big difference because I was the first, no, the second [Black] member of the Church in [this branch]. And there are some who are Black, but not my color! So they are not so visible like me.
>
> HAZEL: Are you conscious of how visible you are?
>
> MATTHEW: Oh yeah! [Laughs] . . . and I managed to bring a new member who was also from [his home country]. They are now a member of the Church. More of my color are coming to church. Because they see me there and they see me with my family, and they hear—of course people will not tell you, but they hear—and they know what's going on in my family. And they want to experience that in their family.

Matthew feels that his identity as a Black African Mormon in Ireland is changing the racial and national makeup of the local Mormon branch; he speaks of how "visible" he is in church, and how his presence makes a "big difference." However, Matthew also indicates an awareness that his religious conversion is being discussed by people he knows in the local Black African community; "people will not tell you, but they hear—and they know what's going on in my family." Matthew thus indicates that his example is changing the religious makeup of the Black African community in the town itself; "more of my color are coming to church."

Matthew works as a hospital porter and serves meals to patients, which brings him in regular direct contact with the majority population. He tells me how the patients assume he might be Muslim because he is Black, and of their subtle attempts to discern if he is Muslim or Christian. He says, "I always go direct to what the patient asked me. When they ask me my country, I tell them. If they ask me my religion, I can tell them, but nobody has ever asked me. But always they ask me my first name. They always ask me. They want to know. Because Christian—we have to do things in a Christian way with love, but there are some people who don't do it that way, but once they ask my name, they know I'm Christian." Matthew knows that his biblical name indicates Christianity to his patients, and for many of them, that is enough.

> The people, once they know that we are Christian, they have that accep-
> tance which comes to them. They start to believe in you. . . . But when
> you tell them a different religion which is not Christian, then they have
> different feeling. It's like when someone tells you they're from Ireland and
> you've been living in Ireland for a long time, you start to see his behavior.
> There are people from neighboring countries like Rwanda and Kenya and
> Tanzania, but someone, you can see him or her in the distance, and you
> know that he is from Kenya. The way he walks or the way she is dressed.
> It is the same with Christianity. Once they know your name, they start to
> study you. Sometimes, if you do things not in the right way, they may say
> "that's not Christianity."

In Matthew's workplace, then, his skin color inadvertently raises questions of his religious identity. He and his patients never mention the words Muslim, Christian, or Mormon, but both understand the unstated query and response that lies behind the exchange. In Ireland, to be non-White is to immediately be labeled as an outsider, and both Matthew and his patients understand this. These processes of identification are common across the island of Ireland, and work by Sidsel Saugestad Larsen (1982) in Northern Ireland has articulated the ways in which coded language and euphemisms are used to navigate public references to religion, because "to display open interest in the religion of anyone present or being referred to is incompatible with the norms of decent behaviour" (Larsen, 1982, p. 138).

For Matthew, emphasizing his Christian identity is a way for him to connect with those Irish people who view him as an outsider by virtue of his skin color. Matthew uses Christianity to move inside Irish conceptions of belonging, just as Suzanne and Seán use their nationality to disrupt the marginalization they experience on the basis of their faith. Matthew suggests that his patients seem relieved to know that he is Christian. However, I suggest that behind the knowledge that he is Christian is an assumption that he is Catholic or a member of one of the mainstream Protestant denominations. Matthew has never told his patients that his particular form of Christianity is Mormonism, and I suspect that if he did, he would be viewed as a stranger once more.

Managing Congregational Identity

A key difference between Appleby's and Sweetwater's congregational cultures relates to their levels of conflict. While Appleby was also a diverse branch, with perhaps ten nationalities regularly attending church, it was described to me by others as being a less "transient" branch than Sweet-water. In Sweetwater, conflicts were often expected to be managed by branch leadership, but branch leadership were also regularly accused of being the source of such conflict, which led to branch leadership being under pressure to manage the difficulties of the branch. Mormonism is a hierarchical faith in which the branch president is usually accepted and respected as the leader of the congregation. Although some of the decision-making is communal because the branch president may consult his counselors for advice and support, ultimately the final decisions regarding the congregation rest with him. Seán explained to me that "the branch president has the final say. He is literally the representative of Jesus Christ locally. If you disobey, you're telling Jesus to take a hike."

Jason, Appleby's branch president, readily acknowledges that the system of leadership in the Church is quite hierarchical but points out that the power that comes with leadership should be attached the leadership role itself, and not the individual person who holds that role. He told me, "It is quite hierarchical. You know like in the army, if you are the lower rank you salute the higher rank. You are not saluting the person, you are saluting the rank." Given this centrality of his role, the branch president can make or break the spirit and functioning of the branch. In a country such as Ireland where wards are few and branches often struggle to thrive, this role takes on even more significance. The stability and success of the CoJCoLDS locally and nationally is greatly dependent on the leadership offered at a congregational level.

At the time of my research, Jason worked alongside Stephanie who was the Relief Society president. Stephanie was one of the youngest Relief Society presidents who had ever been called to the role in the branch. She was in her mid-twenties when I first met her, and she immediately won me over with her youthful optimism, her pop culture references that peppered her talks in church, and her clear desire to create a modern and fun version of what Church leadership could be. She was a second-generation Mormon—her parents converted in their youth. Stephanie was one of the few younger members I spoke to who had always grown up in the church and who knew no other way of life. For my interview with Stephanie, we went to a small Italian restaurant in the center of Appleby on a rainy winter's night midweek. We had a pleasant evening of good food and conversation, while my recorder ran unobtrusively on one corner of the table. Over dessert she told me about her belief that strong and effective local leaders, who really connected with members, were vital to the success of a branch:

> If you have a strong . . . Jason is a great branch president—so good. Previous to that we had another two who weren't that great and you could feel

the branch kind of dwindle. . . . Jason is such a get-go person . . . he is really motivational. . . . Because we had a branch president before, and he was an older guy so he kind of wasn't good at the computer stuff, and you would ask him for things that he would be all like "what are you talking about?" Things like that when you look back at that, you think, well, that wasn't great. And this is fantastic.

According to Stephanie and others from Appleby, Jason connected with branch members. He took time to get to know them and understood their experiences. I began to wonder how much of this might be related to Jason's being a White Irish man, someone familiar to the majority White Irish branch members. Would a racialized non-Irish leader be viewed in the same way, or would he be positioned as "the stranger" (Simmel, 1971) within the congregation?

I had a hint at the answer from Jason himself, who told me that he worried about his own unconscious bias in the allocation of "callings." An important way that members serve the organization of the branch and assist each other is through carrying out their callings, the voluntary work in the branch that they are personally called by God to carry out. Callings are allocated from branch leadership through a process of personal revelation from God. The branch president prays to Heavenly Father for assistance in deciding which member is the most appropriate person for that calling at that time. The most appropriate person may not always be the most experienced or best qualified. Rather, revelation from Heavenly Father means that those who are called to a role may also be those who are in need of a purpose, or those who are struggling in their personal lives. The nature of callings is that "every Mormon is the preacher, teacher, exegete, and definer of meaning before an audience of peers, who at a moment or a month later may switch positions with him" (Leone, 1979, p. 168). This is because once called, an individual may be released from that calling at any time.

Jason told me that there was one man in church who was an active member and living an honorable life. In spite of this, Jason had not yet had an urge to call him to a position in the branch and wondered if, in spite of himself, cultural or ethnic differences might be causing him to hesitate. I felt this to be an honest admission of the thoughts that must cross many leaders' minds as they evaluate their own leadership. It seemed to me that Jason was wondering if he and the man in question shared more cultural commonalities, might he find it easier to know that a calling was right for him. Jason's admission revealed to me that which some Mormons were reluctant to speak to me about—the interrelationship between the sacred and the profane (Durkheim, 1915).

When I reminded the participants of my research that I was a sociologist and thus interested in the social, cultural, and structural influences on religious life, I sometimes struggled to get some participants to speak about such matters. For example, Donal was an elderly man in his seventies living alone in an isolated and rural location. As I learned more about his life sitting at his kitchen table, I came to understand just how much some Mormons attributed meaning to their actions and decisions through Heavenly Father alone. Donal's decision in his twenties to join the Church as a young convert, his decision to return home to Ireland after many years living abroad, and his feelings on gender equality in church, were all mediated through his worldview that "the Lord sets the standards, not the man." Donal told me: "A lot of people don't really take Jesus Christ as real as me or you or anybody else. He truly is here. He died on Calvary's Cross, rose from the dead, [on the] third day he ascended into heaven where he is seated to the right hand of the Father. He's fully in charge of this earth, believe me he is. Man might think he is, but he's not." In contrast, I knew Jason had taken sociology classes during his undergraduate years. I wondered to what extent this may have given him greater insight into how cultural and structural experiences of race, migration, and exclusion may be influencing leaders' decisions regarding the allocations of callings, particularly his ongoing uncertainty about the readiness of particular individuals.

In the well-established Appleby branch where many members were White Irish, the process of allocating callings was fairly well managed and caused no significant effects on the atmosphere of the branch during my time there. Appleby had less ethnic and national diversity than Sweetwater, but at the time of my fieldwork two men who were not White or Irish held the Sunday School president calling, one after the other. This may demonstrate that efforts were made to ensure not all leadership roles were held by the majority White Irish members. In the diverse Sweetwater branch, however, the allocation of callings was a divisive issue and caused much branch conflict. One ongoing dispute related to allegations from Suzanne and her family and friends that branch leaders are not truly praying to Heavenly Father for revelation and inspiration about which member should be called to roles. They alleged that instead personal alliances infiltrated the process of calling members.

Suzanne and her husband Michael strongly believed this to be the case. When I asked her if the branch president, a man who I will refer to as Mackey, is inadvertently placing people into callings who reflect his own worldview, she said:

> He loves Americans, like that is a fact. Any American who comes to the branch gets a calling immediately. . . . And it's not about bitterness, it's not

that I need to be in a calling, no, no, no. Lots of responsibility and you don't always want that. . . . You have to be careful, *they* have to be careful, when they are in that role, to think "Are we really praying about everybody here and going with who we feel?" not like "Well, we think that they should do the calling because they've been years in the Church, because they are American, and they know a lot of stuff." It doesn't work that way. It *shouldn't* work that way.

Despite Church efforts to create a global church, the hegemonic association between Mormonism and the United States has not disappeared in the contemporary era. It remains an international church intimately bound to the United States. In chapter 6, I will illustrate how this association works to privilege US Mormons in non-US contexts, and functions as a form of cultural colonialism. Suzanne's comments here reference such patterns, by implying that Mackey idealizes US Mormonism and as a result gives preference to US members in church. These types of disputes are further complicated in Sweetwater by its increasing diversity. The majority of members are now not Irish born, and a significant minority are also not White. This diversity is a change for Sweetwater; elderly Mavis told me that Sweetwater branch and its closest neighboring branch were majority White Irish until relatively recently. Irish members of the branch such as Suzanne and Mavis feel marginalized as a minority in a now diverse congregation. In contrast to Jason in Appleby, in Sweetwater some members were disappointed at the performance of Mackey as branch president. He has since been released from the role after about five years of service.

Mackey's most strident critics were some of the Irish members of the congregation; particularly Suzanne, her mother, Mavis, Suzanne's South American husband, Michael, and some of Suzanne and Michael's Irish friends. I heard criticism about the branch president from others also, such as a North American Mandy and South American Maria. Unhappiness with Mackey's performance as branch president was therefore not solely experienced among the Irish. However, those other complaints to me about Mackey were less forthright than those of the Irish group, which suggested to me that the Irish members were opposed to something significant regarding their understanding of how he performed his role. The criticisms from the Irish were wide-ranging—they claimed Mackey was too traditional in his attitudes toward women, that he didn't make enough effort to support social activities in the branch, that he was biased toward the North American members of the branch, and that he was overly concerned with his home country in Southeast Asia and not enough with Ireland. The vocal nature of the Irish group's complaints meant that it was commonly known in Sweetwater that some members were deeply unhappy with their branch president, leading to poor relationships between some members. The Southeast Asian members tended to sit and socialize together in church and at social events, leading to obvious divisions along ethnic and national lines, which I felt was at least partly attributable to the discord surrounding the position of Mackey as branch president.

Additionally, this problem brought about disputes in church that were ostensibly about other issues, but appeared to me to be rooted in this particular issue. Suzanne and her friends enjoyed what they told me was a better social life in church under the leadership of the previous branch president. Suzanne told me that Mackey's response to these complaints was to point out the small space available in the building and the poor kitchen facilities, which he said made social events in church difficult. I strongly agree with Mackey that the Sweetwater building was not ideal for large events. The building was mainly dominated by just one room: the chapel space, which was then subdivided into smaller rooms when needed using folding partition walls. The kitchen consisted of little more than a sink and some kitchen cupboards at the back of the chapel space. Conflicts therefore arose between members about what was achievable within the constraints of the building's cramped facilities. Behind these disputes about facilities lay another, more complex issue. Over dinner one evening in her apartment with her mother Mavis and husband Michael, Suzanne told me that they believed the true reason for the lack of social events in church was that Mackey was not as committed to holding parties and other social events in church as the previous branch president had been, and that he did not give due appreciation to the role of social bonding in the maintenance of a successful congregation. Therefore, ultimately, conflicts about facilities were not really about facilities at all, but about the nature of leadership.

The validity of the criticisms of the Irish group does not concern me so much as what these concerns represent. In her studies of congregational cultures, Penny Edgell Becker (1999) argues that congregational leaders can reaffirm the current path of the group or shift the congregation onto a new path for the future. In Sweetwater, I suspect this is the true cause of the concerns with Mackey as branch president. Suzanne and Mavis agreed that the current president was being compared to the previous leader. Suzanne tells me that "you would have had that before [a 'good' branch president] so you've had that with other priesthood and other bishops, you felt it, and all of a sudden it's not there anymore and it's, like, I miss that." Suzanne's explanation demonstrates that the current branch president has changed the path of the congregation in a way that causes concern among some segments of that congregation.

As someone from Southeast Asia, Mackey was racially marked as different from the mainly White Irish group encompassing Suzanne and her family and friends. It is possible that the branch president's visible difference made his distinction from the previous White European president more acute, and aided perceptions that he was also culturally different from the mainly White Irish group. Evidence of this came from Suzanne's husband, South American Michael. He cited the cultural background of Mackey, his wife, and another couple from the same country in his justification for his concerns regarding Mackey's leadership performance:

> Maybe he has a problem with his own culture, because I remember he always talks about [his home country]. He never stopped talking about [his home country] and for him, his wife has to always be very patient. Say like, when you are in the airport and you are going through security.[1] He's standing there with his arms crossed, and she is using all the bags, and getting the buggy[2] put through, and he is just standing there, you know what I mean? And that is just his culture. The other couple—I went to do something for Suzanne at about six in the morning, and she was almost finished doing the breakfast for her husband and I said, "Is that for you?" and she said "No, it's for him, he likes to have breakfast at six thirty!"

Michael appears to be suggesting that the branch president's cultural background is the cause of his dislike of him. It is interesting that South American Michael, as a fellow immigrant to Ireland, is so forthright in his articulation of these cultural differences. Connecting the gender roles within Mackey's marriage to Mackey's "own culture" serves a dual purpose of racializing Mackey as Other, and of dismissing Mackey's leadership style as being about cultural difference. That this meaning-making was being produced by Michael, a man who himself has been racialized due to his own status, intrigued me. How could Michael have so little empathy for Mackey, a fellow migrant who like Michael sometimes struggled to be accepted?

Getting to know Michael over the course of my time in Sweetwater, I came to understand that despite being a proud South American, an embrace of Irishness and Irish culture more generally was very important to Michael. On St. Patrick's Day, Ireland's national holiday, Michael arrived at the branch party dressed head to toe in a bright green suit and a leprechaun tie. He and Suzanne were also big fans of traditional Irish music, and they traveled all over Ireland to follow one well-known traditional Irish band at their live appearances. He frequently mentioned his love of Ireland in casual conversations with me, and seemed to me to be eager to demonstrate his accumulated "cultural capital" (Bourdieu, 1986) regarding Ireland. Michael appears to have fully embraced a particular form of Irishness, and it shapes his understandings of who he is as a non-Irish person in Ireland.

Michael's reference to Mackey's "problem with his own culture" is about the extent to which Michael feels the branch president has or has not embraced Irish culture. Though a central argument of this book is that neat descriptions of both Irish and Mormon culture are simplistic, reductive, and unhelpful for appreciating the complexity of both modern Mormonism and modern Ireland, it is clear that many of the Mormons I spent time with *did* engage in discourse of this kind. This discourse operated as a way to make sense of their multifaceted identities. In Michael's case, he appears to have adopted particular aspects of Irishness as his own—an informal conversational style, a love of traditional Irish music, and certain idioms and phrases, as a way to integrate himself into Irish society. His assessment of Mackey as branch president seems to be connected to his evaluation of Mackey as a different type of migrant than him; one who doesn't strive to assimilate himself within the dominant culture. Thus, it does seem that the ethnic and national diversity of the Sweetwater branch has negatively affected the cohesiveness of the congregational community. Suzanne says of the branch, "because it's kind of international you don't always have that kind of unity."

It should be noted that this assessment by Suzanne is not shared by all in the congregation. Fellow Irishwoman Claire told me she didn't think that increased diversity was the cause of Sweetwater's tensions, telling me, "I don't think so, to be honest, because it's been very multicultural for a long time and that's been quite a nice aspect of it in my experience. I don't think that at all, to be honest . . . that has always been part of the branch's makeup. It might be more to do with just a couple of, yeah, a couple of clashes maybe, in the current group." Noting that Mormonism is hierarchical and rule-based, Claire suggested that it is this rigidity that some members might be struggling with. Regardless of the root cause, it seems the difficulties of the Sweetwater branch president are emblematic of the challenges inherent in maintaining tradition and building community in a contemporary congregation.

Suzanne and those who are unhappy with their branch president hold a particular conception of leadership, which sometimes comes into conflict with others who conceive leadership in other ways. Suzanne and her mother Mavis told me they see the role of branch president as someone who "listens" and "cares"; someone who supports the personal and collective wellbeing of the congregation. This comes into conflict with other

Sweetwater members such as David from South America, who argues in relation to leadership that "the Church is not a democracy; it is a theocracy. So, whatever happens, it is not by popular vote. It comes from above." Yet, as the head of the congregation and Christ's representative locally, the attitude and behavior of the branch president becomes a communal concern; he does not simply lead the congregation, he represents them. The differences represented here by Jason, Suzanne, Mavis, Michael, and David regarding what makes a good leader illustrates that the role of the branch president can become a contested symbol of congregational identity.

At its heart, however, I contend that these kinds of conflicts reflect a lack of agreement within the congregation about "who we are" and "what we do here" (Becker, 1999, p. 3) in the face of rapid social change both inside and outside of the congregation. The nature of religion in Ireland, and of Irish society more generally, are changing rapidly. The congregational conflict in diverse Sweetwater is therefore emblematic of life outside the congregation, where old traditions are being cast off or adapted, and new ones created. As Nancy Ammerman (1998) reminds us, "congregations are also, of course, shaped by the larger secular culture in which they are located" (Ammerman, 1998, p. 78). Some such as Jason appear to be mindful of this, and engage in reflexive practices that illustrate an awareness of the interrelationships between the world outside of Church and the world within. Others appear to frame understanding around a hierarchal notion of Church leadership and the role of Heavenly Father in guiding people's actions and decisions.

We can also see in these grassroots conflicts a reflection of the global Church. Just as in the wider Church around the globe, we can see that the Sweetwater branch is struggling with rapid change. It is negotiating shifts in power between minority and majority groups. It is learning how to integrate diverging priorities and values and figuring out how to allow marginal voices to be heard. It is learning how to facilitate racialized groups to lead, and how to accommodate those who are fearful of change, and who see the old way of doing things falling away. Thus, rather than being an example of a branch that hasn't managed to make congregational life work, I see Sweetwater as emblematic of the Church itself. Its struggles are the Church's struggles, and having seen them up close, I understand how difficult they are to overcome.

Celebrating St Patrick's Day, the Mormon Way

A social event within the Sweetwater branch represented many of the themes discussed within this chapter. My time in the Sweetwater branch coincided with St. Patrick's Day, Ireland's national holiday. The branch held a party in the church building on the Saturday night closest to St. Patrick's Day. This would not have been unusual; most branches, including Appleby, hold their own St. Patrick's Day parties each year. Abbey was the Relief Society president at the time. This meant that she had responsibility for coordinating the party and allocating its budget; the Relief Society president normally manages all social events in the branch. However, it is usual for the practical planning of such events to be delegated to a willing member of the Relief Society, and in this case Suzanne took on the planning of the event.

The Irish group in Sweetwater comprised about nine regularly attending members within a congregation of roughly fifty members from all over the world. The party offered an opportunity to see how Irishness would be approached by the various diverse groups present. The party was a great success, and was well attended by the various nationalities within the branch who seem to have enjoyed the traditional Irish music playing in the background and the Irish-themed party games. On the evening of the party, I arrived early and helped the missionaries put up the last of the green-colored decorations on the walls, and to arrange the folding chairs around the perimeter of the room in a way that facilitated sociable conversation and space for the children to play and dance. Despite putting in a significant amount of work in preparation, on the evening of the party Suzanne was delayed by about thirty minutes. Rather than keep everyone waiting for Suzanne's arrival, Abbey decided to formally welcome everyone and to get the celebrations under way. I found out afterward that this decision caused great offense to Suzanne, who felt that her fears of the North Americans "interfering" (Marilyn, Sweetwater) were being proved correct. No doubt her anger was heightened due to the party being a celebration of all things Irish in a congregation where the Irish were a minority.

Once the party got under way Marilyn, Marilyn's nonmember friend Evelyn, and I went to get some food and brought it back to our seats where we continued to chat. The congregation had been asked in advance by Suzanne and Abbey to bring "Irish" food to the party. It was emphasized that if they were unfamiliar with traditional Irish dishes, they could choose to bring food decorated in Irish colors or with an Irish theme. As a result, there was a wide variety of foods laid out on the long table. People brought leek and potato soup, Irish stew, Mikado and Kimberley biscuits, Jacob's cream crackers with cheese and jam, and shepherd's pie. There were also plenty of sweets and cakes decorated with green food coloring, including my own.

The congregation had been encouraged to dress up for the party and people of many nationalities had come wearing costumes or incorporated the color green into their outfit. Some of the men were wearing comedy ties, and many Southeast Asians gathered in one corner to use face paint to draw shamrocks, green hearts, and the Irish tricolor on their faces. Suzanne's husband Michael arrived dressed head to toe in a bright green outfit. Seeing such a display of enthusiasm for costumes, I felt a little self-conscious that my only sartorial concession to the theme of the night was to wear a gaudy pair of green, flashing earrings that said "Irish." However, I was conscious of the intergroup disputes in Sweetwater, and I had not wanted to wear a costume or other clothing that would mark me too clearly as Irish and therefore a part of the Irish group in church, as I was trying to maintain relations with all the various groups. Simultaneously, however, as one of the few Irish people regularly attending church, I felt an obligation to get involved and mark my nationality.

Suzanne had organized party games, and particularly used a game of bingo to educate the diverse congregation on aspects of Irish history, culture, literature, and language. I played the bingo game with Mandy and her three children. Suzanne put a lot of effort into the game: she had hand-drawn the bingo cards beautifully, and each square on the bingo card related to an element of Irish culture, history, or language. She included items in each square such as a dolmen (an ancient Irish tomb), a crannog (an ancient dwelling), an Irish wolfhound, Newgrange (an ancient burial ground), and Irish authors such as Bram Stoker and James Joyce. She also included a square that represented the cross of St. Bridget, a well-known Irish saint within Catholicism. Other squares included Irish words like "ceol" (music) and "slán" (goodbye). Suzanne also took the time to explain each reference as she called out each new bingo square. I talked to the children and to Mandy about these various references. Having been in Ireland for just a year, they were interested in learning more.

I was intrigued to see Suzanne's inclusion of the St. Bridget's cross in the bingo game. Mormonism does not celebrate saints, as Catholicism does. Additionally, Suzanne herself converted to Mormonism from the Church of Ireland, rather than from Catholicism. Nonetheless, she is clearly familiar with St. Bridget and feels her to be a significant enough character for Ireland's national holiday that she chose to include her in the bingo game. Similarly, St Patrick's Day is a Catholic religious holiday celebrating a figure of Catholic significance, despite its conflation with Ireland's national holiday. The broad acceptability of this within Irish Mormonism reveals the ways in which Catholicism and national identity are entwined in Ireland and the acceptance of this by small religions such as Mormonism.

The party culminated with the singing of the Irish national anthem, made more difficult by the fact that the anthem is in Irish, a language unfamiliar to almost all the non-Irish people present. Suzanne came up with a solution for the multinational congregation. As we all gathered in rows facing the front of the room, Suzanne handed out a phonetical version of the national anthem to everybody. Once the backing music began, we all stood up and sang. Most of the adults didn't know the words and I noticed as we began to sing that many of them looked a little nervous. Abbey, who had come over to sit down beside me, was joking about how bad everyone would be at this task.

Yet, once we had begun, I noticed that the children, many of whom were ethnically Southeast Asian but born in Ireland, were singing very enthusiastically and full of pride, and they clearly knew all the words. In fact, in many ways they led their parents and other adults through the anthem. As an Irish person in this environment, I felt a certain obligation to calm the nerves I saw crossing the faces of some of the non-Irish members in expectation at having to sing in Irish. Cracking jokes and keeping the atmosphere around me lighthearted, I tried to create a space where the non-Irish surrounding where I stood (mostly North Americans) felt more relaxed. During the anthem, I made sure to sing out loudly, to help those around me who were unsure. At the end, I told Abbey that she had succeeded in singing her first ever Irish song and she smiled broadly back at me, obviously proud of her effort.

The singing of the national anthem did serve as a good reminder of just how few Irish attended the party, with perhaps just seven other Irish people present among a group of forty. However, it is important to note that for most Irish members, this nonattendance would not have been a deliberate snub to the party and its symbolism. The Sweetwater branch had very few regularly attending Irish members, being a diverse branch in which Irish members were a minority. Therefore, the small numbers of Irish present reflected the small numbers of Irish attending church within the branch more generally. Suzanne's careful preparation of traditional food and music for the event, and her attempts on the night to educate those of other backgrounds about Irish culture, history, and language through games, reveal that as one of the few Irish in the branch this celebration represented for Suzanne far more than a simple party. For Suzanne, the party offered an opportunity to bond with others under the umbrella of an Irish identity, and to invoke Irish traditions despite the very nature of the branch and its congregation being proof of Ireland's rapid change.

Additionally, the embrace of face-painting the Irish flag by the Southeast Asian adults, the ease with which their children sung the national anthem—being already familiar with it from school—and the abundant use of Irish costumes by South American Michael and others, all show how Mormons in Ireland can utilize Irishness to create a sense of belonging despite their minority status. In this case, it appears that the congregation could coalesce around an Irish identity, and it became a way for them to overcome some of their challenges as a group. For both ethnic minorities and White Irish, one strategy in managing multiple minority status appeared to be to embrace a sense of Irishness. One might not identify with the majority based on religion or ethnicity, but through an embrace of an Irish national identity one can nonetheless begin a route to finding commonality with the majority by adopting elements of the Irish collective memory as one's own.

Issues such as leadership and heavenly inspiration may not at first seem like obvious ways to better comprehend the simultaneous processes of disruption and maintenance of Irish cultural hegemony taking place in Mormon homes and congregations across Ireland. Yet, the experiences of adherents such as Seán, Suzanne, Michael, Mackey, and Matthew illustrate how Mormonism comes into conflict with dominant understandings of Irishness, and how local branches have become symbolic spaces where tensions over the nature of the cultural milieu of church come to the fore. As a multicultural and multinational branch where White Irish members are now a minority, Sweetwater represents these tensions but is not the only congregation in Ireland, nor in Europe, where such tensions exist. Rather, Sweetwater is emblematic of wider difficulties in diverse religious congregations both within Mormonism and other denominations. Sweetwater's adaptation to be a diverse religious community in a relatively short space of time has forced both Irish and non-Irish members to confront what it means to be Irish and what it means to be a Mormon *in Ireland*. These challenges demonstrate the difficulties in maintaining a common Mormon culture in a modern world of increasing diversity, and in an era of a global Church present in a multitude of cultural landscapes. Danièle Hervieu-Léger (2000) suggests that the collective memory of the religious group can be sustained through the legitimization of tradition. However, the narratives and experiences presented here illustrate that who has, or *should* have, the power to legitimize these traditions is questioned at a local level and is always mediated through personal understandings of culture and belonging.

Members from both Sweetwater and Appleby spoke to me at length about the difficulties inherent in building unity and commonality in diverse or transient branches such as Sweetwater, and in branches that are located far away from many members' homes such as Appleby. Such difficulties are common in a European context, being both physically and culturally removed from the Mormon Culture Region, which supports common values and norms and facilitates sociability. A sense of community does not manifest itself within the group simply as a result of a common religious belief and practice. Cultural differences, political tensions, and rapid social change can all affect community within Mormon congregations.

The narratives presented here remind us that the building of religious community must be very carefully managed in diverse and culturally fragmented locales. Maintaining community in Irish branches and wards is not easy but is vital to ensure that members feel themselves to be a part of something greater than themselves. This is particularly important given the minority status of Mormons within wider Irish society. A strong sense of community could serve as a "sacred canopy" (Berger, 1967) for Mormons in Ireland, which protects against the costs of life as a stigmatized minority. But as the stories here exemplify, this is difficult to create and maintain.

6

We Preach That Culture

Black Suit, Red Tie, Pulpit

Abbey and I were in her spacious dining room, at a beautiful wooden dining table. I grazed on the snacks she had prepared for our interview: fruit, cheese, and crackers. At this point in my fieldwork I thought I had a good handle on who Abbey was as a Mormon. She presented herself as a "Molly Mormon": North American, married with children, attractive, beautifully but appropriately dressed, her outfits signaling a quiet wealth, nothing ostentatious. Her children were adorable, well-behaved, and looked like they might have stepped out of a children's clothing catalog. I knew she was smart and articulate, and her discussions in Relief Society had already revealed to me that she was well traveled and well educated. I knew she presented herself confidently, but always suspected that there may be insecurities beneath this veneer. I knew she was well liked in church but that her cheerful and loud personality could rub some people, particularly Suzanne, the wrong way.

Our three-hour-long conversation at the dining table showed me how complex even a Molly Mormon version of Mormonism can be:

> I went to the BYU Jerusalem Center for Middle Eastern Studies and took courses in Old Testament and New Testament, and Judaism and Islam, and took Arabic and Hebrew, and did current Middle Eastern Studies. And then went to Oxford University and studied at Mansfield College for a semester in postwar British and English Literature. PPE—Philosophy, Politics, and Economics—was the course I was doing that study with. And I felt like that was a really important part of my spiritual development,

too. Looking up and saying, "'OK, I want to know what are other people raised with, and where does that come from, and what kind of identity comes from believing in this, and how is that belief expressed." And I just I think there is so much good and so much truth and so much kindness and so much love in almost all organizations. I mean, I know that there are organizations that aren't, but I think that it was a really wonderful thing to be able to study.

HAZEL: Did it make you reflect differently on the LDS at all?

Yeah . . . but I think that came early on, as my mom started looking into to it, too. She abandoned faith in a Christian god, or in Christ, and started looking into Daoism and Hinduism and Buddhism mostly. And I really love meditation and I love yoga, and that was, I felt, a really strong connection with that. And as I got into yoga and meditation, there was almost this impression that I would have of myself, if I was to put it in picture form. It would be that, you know, half of me would be represented by black suit, red tie, and pulpit like a General Conference–type address. And the other would be like, sitting meditating under a mango tree in some sari.

Abbey clearly makes use of multiple religious and spiritual traditions to inform her worldview and to create personal meaning. Yet, superficially, she appears to be as typically Mormon as anyone could be. Scholars of religion have long understood that people's professed beliefs and presentation do not necessarily reflect their practice (McGuire, 2008) and that a better way to understand people's religion is to look at how they live their religion in the everyday (Ammerman, 2007). Likewise, we know that hybridity (Werbner, 1997; Cieslik & Verkuyten, 2006; Roudometof, 2018) or syncretism (Pandian, 2006; Schwadel, 2010; Dy, 2014) of religious and spiritual beliefs and practices often create a person's worldview. This is to be expected in contemporary societies where information about other traditions is amplified through the media and new technologies (Lövheim, 2007; Lövheim & Linderman, 2015). In this respect we know that Abbey is not unique, and indeed later in this chapter I provide other examples I encountered throughout this research that demonstrate that modern Mormonism certainly incorporates those who find spiritual meaning in many locations within and outside of Mormonism.

Yet, the dominant stereotype of the Church that still persists is the one that Abbey, publicly at least, adheres to: black suit, red tie, pulpit. The Church has gone to great lengths to emphasize that it is a global religion, and that the diversity that comes with this is its strength (Church of Jesus Christ of Latter-day Saints, 2014, n.d.-b). However, the participants of this study were very clear with me that despite these efforts, there strongly persists a dominant culture within Mormonism that firmly centers a White, wealthy, and North American worldview. I have demonstrated that Mormonism maintains a continuity of collective memory in a variety of ways. However, these traditions are often intermingled with a dominant view of Church culture that is not passively accepted by members living outside the United States.

In challenging what some participants named "Church culture" in conversations with me, Mormons in Ireland question the assumptions that underlie the "chain of belief" of Mormonism (Hervieu-Léger, 2000, p. 81). Mormons in Ireland are creating imaginings of Mormonism and its spiritual and logistical homeland of Utah that incorporate *both* connection and disconnection with the dominant traditions of Mormonism. Here, I describe what this Church culture looks like to Church members in Ireland, and reveal the disagreement that exists about the usefulness of this culture. I argue that as so much of this culture is built upon ideals of Whiteness and intermingles with US exceptionalism that we should not be surprised if ordinary Mormons outside of the United States experience this culture as a form of colonialism.

Negotiating Commonality in a Global Age

The Church's policy of correlation appears to have provided the Church with a way to expand internationally into a variety of cultures while retaining a common Mormon identity. In this way, correlation assists in the maintenance of tradition and belonging in the global community. Many members I spoke with told me about how nice it is to have sense of "familiarity" when attending church abroad. For instance, Marilyn in Sweetwater is Irish but used to live in the United States. She tells me of her time attending church in California, saying, "Do you know what's fascinating? It's actually the same all over. The same feeling, the same sayings, it's not like being away." Chase tells me that "the core things are the same everywhere." He describes this as "welcoming" and "familiar," and shows that the standardization of the Church is a comfort to those in an unfamiliar place.

Maureen and John Murphy had a similar experience. In our joint interview Maureen told me that no matter what part of the world in which she attended church, she feels a connection to others:

MAUREEN: I feel a sense of belonging there . . . it's amazing how alike the teachings, well, of course the teachings are the same, but the Sunday school program, for instance. If it's done properly, the same lesson being taught in Appleby is being taught in every other place as well on the same Sunday.

JOHN: And that's anywhere in the world.

MAUREEN: So, I've gone to church in Barcelona, I've gone to church in Paris, and the same questions are asked and people give the same answers. They might be in a different language, and you might have a missionary translating for you, but you sit there and laugh because the same questions are asked and the same answers are given.

Maureen and John show awareness of the Church policy of correlation, although it is never referred to explicitly; they say, "if it's done properly, the same lesson being taught in Appleby is being taught in every other place" (Maureen, Appleby). Similarly, Elder McGuire mentioned to me in the Appleby foyer before church one morning that "the Church is correlated so well," referring to the Church as a global organization. Ordinary members, therefore, are aware that this familiarity is constructed, a deliberate Church policy. Clearly, this bureaucratic organization of the everyday religious experience is appreciated.

Correlation does seem to offer a "sacred canopy" (Berger, 1967) in the face of uncertainty by providing a framework for similar teachings, lessons, resources, architecture, and congregational structure. Indeed, Taunalyn F. Rutherford (2016) uses a similar metaphor to discuss the purpose of correlation. Describing correlation as a tent, Rutherford says that "in spite of its worldwide expansion, the church has maintained its insistence on uniformity in administration, emphasizing that all of Zion is one tent. . . . The emphasis of the LDS Church has been on maintaining a centralized and unified structure even when borders were enlarged, cords stretched, and stakes planted around the globe" (Rutherford, 2016, p. 38). Correlation has therefore created a route to belonging for some Mormons no matter where they find themselves, as it blurs national or cultural differences in attitudes and behavior by emphasizing instead what Mormons have in common.

Yet, a conversation with a visitor to the Appleby branch showed me the ways in which place-based differences can persist within the Church despite correlation. I got talking to the visitor, whom I have called Karla, who is originally from Africa and now lives in Ireland. I enjoyed a long conversation with her after the last lesson of the day, a Relief Society meeting, had concluded. The other women filed out of the room as we talked, until we were left alone in an empty room. Our conversation moved to a discussion of how the ideal Mormon life, as contained within Church manuals, may not always match up to the reality of living the faith every day. Karla used a metaphor of a health and safety briefing to employees to explain the difference to me: "The health and safety rules indicate what you are supposed to do, but everyone knows that people don't always follow them in reality."

She followed this up with another example, from Africa. She tells me, "In some parts [of Africa] there is a tradition of a dowry; the husband's family will pay the wife's family for the marriage." This is not in keeping with Church practices but even practicing Mormons pay this dowry upon marriage. She points out that this is part of the culture in some parts of Africa, and Mormon converts do not want to change this upon conversion to Mormonism. Caroline Kline's (2020) research with Black South African Mormon women confirms Karla's argument that women are reluctant to abandon this practice, as Kline tells of an anecdote where one woman manages to rename the practice in ways that allow her to achieve fulfilment of the *lobola* (bridewealth) while also ensuring she is not breaching guidance from Church leaders.

Karla told me this as an example of the ideal versus the reality of life as a Mormon. However, I suggested to her that it also shows that the Church must sometimes have to incorporate, or at least turn a blind eye, to preexisting cultural beliefs and practices in the areas they move into that contradict Church beliefs and practices. She agrees that this happens, particularly in Africa, but less so in Europe. Karla's observation that the Church offers more inclusive treatment of cultural specificity in Africa than in Europe struck me as familiar. Seán touched on a similar idea in his conversations with me. Seán had spent time in Nigeria in his younger years and he noted how the Church there appeared to facilitate an accommodation of national or ethnic culture within the Church in ways that he saw little evidence of in an Irish context—"Nigerians are not expected to behave as anything other than Nigerians." It is difficult to offer a detailed analysis of this phenomenon with just two instances cited by the participants of this research. However, we do know that members such as Seán, Suzanne, Mary, and Anna all report being frustrated that the Church seems not to understand their cultural differences as Irish people. Seán's resentment that Nigerian cultural difference was better accepted in the Church than Irish cultural difference reflects this attitude.

In chapter 3, I outlined Jason's experience managing his son's minority religious status in a Catholic school. There, he mentioned something that connects to this discussion. He said, "There were a couple of Muslims in the class with dark skin, so they were treated much differently because they were seen as an ethnic minority, so they [school authorities] went out of their way. Because we were White Irish from a different background, they just . . . it would be ignored." Once more through Jason's experiences we can see how Whiteness works to mask cultural or religious difference. I have wondered, however, if these comments from Seán and Jason are evidence of White privilege at work. I must be clear that both men did not blame the people of color at the center of their stories; rather they were blaming the Church and the Irish educational system, respectively. Nonetheless, there is a resentment that their status as a White Irish person seems to eradicate any accommodation of religious or cultural difference. There is no recognition in either of their narratives that those at the center of their stories are facing multiple marginalizations based on racial, ethnic, and religious difference and thus may be more deserving of accommodation.

Although my conversation with Karla prompted a lot of thinking on my part about these kinds of issues, at the heart of the conversation was an awareness of religious hybridity in the global age and how the Church should best respond to that. I have heard of a merging of Catholicism and Mormonism during my research, such as congregations visiting the local Catholic Church's Christmas creche or allowing children who are attending a Catholic school to say their prayers at night by blessing themselves in the Catholic fashion. Interestingly, both cases involved second- and third-generation Mormons rather than converts. Sue has engaged in these behaviors with her children despite having never been raised in any faith other than Mormonism. During a talk in Sacrament meeting Sue also told the congregation that she has "liked" Pope Francis's Facebook page and the page of a Buddhist group so that she can receive their updates through her Facebook account. Similarly, Anna tells me that if she is feeling overwhelmed, or wants a break from her busy family, she drives to a local Catholic church that she feels is particularly picturesque and peaceful and sits there alone with her thoughts.

In Sue's case, it appears that as the broader environment is still widely influenced by Catholicism and increasingly influenced by new religions and ideas such as Buddhism, she has absorbed this to some degree. She has adapted her religious behavior to incorporate some of the religious practices of the wider society in Ireland. In Anna's case, as a convert from Catholicism and coming from a traditional Irish Catholic family, visiting a Catholic church is a comforting and familiar experience that she has carried with her into her Mormon life. My conversation with Karla shows that in other regions of the world such as Africa, a merging of Mormon practices with local customs also persists. This creates a broadly correlated Church worldwide, but one that still retains local distinctiveness. From this perspective, Karla's story regarding the continuance of dowries in parts of

Africa is representative of the continuance of cultural tradition, while Sue's experiences show that her Mormon membership does not mean she has rejected the norms of wider Irish society. Rather, she maintains those habits alongside her Mormon beliefs and practices.

Even in relation to some of the Church's most high profile and identifiable doctrinal and cultural markers, significant divergence from the Church exists. About a year prior to my research, Ireland held a referendum on the question of legalizing same-sex marriage, as recommended by a constitutional convention gathered to assess constitutional change. Previous legal interpretation of marriage as referenced in the Irish constitution had assumed it to be heterosexual marriage, though this wasn't specifically referred to. This led to debate about whether a referendum was necessary, but a "cautious government" decided that putting the question to the people would avoid legislative changes subsequently being challenged in the courts (Suiter & Reidy, 2015). The proposed changes to clearly expand the definition of marriage to include same-sex partners was passed by 62 percent of voters. I was intrigued to find that all these months after the event, many Church members cited the result of the referendum when we were discussing Ireland's social change, and specifically when referring to how they as Irish people do not always subscribe to the dominant conservative narratives within Mormonism.

About four or five of my thirty interviewees indicated to me that they voted to legalize same-sex marriage despite the Church's well-known stance on this issue. It is worth pointing out that this group volunteered this information to me during the course of conversation; I never actually asked anyone about their vote directly, so we can only speculate about how the others may have voted. I can only assume on the basis of many conversations about the issue I had with members more generally, in and outside of church, that this is an underestimation, as I spoke with many people who appeared to me to be quite positive toward LGBTQ+ rights and/or same-sex marriage. Intriguingly, as the majority of Irish are self-identified Catholic, and the Catholic Church also opposes same-sex marriage, we can conclude that many Catholic and Mormon adherents in Ireland voted against the doctrine of their religion. This raises interesting questions about the role of authority in the legitimization of religious tradition. If both religions' adherents are remaking religious tradition without referencing the authority of the institutions of their religion, then we must work to understand what *is* the authority that is increasingly being invoked to legitimize this adaptation.

Participants of this research invoked either the authority of their own personal relationship with God or continued to reference the authority of the institutional church, but in inventive and unusual ways. For example, Diane told me that she does not agree with the Church's guidance regarding same-sex marriage. In the following exchange, she first outlined to me the Church's position on same-sex marriage, and then argued that the Church doesn't change in response to people's opinions: "But the way the Church is, it has never changed from the very start to when it was brought back in 1825. . . . You see in different religions they are changing toward the will of the people rather than the will of God. And ours is set out, this is what the Church believes. Same-sex marriage, you know, we believe, the Church, that it is between man and woman and that it is ordained by God and that is it." She then divulged to me that she had broken with Church guidance on the issue of same-sex marriage by voting in favor of same-sex marriage in Ireland's referendum on the issue:

> God says that it is man and woman. But now I voted for it. Because the way I see it is, that for society and people if they are gay, it would make life so much easier for them. There would be so much less suicides, there would be so much less of everything, the trauma that they have to go through, the problems of coming out to their parents. . . . I think I want them to be happy and be fulfilled and have the same life that I would have, and I don't see why they should be different just because they are gay.

As she explains her decision she tells me, "Everyone should be treated the same and our Church is big into that." Paradoxically, despite her clear breach from official Church statements on the issue, Diane remains in favor of the Church's refusal to change doctrine. I asked what her reaction would be if, tomorrow, the Church completely reversed its opposition to same-sex marriage: "Why should they change the religion just to suit the people? I would be thinking that is not what we said yesterday. And I would be thinking why is that changed? and why has God changed his mind because he has just condemned a whole load of other people that did it for the last number of years, so why are other people not being treated the same? I have a big thing about people being treated the same." It appears that Diane disagrees with the Church regarding same-sex marriage and has acted on this in a significant way by being one of the voters who brought about the introduction of same-sex marriage in her country. Yet, she does not want the Church to adapt its doctrine on this issue. How can we understand this contradiction? Diane references the institutional Church to justify her vote, stating that it stems from her desire for everyone to be treated equally, something that she reminds me the Church itself emphasizes. Yet she is also legitimizing the authority of her own personal values—for her, equal treatment matters. In this way Diane is able to legitimize her adaptation of Mormon tradition on heterosexual relationships by invoking the authority of the Church and its position on equality, and her own values.

I found that Church guidance on many matters is regularly disputed, adapted, or even rejected by members. Debates about how strictly one should follow Church guidance, or how loosely that guidance should be interpreted, can be a source of tension between members. After church one Sunday a woman I have called Sofia, two sister missionaries, and I were talking in the bright foyer of the Appleby church building. One of the missionaries was from the United States, the other English. A discussion of the Church's health code known as the Word of Wisdom (WoW) (Doctrine and Covenants, 89, 1–21) occurred. The WoW advises against consuming "hot drinks" (Church of Jesus Christ of Latter-day Saints, n.d.-e). This has usually been interpreted by members discouraging the consumption of tea and coffee, but the WoW doesn't give any further details on which types of hot beverage it means, or whether or not such foodstuffs should or should not be kept in the family home. The Church has refrained from offering clarifications on the WoW, something that has facilitated individual interpretation over Church instruction, while also sowing the seeds for disparate cultural norms to influence how this directive is interpreted. At this stage of my research I knew that the WoW was variously interpreted by members. Some drank decaffeinated coffee, for instance, arguing that it was the caffeine that the Church advised against. In contrast, others refused to keep tea or coffee in their homes, even for guests. This variable interpretation of the WoW is common, with James E. Faulconer (2006) noting that it is common for Mormons to reject tea or coffee because they are caffeinated, but to consume Coke, which is a highly caffeinated drink. It is within this context of variable interpretation of Church advice that the following incident occurred.

While Sofia, the sister missionaries, and I were talking, the topic of tea and coffee arose. The missionaries both said that they don't have tea or coffee in their houses at home. Sofia said she does, for when guests come, so she can offer it to them. I privately observed that she seemed quite flustered in her explanation to us, and I began to wonder if she felt that the missionaries or I were judging her for this admission. As she explained her position, both the missionaries began shaking their heads and pursing their lips disapprovingly, which gave me the impression that they really did not approve of this at all. Sofia seemed aware of this too. She appeared to be taking extra care to justify her practices, saying that people come to visit her from Italy, and everyone drinks so much coffee in Italy that it would be impossible not to offer it to them.

For Sofia, this breach of Church tradition is justified by national cultural tradition. Yet despite Sofia's protestations, this didn't appear to me to be an issue explained simply by national differences. I had heard and experienced many variations on the topic of abstaining from tea/coffee from all the nationalities I encountered throughout fieldwork. Indeed, during this conversation, the English missionary countered to Sofia that despite the traditionally English love of tea, her family still does not keep it in their house. Afterward as I reflected upon this conversation on the long drive home from church, I wondered if the differences about the management of tea/coffee guidance were more about a public expression of faith. Perhaps it is felt by some that the stricter you are with tea and coffee, the more devoted to the Church you must be. This aligned better with my own experiences; those who offered me tea and coffee in their homes or admitted to drinking decaffeinated coffee themselves have been those whom I would consider to be less conservative and rigid in their approach to their faith. Similarly, those who go out on a mission, like the young sister missionaries based in Appleby, tend to be devout and very adherent Mormons, which might explain their obvious disapproval.

Maureen and John told me of other examples where Church guidance is variously interpreted. The Church maintains that the Sabbath day is sacred and suggest it is a day for attending church, receiving the Sacrament, and quiet reflection. Like the WoW, this message is variously received. Maureen tells me:

> We do have some kind of fanatical people in our Church. . . . I've heard people nowadays say, "Oh I wouldn't have the internet in my house, there's too much dirt on it" [a reference to pornography or sexual images], or "I don't allow my children the television on Sunday because it's the Sabbath day" and that, to me, is all rot. . . . Sometimes you hear people standing up and bearing testimony and say, "My testimony of the gospel is the most important thing that I have." And I'm down there thinking "are they mad or what?"

John, who had been quietly listening to his wife speak, laughed loudly at this evaluation, while Maureen continues, "Because like, my testimony of the gospel, it's important to me but probably the most important thing—now I don't mean any disrespect to you—my husband would be the most important thing in my life, my children, my grandchildren. My friends. My testimony is one thing. But it's not the be-all and end-all of everything in my life." Maureen clearly places herself in opposition to "fanatical" members who take a strict interpretation of any guidance that might offer room for interpretation, and rationalizes that a strict interpretation of Church guidance is a form of "fundamentalism."

The experiences of Diane, Maureen, Sofia, and Sue highlight the variability of how Church doctrine and advice is interpreted. These interpretations do not appear to clearly diverge along national, ethnic, class, or gender lines, although it has been suggested to me that the Irish are more "relaxed" (Abbey, Sweetwater) than North Americans. Therefore, although correlation has been broadly successful in providing the global Church a common identity under which to unite, significant cases of divergence and disunity remain in the everyday experience of Mormonism. These divergences emphasize difference within the community and remind us that adaption of tradition will inevitably occur no matter how standardized or tightly controlled the messages are from Church headquarters in Salt Lake City.

Debating Church Culture

Many of the non-Irish Mormons I developed relationships with had often previously lived in other countries. Abbey was well traveled; David and Meredith, originally from South America, had lived in Europe and the United States; while Matthew had lived in three other European countries before settling in Ireland. These non-Irish Mormons were, broadly speaking, more likely to embrace the concept of a global Mormon identity centered around a Church culture and less likely to focus on national identifications above religious identifications. David and Meredith have traveled extensively and are baffled by what they see as Europe's continuing divisions along national and ethnic lines. David mentioned to me the continued divisions within Northern Irish Mormonism along traditional religious and ethnic lines:

> In Northern Ireland, you have heard probably, they normally say "Mormon" and then people will say, "Are you a Catholic Mormon or Protestant Mormon?" I know that many years ago in one of our congregations, people that was [sic] previously Protestant, they would sit on one side of the church and people that were previously Catholic would sit on the other side of the church. So, they were all Mormons, they were all believing the same thing, but somehow, culturally speaking . . . so eventually these people have to be coached, right? To be taught how to be. But it's beyond . . . you *have* to. Your belief cannot be subscribed to your nationality.

With this final statement, David rejects these kinds of affiliations. For him, a Mormon identity is a universal one. By choosing to view Church culture as something that should transcend national differences, David is inserting himself within a community in which he feels a clear sense of belonging. However, David himself is aware that this is not how identity often functions in Ireland:

DAVID: There is a sister in our branch, and she's Irish, and she told us her families aren't a member [*sic*] of the Church so when she was going to get married, she was going to marry in the temple, right? So she decided to get married in the States because she wasn't able to say to the family who were Irish that she was going to get married in England—in a temple in England.

HAZEL: So it was not the fact that she was marrying in the temple that would annoy them, but that she was getting married in England?

MEREDITH: Yeah, it was England. So she said it was enough, hard enough for them to understand that she was being Mormon, "but if I tell them I'm going to get married in England they will go crazy."

These anecdotes are revealing. Local variation in the experience of Mormonism as a lived religion is common. Every congregation brings its own history, myths, and challenges to create a unique experience. David's story of Northern Ireland clearly reveals that religious and cultural differences that existed before Mormon conversion continue in the new faith. The strength of these traditions of belonging ensure that they become part of the Northern Irish Mormon experience. David's mention of a fellow member's religious marriage in a US temple rather than the closest temple in the United Kingdom to avoid conflict with her family also illustrates that old traditions of belonging have lingered in contemporary Ireland because for this family, marriage in England would cause greater offense than the Mormon union.

Despite David's narrative, which actually illuminates the variation present in experiences of Mormonism, he and Meredith are adamant that Church culture is, or should be, the same worldwide. Meredith proudly told me that the Church has its own culture that exists across national boundaries. To demonstrate this idea, she tells me about the family's time spent living in the United States. She recalled the day her children asked her if it was OK to salute the US flag in school, despite not being from the United States themselves. "I said, 'Look, you are here; you have to respect that as a symbol. It's nothing bad in respecting it and in participating in it.' So, you are in their country, and the same when we moved to Italy. So, it's more like we have, the church has, a culture." Her narrative appears to place Church culture in opposition to varying national cultures. She taught her children to respect the symbols of both US and Italian cultures while they lived there.

National culture, she implies, is shifting, and the children must learn to adapt to each country they find themselves in, while Church culture stands apart and remains unchanged regardless of the country one finds oneself in.

David interrupts us to remind me that Church culture is deliberately cultivated because it is directly related to Church doctrine: that all people are children of God and brothers and sisters to each other, regardless of their nationality:

DAVID: We don't have it by chance, we have it because we preach that culture. We preach it on purpose because it doesn't really matter if you are Irish or from South America, it shouldn't matter. If we believe that we are children of God, you know? What the heck matters where you are from?

HAZEL: So, it goes back to the doctrine again?

DAVID: Absolutely. It shouldn't in any way affect our relations. Now obviously if in your culture you kill your neighbors and you put them in barbecues, that is a culture you need to change! But other than that, nationalities are completely irrelevant. They should be.

David accepts and supports the development of a common Church culture, based on the core principles contained within the Plan of Salvation. For him, this commonality across national boundaries is a reaffirmation of religious community.

In contrast, Maria, also from South America, strongly disputed this perspective of a universal Church culture during my interview with her. Having lived in South America, the United States, and Ireland, she has also experienced Mormonism in a variety of countries. We talked at her apartment, which she shares which her South American husband. Like David and Meredith, she moved to Ireland for work purposes, so that her husband could avail himself of a job opportunity. A young Mormon in her twenties, Maria is always immaculately dressed and unfailingly polite. When I arrived at her apartment, I was unsurprised to find that her home was spotlessly clean and organized, with a plate of cookies sitting on the table waiting for me. This was all in keeping with what I had imagined Maria to be, a model Mormon who would strongly identify with a common Mormon identity that crosses borders.

However, Maria rejected any claim to a universal Church culture, telling me:

I think every country, every branch, every ward is different. Yes, you will have the same classes and things but, no, it is never the same. It is an adjustment every time you change. At least for me . . . I feel like we are taught that, so we repeat that. We repeat the "oh everywhere is the same, we are the same." Maybe we like to think that, so we think that wherever we go we have a place, something to hold onto. But I don't think it's true. You are just, it is different, everything is different.

Maria's suggestion that Mormons are simply repeating what they have been told and taught regarding their inherent commonality is a bold statement, but it stems from her personal experiences in multiple wards and branches across three continents.

Despite the variety of views concerning a global Church culture, there can be said to be key Mormon values that most, if not all Mormons, agree exist. One of these is the ongoing need to progress and to strive for perfection. Mormons are taught and frequently tell each other that they must aspire for perfection. The Church's values stem from doctrinal instruction; the Plan of Salvation indicates that learning to consistently make the right choices aids in an individual's eventual salvation (Church of Jesus Christ of Latter-day Saints, 2008, p. 9). This has many positive effects for members, as they try to improve themselves spiritually and temporally in preparation for the next life. Meredith tells me, "One thing that I like about the culture of the Church is that we try to, we aim to excellence. We don't aim to bad [sic]. We should do that in our lives; if we are studying we should aim for more, if we are workers we should aim for excellence."

However, in that same interview with Meredith, David asked me, "Have you ever heard about the problem of perfection in our church? Sometimes people will worry about not being perfect and everything. . . . Sometimes people feel guilty for that because they made a mistake, to compare themselves to this perfect ideal that you should achieve in the family. Sometimes some Mormons have that problem." Here, he touches on the negative effect of striving for perfection within Mormonism, which is the pressure members feel to do things correctly, all the time. The conversation continues by my observing what I see as the paradox of perfection:

HAZEL: I think it's a cruel irony, actually, that the Church emphasizes all the time that you don't have to be perfect *yet*, and yet I think because you're holding yourself to high standards, you are then disappointed when you're not doing better than you think you should be.

DAVID: But it is your own personal problem, because nobody will say anything. It's not like we are saying "if you are not perfect, if you not like this all the time, you are doomed."

David insists that this problem of perfection is a "personal problem" rather than a problem of Church culture, and that it is not Church members who place these pressures on others.

Maria once more presents a different interpretation. During my conversation with her she argued that in fact Church members *do* exert pressures on others to live up to the perfection ideal. She told me of her troubled relationship with Mormonism, centered around her teenage years when she had "gone off the rails"—drinking heavily, having sex, and associating with drug dealers. She has since abandoned those behaviors and is now active in the Church once more, but during that period her Mormon parents threw her out of the family home. She recalls this period of her life:

> When I went inactive and crazy, drinking and all this stuff, they turned their backs on me, nobody talks to me. Nobody wanted to be close to me because I have a tainted . . . because I was wicked. . . . I went to the bishop and I asked for money. I explained the situation, I told him I don't have any money, I have 200 pesos, which is about 20 euro, and he said, "I can give you that; that is all I can give you; you have your parents' home; you can go back," and so maybe that's why I have that issue with the Church because everybody turned their backs on me, didn't even want to know me. Like my best, best friends were like, "no."

Maria's story confirms what David has said regarding there being a mistaken pressure to live up to what Maria calls "a perfect ideal," but it also shows that not all members agree with David's inference that there is no judgment from other members of the Church in not living up to these standards.

Importantly, Maria's story took place while she was still in South America and so I asked her if she feels this is a universal trait of a global Church culture—for instance, do these types of attitudes prevail in places like Ireland also? She replied:

MARIA: I know of cases that they were, people were serving in a calling, and because they did something that wasn't well seen, they took them off and they never call them again for anything.
HAZEL: Really? That's crazy.
MARIA: Yeah, yeah. It happens, every Sunday! *Sometimes* it happens every Sunday. It's just bad. The perception is very important, it's a very important thing for them. For *us*, I mean [she laughs at her own correction].

Maria's mention of people being removed from callings, never to be called again, reminded me of something Marilyn had said to me previously:

MARILYN: There is always the same people, the same always. That's a problem, I think, that they had the same people in the same callings. They don't use people who haven't been there for too long, to do callings. I think if they had, then people would be more organized and involved. . . . If one is not in one calling, then they're in the other callings, so it's always the same people.

HAZEL: Why don't they call the newer people?

MARILYN: I think, well, it's more of a cultural thing, I think. Because you will see that in everywhere in the LDS Church. We use the same people in leadership all the time because it's kind of like a mark of your worthiness. That you are worthy, or you are good Mormon, so I will give you a leadership position. And then kind of they keep them because they think, "Well, you are worthy."

HAZEL: Something else that might feed into this is that people have said to me that it is the same 20 percent of people doing 80 percent of the work. But is that not a self-fulfilling prophecy? If you give the same jobs to the same people over and over again, then of course it's going to be the same 20 percent of people doing the bulk of the work.

MARILYN: Yeah, exactly, and there is so many people into great things, but it's just almost not allowed sometimes. Where the suggestions are not taken. It is about worthiness and sometimes we say that we call people as revelation, like you know, from God? But sometimes I think like, it gets in between, the judgment of people gets in between that.

Marilyn's words echo the criticisms offered by Suzanne and the concerns raised by Jason in chapter 5 on the nature of callings. They, Marilyn, and Maria all acknowledge that human judgment plays a part in the allocation of callings. It is clear, then, that the behaviors, attitudes, and competencies that constitute "worthiness" are affected by human interpretation. In the rest of this chapter, I demonstrate how a White, wealthy, and US-focused worldview continues to permeate Church culture. It is clear to me that this worldview must also shape understandings of worthiness.

The consequences of this for a worldwide Church are significant. These dynamics operate at the highest levels of the Church, where a "monoculture" of Church leadership leads to a scenario where "LDS Church leadership appears to struggle with the idea that there might be more than one way to be a righteous Mormon in good standing with the Church" (Cragun, 2020, p. 820). It appears that this monoculture is also visible at the level of local leadership, too, shaping grassroots conceptions of worthiness and, therefore, of leadership. Is the Church reproducing a specific racialized, classed, and gendered definition of worthiness that excludes those members outside of its boundaries? And what are the long-term consequences if this is the case? All this is not to say that Church culture is a uniformly negative force; it undoubtedly has many benefits and admirable effects. It assists in uniting Mormons across the globe in collective responsibility; there are international welfare programs operated by the Church and funded by ordinary members to support the education and missionary efforts of disadvantaged Mormons across the globe. Similarly, Church humanitarian programs for all, not just Mormons, in times of natural disaster and war is the positive outcome of a Church culture that deemphasizes national boundaries and promotes a global community. Yet, as Maria's narrative shows, shared values of Church culture, such as aspiring for perfection, can also sustain troubling trends that appear to cross those same national boundaries.

Maria is an interesting person with whom to discuss Church culture. She confirms the existence of a global Church culture in a variety of ways. In a discussion with me about patterns in church regarding leadership and callings, she comments, "It's more of a cultural thing, I think. Because you will see that everywhere," inferring that there are universally identifiable trends of behavior within Mormonism. She also explains to me that the judgment and marginalization she experienced as a member in South America is also something that is experienced by members in Ireland, showing awareness of how similar aspects of Church life exist in many parts of the world. Furthermore, Maria is what I imagine in my mind as a model Mormon. She is married to a successful and well-respected priesthood holder, she always attends church, she holds an important calling for which she carefully prepares, she is polite and accommodating and never causes offense, intentional or otherwise. She makes an effort with her dress and appearance and appears perfectly composed at all times. Her troubled past within Mormonism and her ongoing struggles to make peace with how those in church treated her contrasts enormously with these other parts of her identity. Commenting on this image, I asked her how these two sides of her could be reconciled and she told me, "I guess I learned. I learned how to blend in." Maria, like Abbey, appears to be a multifaceted person who has learned to reveal only one aspect of who she is—that which is in keeping with the accepted cultural norms of Mormonism.

In understanding Maria's story, I contend that Maria is a good example of the tensions and complexities in a modern Mormon identity. She has absorbed the common cultural markers within the Church about what a good Mormon should be—"I learned to blend in." Yet, her narrative also tells of troubled times for her within the Church, and of her challenges in overcoming her resentment toward the Church. Maria represents someone who has a more complex and nuanced relationship to Church culture than David and Meredith. Despite their similarities—they have all experienced Mormonism in multiple countries, are settled in Europe, originally from South America—nonetheless, there are key differences in how they experience the concept of Church culture. This reflects the complexity in the lived reality of a global Church.

Exploring the "All-American" Global Church

After the initial settlers trekked to Utah in the 1840s, many European members followed them from the United Kingdom, Germany, Sweden, and elsewhere. Since 1910, however, the Church has encouraged members to stay in their home countries to grow the Church, to instead see Zion as "the Lord's people who are of one heart and one mind" (Church of Jesus Christ of Latter-day Saints, n.d.-f), Utah being considered as not only a physical place, but also a way of thinking. Scholars such as Gina Colvin and Joanna Brooks have posed the question of "What relevance does the idea of Zion have for communities at the margins of Mormonism?" (Colvin & Brooks, 2018b, p. 15) and I maintain that it holds enormous relevance, as a symbol that both unifies and divides the global Church.

Despite the ways in that the Church encourages members to see themselves as a common people, many Mormons in Ireland appear to remain acutely aware of differences between themselves and their fellow Mormons. Particularly, I have found that Irish Mormons are aware of, and often uncomfortable with, a particular version of Mormonism that some people described to me as associated with "American Mormons" (Marilyn, Sweetwater), and others as with "Utah Mormons" (Mandy, Sweetwater). In contrast to the members discussed above who had wide experience of Mormonism in many countries, many of the Irish-born participants of this research were more ambivalent about their connections to a global religious group that supposedly transcends national boundaries.

First, Irish Mormons were more likely than non-Irish Mormons to question the myths and narratives of Mormon history that assist in creating a common identity. For example, Seán rejected the Church tradition of commemorating the early Church's trek to Utah in an annual Pioneer Day celebration:

> They expect or encourage people to go along dressed as pioneer and so on. Now, I see that as an impingement on my national identity. I respect what those people did, and I think it was brilliant to march 3,000 miles and be harassed and so on, and I have great respect and great sympathy . . . but I will not be taken in and expected to behave as an American just because it happens to be based in America. No more than I would expect to behave as Italian because the head of the Catholic Church happens to be in Rome.

Second, Irish Mormons were also more likely to articulate differences between American Mormonism and other forms of Mormonism, and to identify this as a barrier to belonging to a global community. Knowing that the Sweetwater branch was struggling with interpersonal disputes like those explored in chapter 5, I asked Marilyn, "Is it hard having a branch that's so international?" and she responded:

> Not to me. It would be with an Irish person that hasn't traveled. Suzanne finds it a problem with some of the Americans, anyway. They drive her mad, but they don't drive me mad because I lived there and I can take it. I think it's, if you come from the island of Ireland and you don't travel, I think you get a bit closed-minded. I hear them in the town, and I hear them in the hairdressing salon, and they say, "them bleeding foreigners taking our jobs" and all this. I think they are so ignorant; they don't realize that without immigration the country is dead.

Marilyn argues that it is a lack of exposure to different countries and a fear of immigration that cause some Irish people, including Irish Mormons, to dislike other nationalities.

Mary Daly also admitted to disliking Mormons from the United States, but tells me that part of this dislike is based on her visit to Utah. For Mary, and unlike Marilyn, travel and exposure to US Mormonism has not made her more accepting of cultural differences. Mary firstly tells me that her family life with husband Bob is "different to typical Mormons, or what I would call American Mormons," because Mary and Bob are more relaxed about the Church and less socially conservative. Mary describes to me the US Mormons she has encountered during time spent in Utah, and those who visit the Appleby branch:

> This is the difference between me and what I would see, which is a lot of the missionary couples. Bob and I will *slag* each other.[1] We wouldn't be "hi sweetie," and it's not that we are being rude to each other or anything. You see a lot of people from the US background and they are they are just really nice, and sweet. It's like when you go to America and it's all "have a nice day." . . . You have to be having a bad day sometimes. You can't have this cheese constantly. So, there is, sometimes, you know it, I would see it as being a difference in culture probably. I'm not saying that every Mormon is like that, and it is stereotypical obviously. But lots of times I don't know, I don't know that the missionaries see anything outside of the Church. I met this lovely couple who reactivated me if you like.[2] I went to visit them [in Utah] with Bob and then they were asked to talk [in church] about their time in Ireland, and they were describing a totally different Ireland than the Ireland that I live in! They were talking about,

you know, everybody being in the pub. They didn't talk about family, and how important family is to Irish people. And then I may have said that I had been reactivated, that I was inactive, and this man came up to me in the chapel in America, and I knew that he thought that I had actually been in the *gutter* you know?!

Mary clearly feels that cultural differences are a barrier to identifying with US Mormons. This is a significant difficulty toward achieving the full inclusion of Mormons across the globe considering the continued American influence within the faith generally, and on Church culture specifically.

Yet, Mary acknowledges that just as her US friends saw a different Ireland to what she sees, her own views of them may also be subjective. "Maybe I'm seeing a different America as well, to what they see. People see totally different things, don't they? So maybe if I was to talk to somebody and say what my perception of America was when I was there, theirs would be very, very different. But that was my perception. And their perception [of Ireland], even though it upset me, was their perception." In contrast to David's insistence that national differences do not matter within Mormonism, Mary reflects upon the subjectivity of her position as an Irish Mormon. She sees and understands the perceived differences between Irish and American Mormonism, but also understands that these supposed differences are always dependent on a particular standpoint.

Simultaneous to an Irish rejection of US Mormonism, there appears to be an Irish idealization of Mormonism and Utah. Many Irish Mormons still move to Utah or other areas of the United States that support high levels of Mormonism, such as Stephanie who is now based in Utah. Others are wistful about the plentiful social and religious activities that are possible within US congregations, yet unsustainable in Ireland. Maureen tells me that "a lot of Irish members of the Church, they move to a place where there are a lot of members of the Church, where all the church programs are operating. Where they wouldn't all be operating in Appleby. We would just have the nucleus of them whereas they operate on a much bigger scale in bigger places." The Irish, then, both reject *and* idealize US Mormonism. These two versions of an imagined Zion coexist simultaneously. It is even possible for one person to incorporate both viewpoints, such as Suzanne from Sweetwater. Suzanne displays much of the complexity regarding how Mormons in Ireland think about US Mormonism as *the* key representation of a global faith community. Given her strained relationship with Abbey, whom it seems that Suzanne may have viewed as an archetypal North American, we might expect that Suzanne, too, rejects the heavily

Americanized aspect of Church culture. The reality is more nuanced. She tells me:

> The Americans are really different to us. There is so much difference. I was in Utah, went to visit in Utah. We always wanted to see what it was like, and at first there was a lovely spirit there, and you feel the presence of the Church there and you can't deny all that. It's just not a place that I would—I wouldn't want to live in America. I just wouldn't, Americans, not the Americans that I know, put it that way. I've never been to New York, never been to Boston, I don't know those kinds of [Americans], I'm talking about Church Americans mostly. But I think it's mostly because, they are brought up in the Church, they have a different viewpoint. They can be a bit patronizing toward those that are not born in the Church and they don't allow for your point of view.

Suzanne believes that "Church Americans" are different not just to the Irish, but perhaps also to others from the United States. She illustrates how some Irish Mormons think that Utah and those who live there are a different and unusual place and people. Later, Suzanne tells me about those Irish who idealize US Mormonism:

> I think people kind of looked up to them and thought about "the American Dream"; you know the Irish still do kind of love Americans. . . . You get a lot of Irish members of the Church wanting to be Americans. We had a friend called Vincent . . . and he was mad about America; he's living over in Utah now. But he had the accent way before. And I used to ask, "Why have you got an American accent?" and he'd say, "Oh, I hang around with the missionaries" and I would say, "Well, I hang around with the missionaries and I don't have an American accent." They have this idealism. But when I was in Utah, and the temples there, you do feel the spirit, I'm not saying you don't. It's like going to Jerusalem probably. You feel the same. You also see, like, we drove into an area of Utah that was all like broken-down cars, and there was Mexicans walking around with big tattoos on them, and you know then that it is clearly not all members over there, and there is a massive difference. It's not all rose beds.

Suzanne represents the dual construction of Zion in the Irish mind. She does feel that Utah is special; she speaks of "feeling the spirit" there and compares it to Jerusalem to demonstrate its sacredness. For her, Utah is a very spiritual place. Yet, she also speaks of not liking the people there, and observes that not all parts of Utah encapsulate a White, respectable, middle-class lifestyle that many Irish Mormons imagine Utah to be as part of their "mental pictures" (Vertovec, 2004, p. 282) of the religious homeland. Both

Suzanne and Mary demonstrate how complex the imagined community of Zion can be, by both identifying and dis-identifying with its people and place.

Confronting White US Mormonism

Further evidence of disunity within the standardized Church comes from areas of the world that have not traditionally been sites of Mormon proselytizing. Rapid growth in South America, Africa, and parts of Asia have challenged the limits of correlation. This growth throws into high relief the White American underpinnings of the faith, which is now more visible as the Church grows in regions far removed from this White American background. In Ireland, too, increasingly diverse Mormon congregations have brought about an increased awareness of the place of race within the religion.

Chase, who is White North American, travels regularly for work and will stay in one country for only up to five years at a time before he is required to move again for work purposes. He has lived in many countries including the Netherlands, the Philippines, and the Maldives. He has also attended church in many more countries as a visitor if he is staying briefly for work purposes. Therefore, he has experienced Church life in a variety of places including the Global South where he has spent time with Church members whose lives are far removed from the all-American ideal that Irish members appear to struggle with. He says of the Church's attempts to universalize the Mormon experience:

> It's been a struggle. I work with a lot of multinationals. If you try and take some US company and bring it over to Africa, it's hard. So, there are some things you want to bring over from that culture that are important to what the company is; this is Apple, this is what we do, this is how we believe. And you bring it over to somewhere like China or Africa, well, it's going to clash a little bit. . . . My brother, he was a mission president in India so he was over in India and over in Pakistan, so the stories he tells about Christians in Pakistan being baptized—that's not only hard, it's dangerous, you can imagine. So how does the Church deal with all these different things? You can imagine for the first long while it was trying to create this identity. When you have people from all around the globe coming in . . . So I think it's a work in progress. But you definitely would see it if you were to go back and look at the manuals and look at the pictures or whatever;[3] I mean the message is the same, but the stories that they use, or the pictures that they use—they have tried to regionalize it to some

degree. . . . But I can tell you from a real point of view, for example, being in the Philippines and teaching lessons, when every single picture image is Caucasian, that's hard.

Before this conversation with Chase I had noticed quite a diverse range of ethnicities and racial groups represented in the Church manuals stocked in Appleby and Sweetwater, which I had interpreted as a positive example of how the Church is increasingly becoming aware of the need to represent all members across the globe. Yet, through his example of teaching lessons in the Philippines using manuals with only images of White people, Chase articulates being uncomfortable with the lack of diversity that still exists in the Church despite its global nature.

Mandy is another White North American in Ireland, and similarly conscious of how the Church includes members of diverse backgrounds. Having attended another ward in Ireland prior to Sweetwater, she told me how diverse the Irish congregations are compared to her experiences in North America:

[Her first Irish ward] is very diverse, there is a couple of families from Nigeria, and there are people who are originally from the Ivory Coast, there are French, and there is German, and so I was really excited about that. . . . Our ward in the States was 100 percent White, there was not even a Latino! I'm sorry—there was one Asian man . . . and his wife was White. And other than that, there was no diversity, so I loved that when we moved here. I was glad to move to Sweetwater, where there is still more diversity. It helps me enjoy church more because I feel as though, OK, this *is* a worldwide Church. . . . And I love to hear the experiences of people who grew up in other countries and what brought them into the Church. . . . So, for me it helps to strengthen my feelings because I feel like when you live in [her previous location], you just feel like the Church is just a bunch of White people. you know?

Chase's concern about the predominate White focus in the Church is clearly also shared by Mandy. Part of what has made her time in Ireland enjoyable, despite the homogenous nature of the majority society, has been the diversity within the Mormon congregations she has attended. It is interesting that Mandy and Chase come from North America, substantially more diverse societies than Ireland, yet they have experienced Mormonism as a White religion and Mandy, in particular, criticizes the homogeneity of the wards she has previously belonged to. In Ireland, they find the Mormon branches to be more diverse than what they have previously experienced. This is despite the wider lack of ethnic and racial diversity in Irish society.

On one occasion during a Sunday School class in Sweetwater I was intrigued to hear the White US teacher I have named Ted describe Church teaching manuals as featuring "the token Asian person" and describe these attempts at diversity as appearing forced. Ted can trace his family back to one of the original pioneers who made the trek to Utah. He now lives in Ireland, and the others in Sweetwater were well aware of his pioneer background. In mentioning Ted to me on one occasion, Marilyn approvingly told me, "He is a [she says his family name], you know, they are one of the pioneer families." I felt that Ted's family background gave him a certain status in Sweetwater. Unlike in parts of the Mormon Culture Region, in Ireland it would not have been common to have descendants from the founding families attending church. Ted's special status is also further evidence of how the founding myths of Mormonism, which are so centered upon a particular place and a particular people, still hold powerful influence in parts of the world that would otherwise be unmoved by such things.

In reflecting upon these commonalities and differences between the Mormon Culture Region and Ireland as we talked in between lessons one day at church, Ted told me that "being Mormon in Utah is like being Catholic in Ireland." In other words, there is a ubiquity to the White Irish Catholic experience in Ireland that is familiar to him due to his experiences as White US Mormon in the Mormon Culture Region. It is within this context that Ted described the "token Asian person" within Church teaching manuals as being a "forced" attempt at highlighting the racial and ethnic diversity of the Church. Ted inferred that the Church was trying to insert a diverse representation of Church members into Mormonism where once there was none, and in the process made this diversity appear forced. Yet, it was an odd comment—surely wouldn't the high number of his fellow attendees in the Sweetwater branch who had an Asian background feel that this representation was not forced, but simply a representation of their lives? And as Chase has noted, in Southeast Asian congregations it is White images that are jarring, not Asian. It seemed to me that Ted did not fully appreciate this global reality but rather was viewing Mormonism through a Utah-focused lens, which represents just a small microcosm of the overall Mormon ecology, yet which holds an outsize influence over the whole.

Undoubtedly, though, Ted, like Chase and Mandy, seems self-conscious about diverse representation in a traditionally White church that is becoming increasingly racially diverse. All three White North Americans are consciously engaging with ideas of race and representation, and their reflections are significant. The Church is consciously attempting to move away from its predominate Utah-American focus to ensure global growth.

Ted, Chase, and Mandy are aware of the Church's increasingly multicultural focus. This new focus is a break with Church traditions that put much effort into mythologizing the pioneers, those White North Americans and Europeans from whom Ted is descended. This change indicates an adaptation, or even a rupture of Mormon traditions of belonging. As Jason previously noted, the Church now supports the idea that *all* converts to Mormonism are pioneers. This shift in the interpretation of pioneer—from White North American and European founding member to global converts of all backgrounds—broadens the scope of belonging for the modern age, but it seems clear that there is much more work to do to embed this worldview into the Church.

He Said He'd Think About It

Despite divergences in constructions of Mormon identity, there still remains a sense of community based on faith and culture. When I was based in Appleby, a member of the Church's Quorum of the Twelve Apostles[4] visited Ireland. Elder M. Russell Ballard is viewed by members as a living prophet of God, and so the visit was highly anticipated by Appleby members weeks in advance and they were delighted to hear that I would be attending the event in Dublin alongside people from all over the country who were traveling there for the event. My fieldnote record of that night reveals a community that rarely gets a chance to come together and that revels in those rare opportunities. Crucially, it tells of an event that is centered around one person who is viewed as God's representative on earth and who also exemplifies US Mormonism. Living and working in the place of his birth, Salt Lake City, Utah, Elder Ballard is a White, wealthy North American with an illustrious familial legacy in the Church that stretches back to the prophet and founder Joseph Smith. He is pioneer stock. Yet, while firmly representing a stereotypical version of Mormonism that many Irish Mormons reject, I found that he nonetheless retains the ability to unite Mormons in Ireland of all ages, ethnicities, and backgrounds in an experience of collective effervescence (Durkheim, 1915).

The event took place in the Dublin stake center. The stake center functions as an administrative center, but the building itself also generally houses a large congregation by Irish standards, of about 150 active members. Below, I have reproduced some of my fieldnotes as I wrote them on the night. Some were jotted in my notebook during the various talks, and full notes were written up once I arrived home after the event, exhilarated from the atmosphere of excitement that permeated the gathering. I hope that these notes provide not just a factual record of the evening, but sense of the atmosphere and high emotion that we all felt.

When I arrive at the event it is very busy with lots of cars waiting to get in. There are cars parked all over the grassy areas and crammed in together. There are hundreds of people here, and it's very noisy with everyone talking. It feels that there is an atmosphere of a reunion here; everywhere people are shouting "hello," "hi," shaking hands, hugging, and talking in groups. I feel a bit overwhelmed to see so many Mormons all together as I am so used to the small groups in Appleby. I look for Appleby people and can't see any, but then at the very back of the room I see Jason and Catherine, and I go and sit with them. As I look at the pamphlet for the event that we have been given, I can see that it uses American English spellings—"savior," "center" etc.—and I wonder who was responsible for creating it. It immediately jumps out at me as an obvious error.

It occurs to me that I am underdressed. Everyone else seems to be dressed up in some way. I see Diane further up the room, and I notice she has her hair down and appears to be wearing more makeup than usual. Jason is wearing braces with his shirt and tie, and most of the men are in three-piece suits. As I'm chatting with Jason and Catherine, Elder Ballard arrives and takes a seat. There is a murmur through the crowd at this, and Catherine says very excitedly, "Oh, there he is!" There are some speakers before Elder Ballard gets up to talk; the wife of the European Area president says, "I can feel the excitement, anticipation, and reverence" that is here for this event. She says she saw people lifting up their children so they could get a glimpse of Elder Ballard, and about them being so excited to be here.

The European Area president gets up to speak directly before Elder Ballard. He tells a story about planning Elder Ballard's schedule for his visit here ensuring to leave him some free time, but that Elder Ballard filled up all his free time by adding in other appointments. He says it is "a signal and a symbol not to settle." He says that he has been talking to people here who told him of traveling to the UK for the temple visit this weekend. He says he has also heard stories of people who have traveled for fifteen hours for a fifteen-minute visit to the temple. He pauses, and repeats that slowly, and then starts crying. He says, "That's a great symbol too." I can feel goosebumps on my arms, and I have a sense that everyone is taken with the emotion of this, though I can't really say why; it's an atmosphere in the room. He says that he prays that we will receive blessings out of all proportion for that fifteen minutes.

Elder Ballard finally comes to the podium. Catherine puts her hand on her heart and she is taking big breaths; she seems very overwhelmed. He says, "God bless us to be active, vibrant, and excited members." He starts to say, "here in Belfast" but catches himself as he gets as far as Belf . . . and turns it into "here in Belfast, Dublin, here in Ireland." I know he made the mistake because I heard his hesitation, and I had that feeling of dread in my stomach when I felt he was about to say the wrong place. This causes me to think about the focus on Northern Ireland by the Church in its early years, and I'm wondering if this might be an example that the oversight of the Republic of Ireland has lingered. Like the American spellings on the pamphlet, it makes me uncomfortable. Afterward, the Dublin stake president gives the closing prayer. He says, "This is the most important meeting that is taking place in Ireland" and "an Apostle of the Lord is in our midst."

I walk out with Teresa, whom I bumped into along the way. We have to go into the long narrow corridor and there are hundreds of people there. It is difficult to make our way through the crowd. When we are near the end of the corridor, she meets a man she knows who says that he hugged Elder Ballard but that he has left the building now. Teresa turns to look at me and her face is devastated. She looks so upset that she missed him and I feel awful for her. Before we leave, we meet Diane with some others; she says that she got to shake Elder Ballard's hand. She seems delighted, so smiley and happy. I ask, "What did you say to him?" and she says she asked him if they could have a temple in Ireland. The others laugh and exclaim "No you did not!!" and she says she did, laughing with us. We ask, "What did he say?" and she says, "He said he'd think about it."

The sense of pilgrimage and reunion that permeates my account reminds us of how the Church leadership centered in Utah can emotionally move and motivate members around the globe. The large crowds, the long distances people traveled from all over the country, and the effort that people took with their appearance shows us that this was a very special event. Quite revealing is Diane's gleeful admittance that, given what may be her only chance to speak to one of God's prophets on earth, she asked him to provide a temple for Ireland. The temple serves as a significant symbol for the dispersed faithful across the globe, and the granting of a temple perhaps interpreted as a reward for loyal and faithful perseverance in the face of opposition and marginalization. Additionally, despite the joyous reception for the US prophet from Utah who is a clear reminder of both the global nature of the Church and its continued North American influence, ultimately what matters to Diane is a local issue. Her request of a temple reveals that for Mormons in Ireland, local experiences intimately shape their understandings of Mormonism in the global age.

There can be no doubt of the significance of the United States, and Utah particularly, in the minds of Mormons across the globe. What I believe can be disputed is a simplistic narrative that the Mormon Culture Region and the Church culture that came from it is received entirely enthusiastically worldwide. I have shown in this chapter that Utah and Church culture are defining components of global Mormon identities, but that they are often used to define who a global, modern Mormon is *not*, as much as they are used to define who they *are*. This complexity in how members across the globe understand Mormonism contrasts with the efforts of the Church to maintain historical traditions in the face of changing Church membership.

The Church's policy of correlation ensured a common church experience across the globe from the 1970s onward and serves a practical and symbolic purpose in continuously re-creating a common identity. The Elder Ballard visit to Ireland and similar events achieve the same function. Religious institutions operate a "complex strategy" to "maintain their visibility in a cultural and symbolic climate, where their message is under threat of dilution" (Hervieu-Léger, 2000, p. 174). This strategy incorporates a "marrying" of "the emotivity of belonging with a reasoned appeal to ethico-cultural heritage" (Hervieu-Léger, 2000, p. 175).

Both correlation and visits from Church leaders such as Elder Ballard can be said to be part of these "institutional top-down attempts to revive consciousness of a chain of belief" (Hervieu-Léger 2000, p. 175) as the Church expands globally and becomes ever more diverse. If these are deliberate revivals of the chain of belief by the Church, then this implies that the chain may be weakening in the modern age of a diverse global Church. Maintaining a collective memory of Mormonism in this context will be difficult, forcing the Church to engage in more measures such as those that are actively designed to reassert Mormon belonging on the basis of shared religious heritage and traditions.

Despite these measures, I have shown in this chapter that a global Mormon identity is regularly disputed, negotiated, or even rejected by members. This is evidenced particularly by Irish members who hold a complex relationship to US Mormonism, but is also evidenced by the divergences of opinion regarding the existence of a global Church culture. This internal "division and dissent" (Werbner, 2004, p. 896) symbolizes a global Mormonism in which disunity and dis-identification are as much part of the experience as commonality and co-responsibility. For example, although Irish Mormons are influenced by Utah and US Mormonism, this may not always be in the way the Church might hope. US Mormonism is utilized by Irish Mormons to define what they are not, and in the process to create something new—a form of Mormonism that is distinctly Irish.

Specifically, some Irish Mormons construct themselves as more relaxed in their demeanor and more liberal in their beliefs than US Mormons, thereby creating a version of Irish Mormonism that disrupts Church culture. While this was not articulated by all participants, people such as Suzanne, Mavis, Mary, and Anna referenced these differences. By broadening their definition of marriage to incorporate same-sex couples, many Irish Mormons are also challenging the Church's well-defined boundaries on family issues in ways that may over time come to influence Church policy and doctrine. The Church may need to accept that the plurality of views within its own membership on family issues is stemming not from a desire to disrupt or undermine the Church (for example, Diane is a committed and worthy member, and very explicitly stated she does not want or expect the Church to change its doctrine on LGBTQ+ couples), but because views are shaped by diverse cultural landscapes across the globe that may differ from the cultural milieu in which such doctrine is created.

Thus, Mormons in Ireland are creating adaptations to Mormonism that better suit their lived experiences. On this basis, there is much complexity in the experience of global Mormonism and Church culture. As the Church consciously attempts to constitute a global identity, Mormons in Ireland regularly disrupt it. Informed by these and other ideas, below I offer a concluding discussion of the themes of tradition, community, and identity that emerged through my time with these congregations. I reflect upon ideas of tradition and collective memory in religion in contemporary Ireland to shed light on the future of global Mormonism as it continues to transform.

Reflections for the Future

I See My Father. He Is There.

Matthew was sitting in front of me in a large and dark boardroom at my workplace. We were seated around an enormous table that could easily fit fifteen people. This, coupled with the fact that it was a typical early morning in an Irish winter—dreary, cloudy, and not yet fully escaping darkness—gave a rather grim atmosphere for our interview. Matthew was nervous but as he settled into telling me about his childhood in East Africa it felt like we were starting to overcome our foreboding surroundings. As we talked, I came to understand that his father played a central role in Matthew's worldview and in his conception of his own identity. Reflecting on the interview afterward, I also realized that Matthew, in many ways, encapsulates the Irish Mormon experience. He is a suitable person to teach us about the complexity of Mormonism in Ireland, about the marginalization that sits at its heart, about the struggle for belonging, and about the strong need to maintain a chain of belief in the midst of upheaval.

For Matthew, his father's active religiosity as evidenced through his work as a preacher has been fundamental in shaping Matthew's religiosity:

> I was born in [his country of origin] and I grew up with my grandma and grandad. By the time I was born, my mum was only sixteen years old and my dad was eighteen. So both of them, they were young. They were too young to start a family; that's why I was taken to stay with my grandparents. Initially my grandad and my grandma—what I was told was that we were Muslim before. But when my dad grew up, he went into a Protestant school. From there, he practiced the Protestant religion. Then he started

preaching at the age of fourteen, I think, seventeen, eighteen. He became a reverend and up until now he is still a preacher.

Matthew tells me about his move to Ireland, his children, and his conversion story; how he came to be Mormon:

> In 2008 there was a church which was for an American pastor. It was called Joyful Day, so when I came here, I joined Joyful Day. Then after that in 2014, 2013, I met the elders, [as] I was going to Aldi [a supermarket]. But all along I wanted to exercise my faith direct, not indirect. I just want people to know what my faith is, because I have something in my mind that I can do what my dad did, does. And not to *be* a Christian, but to practice Christianity and to teach. Because when I was in [his country of origin] I used to go with my dad teaching people. So, I was finding where, which church I could get that opportunity. So when I met the elders they struck me, I definitely had to stop because it was in my mind to know what they're talking about . . . they asked me if I would mind taking a copy from them of the *Book of Mormon* . . . they asked me to pray and to know that the *Book of Mormon* is true. So, when I came back home, I told my wife, and my wife was not buying it! [Matthew and I laugh at this aspect of his story.]

Further into our conversation, Matthew once more raises the topic of his father. He tells me that despite of, or perhaps because of, his obvious admiration for his father and his preaching, he has still not told him about his conversion to Mormonism:

> MATTHEW: There's something that is funny for me and my dad. My dad has been living in the States since 1990 and has never come back home. I was reading one book, it said that two companions were just on the phone and they had to pray to each other, but sometimes I can't talk to my dad on the phone, and sometimes we don't get such conversations or prayers on the phone. My dad, he doesn't know that I'm a member of another church. The Mormon Church. It has never come to my mind that this is the time to tell him that I have converted from this church to this church. I feel comfortable the way I am, and I think that he also feels comfortable where he is.
>
> HAZEL: Do you think that it would disturb him or upset him to know that you've joined another religion?
>
> MATTHEW: [There is a long pause as Matthew considers my question.] It can, but as I am a grown-up man with a family, I think you cannot show it direct. I prefer for my dad to see to see me physically, and my family, and the way that we behave, and then when I tell him that I joined this church he will know that it is a true church. Because I want my dad to convert to the Mormon Church, which is I think is very impossible unless he sees, he appreciates what we do.

Matthew tells me that one of the things he enjoys the most about his religious practice is that the Church facilitates him to give testimony, and to teach others. It is clear that he feels a connection to his father through this:

> I remember there was one member of the Church he had been a member of the Church for a long time, over fifty years, and he came to me, he didn't know about my father. He came to me and said, "There is something, as though I have seen a new something behind you, in the way that you talk; it is quite different. And I think there is a dream in you." But I think what he was talking about, what he was referring to, was the experience of my father because every time that I come talk in front [at the pulpit] I see my father. He is there. And I see the Heavenly Father helps me to do that, but I also see that I like to talk like my father. Because my father was a very good speaker in the church and is still a good speaker in the church. . . . It is something that I can't leave; I feel that I have to teach; I feel that I want to. I want to do this.

Matthew's narrative represents so many of the themes raised in this book. As a Black African in Ireland, he represents the diversity and complexity of the Church in Europe where many congregations are predominantly made up of racial, ethnic, and national minorities. As a racialized religious minority he experiences multiple forms of marginalization from the dominant routes to belonging both inside and outside of his religion. His story of conversion reminds us that many Mormons in Europe are converts, and as a consequence are navigating that specific form of Mormonism that incorporates stigma, guilt, and the difficulties associated with part-member families. Unlike the rhetoric from the Church, which acknowledges that some members may be facing these difficulties, in Ireland as in many regions across the globe this is the *norm* and is part and parcel of the Mormon experience. These converts know no other form of Mormonism despite the hegemonic ideal that they are consistently presented with. These two realities coexist uneasily with each other. The reality of many Mormons' lived experiences contradicts the idealized rhetoric that emerges from the Church, yet it is also shaped by it. If Church culture was more representative of lived experience, stigma, guilt, and exclusion would not form part of the ordinary Mormon experience as it does. Thus, the lived experience of Mormonism in Ireland is directly shaped by the same Church discourse that marginalizes it.

Matthew's story also centers around family and tradition. In his telling of his relationship with his father, it is clear to see that he has placed himself into a lineage of religious practice through teaching. In his father he sees encapsulated that which matters most to him: religiosity through doing, and not just being. This also operates in reverse; through his faith, which incorporates testimony and teaching, he connects with his father and his family from whom he has been geographically and culturally separated for many years. Here, we can see Danièle Hervieu-Leger's "chain of belief" at work. Matthew has left his father's religion and joined one that has few historical or cultural ties to his home country and culture. Superficially, this may appear to be a rupture of religious tradition, further evidence of the breakdown of religious transmission as a result of the fragmentation of collective memory under modernity. Yet, Matthew brings his connection to his father and his father's faith *into* Mormonism. By referencing the tradition of his father's teaching and the authority of that work, he inserts an adapted chain of belief into his own experience, and into Mormonism. The preacher's son from East Africa has found himself in Ireland, determined to bring his father into Mormonism both literally and symbolically. Every time he gives his testimony, teaches a Sunday School class, his father is there.

In this book I have provided an ethnographic account of a religious minority in Ireland, hoping to illustrate that even in countries that have modernized rapidly, such as Ireland, religion continues to exert a powerful influence and is primary in shaping the worldviews of many. I confirm that the memory of religion does not disappear, nor become unimportant in modern societies. Rather, that memory adapts to create new religious experiences, which are simultaneously informed by the old. By examining these ideas through the unique case study of Mormons in modern Ireland, we see how a collective memory of religion can be challenged, disrupted, and reshaped, just as Matthew has done.

Such adaptations of tradition are evidenced at two levels. First, through Mormons' engagement with their own faith and understanding of their religious community. Second, through Mormons' engagement with Irish society, a society still heavily informed by Irish Catholic tradition. At both levels, I have emphasized the difficulties inherent in maintaining religious tradition and the remarkable resilience and adaptability of such tradition. Through complex understandings and negotiations of ideas of Irishness and community, Mormons in Ireland simultaneously challenge and continue religious memory. As has been demonstrated throughout this book, themes of tradition, community, and identity are critical. For this reason, I have structured the following discussion around these three themes, discussing in greater detail how each of these is central to the Mormon experience. These discussions bring to the fore the underpinning theory that has informed the previous chapters and point toward the continuing challenges for the Church as it progresses further into the twenty-first century.

Adapting Tradition

Conversion to Mormonism does not entail an outright rejection of the traditions of the majority society. Rather, the continued emphasis on family, community, tradition, and Jesus Christ, held in common between Catholicism and Mormonism, allows for a continuity of previous tradition to emerge within the experience of a new religion. For some converts such as Margaret from chapter 4, conversion to Mormonism can be lonely and difficult to manage within the family as a sole convert. Research into various facets of Mormonism across Europe also identifies that European converts struggle with the responses of family members postconversion and that the culture and structures of the majority society in Europe often make the Mormon experience more difficult. Margaret's experiences reflect the reality that conversion to Mormonism is a break with previous tradition, both within and outside of the Irish family. In this way, Mormon conversion is a threat to the Irish social body, and converts often experience some form of isolation postconversion.

Yet, conversion to Mormonism also involves a continuity with what has gone before. The experience is invariably filtered through a lens of Irish Catholicism. Although the reasons for conversion vary, some such as James in Sweetwater are seeking a return to more conservative traditions, which they feel have been lost as Ireland modernizes. Others, like Maureen, are seeking to reject those same traditions. However, most converts from Catholicism still use Irish Catholicism to make sense of their religious experience. There is, then, a continuity of the influence of Catholicism that continues to shape understandings of religion postconversion. While research has shown this process at work with other converts from Catholicism in Ireland (Sakaranaho, 2003; Ganiel, 2016a, 2016b), we can now say that this also holds true for Mormon converts from Catholicism in Ireland. The continued influence of Irish Catholicism on other religions in Ireland, therefore, cannot be underestimated. Irish Catholicism remains a potent force in modern religious experience in Ireland, even outside of Catholicism itself.

On that basis, I think it is short-sighted to judge the decline of Catholicism in Ireland only through traditional indicators of religiosity such as church attendance or self-identifications. There also needs to be a greater investigation of the ways in which Catholicism continues to affect the wider religious landscape in Ireland, by exploring the place of Catholicism within other religious experiences. Mormons in Ireland experience life in a country in which Catholicism is expressed by the majority as a cultural marker of Irishness with little religious meaning, where many do not attend church or adhere to Catholic teachings. Those such as Maureen and John are also regularly reduced to just their faith by members of the majority. Their religious beliefs are constructed by others as the most significant part of their identities, no matter how much this is disputed by the individual. In contrast, these Mormons often see their religious identity as being just one aspect of a complex personhood. What does this tell us about Ireland and its relationship to religion? Mormons in Ireland become representative for the majority society not just of Mormonism, but of religious tradition generally. Although Mormons belong to a different religion than the majority, they are still maintaining the presence of religion in Irish society. Compounding this, they are often expected to do so by members of the majority who police Mormon behavior according to what they think is appropriate for members.

Regarding secularization, numbers identifying as Catholic and attending Mass have been consistently dropping for many years. It is also clear that the Catholic Church has lost a good deal of authority, no longer influencing the Irish political system to the degree it once did, and increasingly represented as just one voice of morality in a society that is becoming more religiously diverse. This has resulted in a significant gap between the teachings of the Catholic Church and the beliefs and behavior of Irish people. Yet, declines in attendance and self-identification are from an unusually high level of identification and participation. Numbers of people identifying as Catholic remain high, and Catholicism is still influential in shaping Irish people's sense of self. Despite the preponderance in modern Ireland of a cultural Catholicism that has little religious meaning, I have shown that Catholicism does remain influential for individuals even after conversion to another faith, and therefore has the capacity to shape minority religious experience in Ireland. Similarly, the small presence of Mormonism itself, alongside the growth of other religious minorities, also offers proof that religion can adapt in unusual ways within a wider secularization process. My fieldwork has shown to me a small but vibrant and committed Mormon community in Ireland, whose religion is central to their understanding of themselves and the world around them. They are part of a changing religious landscape in Ireland.

This raises the question of what that changed relationship to Mormonism might look like. Based on the experiences recounted here, it appears that a more privatized form of religious adherence might be becoming more common. My research demonstrates high levels of concealment of religious identity, and a reluctance among the participants to discuss religion in public contexts. This indicates that Ireland's traditionally public form of religiosity, which infiltrated almost all aspects of Irish life, might be coming to a close. While the privatization of faith is often cited as an indicator of a secularization process (Wilson, 1966), this book also illustrates that a private religious expression can still be influential in public life. I have shown that it still retains the power to shape family formation, marriage, and educational choices, for instance. It also remains influential in shaping how people see themselves in the world, and, therefore, their interactions with the world.

In the era of global Mormonism, Utah's dominance in shaping Mormonism may be waning. Increasingly, Mormonism is experienced in ways that are more reflective of Dublin, Delhi, or Dakar, than Salt Lake City. This process is evident even within the Mormon heartland (Embry, 2000). This means that Mormons will increasingly find themselves to be adherents of just one religion living among many. Where religious diversity is celebrated, this may be an opportunity for the Church and for Church members in these regions. However, as Ireland is a country where religious diversity is not celebrated, a greater privatization of Mormon faith there is likely, and efforts will be needed in the Church to acknowledge this and to support adherents about the realities of their religious experiences, which involves marginalization and stigmatization.

Historically, Mormonism's violent and tragic origins have been used to sustain a collective memory of Mormons as a persecuted people (Bowman, 2012) and this has been connected to the stigmatization of the Church and its members, as proof of the Church's unique and special place in the world (Widtsoe, 1988). It has been an effective tool to sustain Mormon collective memory as adherents face societal change. However, supporting this narrative in contemporary times may further demoralize recent converts who have already challenged family and cultural norms through their act of conversion. Many US members live within the Mormon Culture Region, which means that although they may be stigmatized within wider US society, they do still have the social, cultural, and structural support of fellow members and institutional structures within their communities to assist them to cope with this.

The majority of global Church members do not have this privilege. They are absorbing a persecuted and "peculiar people" narrative, disseminated from the institutional Church, with few supports to manage the effects of this on their sense of self and their relationship to their wider communities. Jana Riess (2019) has demonstrated that a Mormon continuity of belief is supported through relationships and that social networks are important.

Among those with a strong Mormon social circle, a narrative of persecution that necessitates being apart from the world creates a self-fulfilling prophecy, which further strengthens such ties. But most Mormons across the globe do not live in self-sustaining Mormon communities and this narrative further disconnects them from the society they live within. It isolates them from their friends and families as they grapple with the disconnect between their experiences and the dominant Church narrative.

However, although I find that significant variability of traditions exists at a congregational and individual level, nonetheless the lineage of belief within Mormonism is strong. The variability and adaption of Mormonism found throughout this research is proof of the persistence and adaptability of tradition in modernity. Adaption of Mormon traditions in countries far from the Mormon heartland show that despite the struggles associated with global Mormonism, the faith is also capable of remarkable adaptability and resilience as it embeds itself into a variety of societies in which other faiths are already established. This adaptability is evidenced in my research, which found that Mormons in Ireland have accommodated the dominant opinions on social issues in Ireland into their own experience of Mormonism. Although the Church denounces same-sex marriage, I found that many Mormons voted in favor of legalizing Irish same-sex marriage, aligning themselves with the majority who voted in favor. This means that Church members are not following its guidance on matters of doctrine and culture but importantly, these adherents do not see themselves as any less Mormon for this. They still place themselves within a Mormon tradition of faith. The challenge for Mormonism may be that even though adherents do not see themselves as any less Mormon for these adaptations, their institutional Church may. To a nonmember such as myself, this appears to be a one-sided standoff, with the Church refusing to adapt to changed circumstances while the Church's members have already moved on. This appears reminiscent of and ironically similar to the relationship between the Catholic Church and its adherents in Ireland. Although the Catholic Church has also refused to adapt to changing times and cultures regarding issues such as female ordination or LGBTQ+ rights, Irish Catholics have nonetheless adapted their own lives and opinions accordingly while still identifying as Catholic.

This trend in both Mormonism and Catholicism in Ireland raises interesting reflections about the role of authority in the legitimization of religious tradition. If both religions' adherents are remaking religious tradition, then we must work to understand what is the authority that is increasingly being invoked to legitimize this adaptation. For the participants of this research, the authority they invoked was often either their own personal relationship with Heavenly Father or the authority of the institutional Church legitimized in unexpected ways. Diane's explanation of her opinions on the Church and same-sex marriage, as discussed in chapter 6, illustrates this phenomenon. Similarly, the diversity of opinion I have found regarding gendered hierarchies within Mormonism disrupts a patriarchal Church narrative on gender, which results in unequal treatment of men and women in the Church. Church doctrine and organization supports a gendered experience of Mormonism, and this has been confirmed in the experience of many women in this research. However, paths toward respect and inclusion can be created and maintained locally, which result in a more inclusive experience of gender within the Church. For example, despite structures in Church organization that prevented Stephanie's full equality as leader within the Appleby branch, she *feels* equal to other male leaders and maintains that the role of the branch president in facilitating an atmosphere of equality is vital in fostering those feelings. This is perhaps in keeping with the position of women in Ireland more generally, and like same-sex marriage, is proof that Mormons in Ireland are adapting religious tradition to better fit the emergence of a more secular Catholic society of which they are a part. Thus, many strands of the dominant narrative about Mormonism, such as Mormon adherence to strict gender roles that subjugate Mormon women and the stereotype of Mormon opposition to same-sex relationships, may be too simplistic to be truly representative of the lived experience of Mormonism across the globe at a local level.

A Community of Continuity and Change

Community for Mormons in Ireland is constructed and imagined, and I have found that community is meaningful for Mormons at three levels. First, at the level of the family, second within the congregation, and finally at the level of a national and/or global community of Mormons. At all three levels, community is experienced in terms of continuity and change. At the level of family, I have found that Douglas J. Davies's (2010, p. 175) concept of "doctrinal kinship" is in evidence within Mormon families in Ireland. Church members show understanding of the importance of family rituals such as sealing and baptisms for the dead for creating community. These rituals support and maintain a familial community of Mormons that is capable of incorporating non-Mormons into this faith community. This community, which exists simultaneously in past, present, and future, is in existence in both temporal and spiritual worlds. In this respect, "doctrinal kinship" is an example of Hervieu-Léger's understanding of religion as a "chain of belief" that is dependent upon a lineage of tradition.

By valuing ancestry and genealogy, Mormon families in Ireland consciously support a familial "chain of belief" that breaks conventional notions of time. Formalizing these connections through rituals such as baptisms for the dead both increases the numbers of family who are spiritually connected and enhances those connections. Children are encouraged to assist in the genealogical work of family history, thereby teaching the next generation of the importance of this work and the ritual it supports. Similarly, encouraging young people to be sealed in the temple ensures the continuance of strong Mormon families by ensuring young people are motivated to marry a fellow Mormon. By being sealed in the temple, a husband and wife's spiritual ties to each other and to any children born to them are secured. "Doctrinal kinship" therefore assists in the continuity of religious memory, which is maintained through the family.

Despite Church encouragement to marry within the faith, small numbers of young Mormons in Ireland mean that achieving this objective proves incredibly challenging in an Irish context. This has been referred to in other European contexts as "the marriage challenge" (Decoo, 1996, p. 106), and the breadth of this problem for Mormons in Europe has been further confirmed in my Irish-based research. Young Mormons are likely to emigrate in search of a spouse, or to marry a fellow Mormon from outside of Ireland. These practices represent a changed way of forming the Mormon family that sits in contrast to the idealized Utah Mormon family, which is often formed through marrying a fellow member in the local area. These Irish adaptions to the ideal Mormon family are directly related to the circumstances of the Church in Ireland as a small religion. However, this pragmatic way of ensuring the continuance of Mormon family has the unintended consequence of diluting the numbers of "Irish" Mormon families in Ireland. Those who emigrate in search of a Mormon partner decrease the numbers of Mormons in the country. Those who remain but marry a Mormon of another nationality (in Ireland, often the United Kingdom or United States) bring a non-Irish influence into their family, which might perpetuate the majority's stereotype of Mormonism as a "foreign" religion. This trend also might serve to undermine any perceived commonalities between Catholicism and Mormonism, which can be helpful in the recruitment of Irish converts.

When reflecting upon community at the level of global Mormonism, we must consider that Mormons in Ireland who are not Irish-born, such as David and Meredith, are particularly likely to identify and support a global Church culture that crosses national boundaries. Supported by the Church policy of correlation, Church culture is a route to belonging for these Mormons. Given the double marginalization that these Mormons experience in struggling to belong based on either Irishness or Catholicism, identifying with a global Church culture allows these Mormons to create and maintain a global community in which they feel a sense of belonging. However, by examining Church culture within the context of Irish Mormonism and at a congregational level, we can see that this concept of a global community is disputed, negotiated, and even rejected. Within congregations, local experiences often shape the atmosphere of the congregation to a greater degree than the correlated version of Church life that the congregations are obliged to implement. Additionally, Mormon sports teams, discos, crafts groups, book clubs, and other common social outlets, which are ubiquitous in the Mormon Culture Region, are either rare or nonexistent in Ireland. Therefore, core functions of Mormon congregations such as a full and active social calendar to support a Church culture are modified or abandoned at a congregational level in Ireland.

Irish-born Mormons are particularly likely to reject or dispute aspects of a global Mormon community. Although US Mormonism and its home in Utah exert considerable influence on Irish Mormonism, this brand of Mormonism is not merely viewed as something to envy, or to aspire to. I have found that Irish-born Mormons such as Seán, Suzanne, and Mary often subvert or reject the traditional American version of Mormonism that has shaped Church culture. The narratives on US Mormonism in chapter 6 indicate that Irish Mormons use US Mormonism as an Other—a way to identify who they are by identifying who they are not. They describe US Mormonism as "serious," and as "cheesy," and describe Irish Mormonism as being more laidback and authentic in its outlook and behaviors. Therefore, in rejecting aspects of US Mormonism, Irish Mormons create their own version of Mormonism that takes account of their local experiences in the Church and that has adapted to the majority Irish society in which they find themselves.

Simultaneously, US Mormonism influences the Mormon worldview and affects patterns of behavior in Ireland. The Mormon expectation of early marriage and childrearing leads Mormons in Ireland to have particular conceptions of marriage and family, which often causes them to marry and become parents earlier than the national average in Ireland. Opposite-sex couples in Ireland are now marrying at approximately thirty-seven years of age (with same-sex couples marrying later, at forty) (Central Statistics Office, 2021), but I have found that members of the LDS Church in Ireland are likely to marry approximately ten to twelve years earlier than this. While marrying in the mid-twenties may be considered "old" in parts of the

Mormon Culture Region, Mormons in Ireland are constrained in their marriage behavior by the small numbers of prospective partners in Ireland. The inability to keep up with the ideal of Mormon family life can be experienced as stigmatizing, and shameful. Nonetheless, marriage remains a key priority for Mormons in Ireland, whose patterns of attitude and behavior around marriage is undoubtedly shaped by Church culture. For example, Stephanie told me how important it was for her to marry within the Church, and of her efforts to study at BYU to achieve this. After my fieldwork Stephanie *did* move to the United States and is now married to a fellow Mormon there. The active effort and planning that Stephanie invested in ensuring her own eternal family demonstrates that US Mormonism and Church culture is influential for Mormons in Ireland in shaping their understandings and experiences of family.

Importantly, the relationship with US Mormonism and Church culture functions as a dialectical process; US Mormonism influences the attitudes and behavior of Irish Mormonism while Irish Mormonism in turn reshapes what Church culture looks and feels like across the globe. As discussed in chapter 2, Jehu Hanciles (2015) has argued that a truly global religion will be capable of multidirectional transformations. As evidenced in this research, the Church does not appear fully comfortable with the direction of change being pushed back toward Salt Lake City. The organization of the Church still works to ensure that transformations occur from the center to the periphery. Yet, at a local level we can see small efforts to change this, to create change that pushes back in the other direction. Seán emphasized his struggles to engage with what he sees as a US focus in the Church, and his desire to create an Irish version of Mormonism. His efforts to have Ireland's differences from the United Kingdom recognized, and his giving prayers in church in Irish rather than English, illustrate his active efforts to reshape Mormonism to reflect a sense of Irishness. Suzanne enacts similar acts of rebellion at a more local level, working hard to bring Irish culture into her multicultural branch. Jason has reflected carefully on his position as a White Irish man in a position of authority, and considered how this may shape the decisions he makes about callings. Diane and others reject the teaching of their Church in their everyday behavior by, for example, voting yes for the introduction of same-sex marriage. Likewise, it is clear to me that White North Americans such as Mandy and Chase have been changed by their experiences in diverse branches such as those in Ireland. It has transformed how they conceive of what the Church is, and who the Church is. When they return to North America it is likely that they will bring this worldview back to their home wards. I suggest, therefore, that the local adaption and interpretation of Mormon habits and customs challenges dominant constructions of *both* Irish religion and Mormonism. Mormons in Ireland are renegotiating what it means to be Mormon in the global Church. This confirms the work of Taunalyn F. Rutherford (2016) and Melissa Wei-Tsing Inouye (2014) who observe that local Mormonisms can, and perhaps should, notably differ from the Mormonism that emerges from Utah and is proselytized around the globe.

Based on the findings discussed here, all Mormon adherents should consider how the standardization of Church experience worldwide is often perceived as Americanization outside of the United States. This may be particularly pertinent for Mormons based in the United States, but international Mormons should also take note, as I have observed a valorization of the United States in Irish branches, to detrimental effect. It would be useful for all Mormons to consider how marginalized members of their wards and branches might interpret their words as exclusionary. While celebrating the Church during the giving of testimonies, for example, members could ensure they do not articulate the religion as an especially North American faith, or that the specifically US origins of the Church are somehow cause for celebration. When local Church leaders promote Pioneer Day, are they cognizant that despite their efforts to rebrand its meaning as symbolic, the US legacy remains? When international congregational leaders plan social or church events to celebrate important dates in the US calendar, but not important dates in their own nation's calendar, does this uplift the United States above other nations? How does this work to perpetuate the idea that international Mormons are less worthy of belonging than US Mormons?

Perhaps most importantly, every Mormon who goes out on a mission should work to educate themselves deeply about the region they have been called to. I have been told by active and returned missionaries that the Church's institutional efforts in this regard are not what they should be. These missionaries have told me how intimidating it is as a young missionary to arrive in a country like Ireland, which has a complex religious and political history, and to realize you understand almost nothing of this. As an international religion that places such focus on missionary work, the Church has an obligation to make sure that its (often very young) missionaries have received detailed and thorough cultural competency training that goes far beyond language skills. I would call on the Church to work toward rectifying this problem immediately.

However, individual missionaries also have a responsibility to the communities that they are about to immerse themselves within. If the Church does not adequately equip missionaries with the history and cultural knowledge necessary, then missionaries should work to ensure that they develop this knowledge themselves, and lobby the Church to ensure that the relevant training for missionaries is implemented in the future. This is more feasible for some than for others; for example, some missionaries such as those from the Mormon Culture Region have more economic and cultural power than many of those from the Global South. Greater economic freedom facilitates them to devote more time to such endeavors, and greater cultural power gives them and their families the cultural capital to better challenge Church leadership to do more.

Claiming Identity

This book illustrates that Mormons in Ireland have diverse experiences of their religious, national, racial, ethnic, and classed identities. Both Irish-born Mormons and other Mormons who are living in Ireland engage in concealment strategies, which are either deliberately designed to, or have the effect of, hiding their religious identities from those in the majority society. I suggest that this concealment of Mormon identity has the unintended consequence of creating a continuance of the dominant Irish Catholic narrative. By obscuring their identities, Mormons in Ireland are inadvertently concealing the breadth of religious diversity that exists in Ireland. The presence of Irish Mormonism is an indication of the level of change that has occurred within the religious landscape in Ireland; yet, simultaneously, their concealing strategies continue to perpetuate the Irish Catholic tradition.

The experiences of Matthew reveal that experiences of Irishness differ between White Irish-born Mormons and those Mormons in Ireland who are not White and who were not born in Ireland. This is due to the ability of White Irish-born Mormons to "pass" as Irish Catholic in wider society in a way that Matthew finds more difficult due to the strong relationships among categories of Whiteness, Irishness, and Catholicism in Ireland. Irish-born Mormons also often have greater familiarity with Irish Catholic traditions and customs still present in the majority society, compared to those Mormons who have arrived in the country as adults more recently. Importantly, Irish-born Mormons feel themselves to have been rejected by the majority for their religious beliefs, due to the continuity of national and religious identification of Irishness with Catholicism. My research has identified that an equation of Irish with Catholic is still central in Irish society. This is supported by state institutions such as schools and the army and results in Irish-born Mormons such as Seán feeling marginalized and stigmatized within their own country.

However, I have also found that White Irish-born Mormons are sometimes not considered different enough from the majority to deserve any accommodation of their religious differences. As Grace Davie (2000, 2014) has observed, managing religious pluralism in modern Europe is complex. White Irish Mormons such as Suzanne in Sweetwater feel themselves to be perceived by the majority as less than Irish due to their religion. Yet, they also feel themselves to be unable to have their religious differences respected, in contrast to other religious minorities who are ethnically and racially distinct from the majority. For example, Jason's description of his son's experiences in school demonstrates that White Irish-born Mormons are often caught between being different enough to be viewed as having betrayed a sense of Irishness, but not so different to be deserving of accommodation of those differences by the state.

Matthew's experiences as a Black African Mormon living in Ireland demonstrate multiple forms of marginalization. He is unable to identify with any of the three main markers of Irishness: being born in the country, being White, and being Catholic. To navigate this reality, Matthew utilizes a strategy of emphasizing his Christianity to create a path to belonging in Ireland. Participants such as David and Meredith from South America are not racialized as different to the same extent as Matthew is. Yet, their strategy of deemphasizing the importance national identification allows them to downplay their own differences from the majority. These Mormons must carefully navigate a majority society in which they are perceived as different in multiple ways.

Embracing a form of Irishness appears to be a pathway to belonging and integration within the congregation, and within the wider society. This is true for both Irish-born Mormons and Mormons of another nationality who are living in Ireland. The St. Patrick's Day branch party in Sweetwater illustrated that in diverse congregations whose members may struggle to find points of commonality with each other aside from their faith, Irishness serves as a unifying anchor that brings commonality and stability to the group. Likewise, the narratives of Suzanne and Michael in Sweetwater show that within wider society, a celebration of Irishness assists in diminishing the majority's stereotypes of Mormonism as a foreign religion.

Based on these insights I conclude that continued strong national and religious identification with Irish Catholicism leads to significant exclusion of religious minorities in Ireland. Catholicism continues to be a key cultural marker of Irishness, which identifies those who are not Catholic as less than Irish. The ubiquity of the Irish Catholic narrative means that people with alternative experiences of religion in Ireland are pushed to the margins, forced to engage in concealment of a key part of their identities. Given the marginalization of Mormon experience as demonstrated in my research, we must consider whose religious identities are legitimized in Ireland, by whom, and why. The stories of the participants of this research raise important questions of how religion, race, and ethnicity work with and against each other in complex ways. Given Ireland's continued growth of religious and ethnic diversity, these questions will become even more relevant for the future. This confirms scholarship discussed in chapter 2, which illustrated that the Church's marginal success in modern Europe partly pertains to the wider religious landscapes in which it sits, where individual European countries have longstanding and entrenched preexisting relationships with religion that are difficult to transform. On the basis of that previous evidence and this research, I believe that the Church will struggle to gain a strong foothold in Ireland in the future as long as the wider societal context of strong national and religious identification remains relevant.

Writing this book has given me cause to reflect upon the research process and my conclusions. Born at the end of 1980, I grew up in an Ireland that was changing rapidly, both economically and socially. By the time I entered university, Ireland's Celtic Tiger period had begun, bringing with it high levels of immigration, which accelerated these changes. I was a Celtic Tiger cub; one of many in a generation entering adulthood in a new Ireland. Yet, my generation was still old enough to remember before—the old Ireland. As I began this research I was exploring a country almost unrecognizable to that of my childhood. My awareness of Ireland's transformation fueled my interest in this project. I knew how *I* had experienced these changes, and I understood my own position as an Irish-born, White, middle-class, atheist woman living in this society. But what of others? What did I know of them? It was these questions that propelled me toward Mormonism and into the chapels, homes, and lives of the people who informed this research. They welcomed me with open arms, and were pleased to show me what they felt I needed to know about being Mormon in Ireland, and about being Irish in Mormonism.

They understood, as I do now, that Mormons in Ireland *are* the Church. They are part of its increasingly diverse population and cannot be simply and neatly categorized. Some, like Maureen and John in Appleby, were quietly attending Sacrament meeting in the 1980s of my childhood in someone's home in a housing development due to the lack of a church building. Others, like Matthew, are recent arrivals to both Ireland and Mormonism and find themselves caught up in Ireland's and Mormonism's transformation. *All* the participants of this research demonstrated to me the importance of belonging, and the complex ways in which religious memory is used to support and to challenge it. They opened my eyes to the diversity of Irish experience that was sitting right in front of me, and for that I am most grateful.

Notes

Introduction. Positioning Mormonism within Irish Religions

1. Throughout this book I use the term "Ireland" to refer to the Republic of Ireland. The research that has informed this book was conducted in the Republic of Ireland. Though mention of Northern Ireland is made throughout this book where relevant, that region was not the focus of the research project. Further explanation of terms such as "Northern Ireland," "Republic of Ireland," and "the island of Ireland" is available in chapter 1.

2. Although the CoJCoLDS has recently asked that members be referred to as "Latter-day Saints" (LDS) rather than Mormons, I use the terms "Mormon" and "Mormonism" here for a variety of reasons. Primarily, my decision is centered around how the participants of this research self-described themselves. The vast majority of participants used the term "Mormon" to describe themselves and other members, and many were actively supportive of the term by arguing that this is how other Irish people recognize their religion. In a society where the recognition and understanding of their religion is an ongoing issue for members, the familiarity of the term among the majority population was important to many of them. Though the CoJCoLDS has argued that Church members want to be referred to as Latter-day Saints, that has not been my general experience in an Irish context. Additionally, as a scholar within the field of Mormon Studies, my work encompasses the study of wider cultural components of Mormonism and does not only address religious or doctrinal aspects under the authority of the Church. Outside of the doctrine of the CoJCoLDS, there is a fascinating and diverse culture of Mormonism that encapsulates influences that stem from the CoJCoLDS but also from other Mormon faiths that are not affiliated with the Church. Casual readers may also be interested to know that the CoJCoLDS was heavily promoting the religion through a campaign called "I'm a Mormon," which ended as recently as 2018. For more on this in the United Kingdom and Ireland see https://news-uk.churchofjesuschrist.org/article/im-a-mormon.

3. This is the full name of the Church, which I abbreviate in this book to "the Church" or "the LDS Church." The acronym CoJCoLDS is also often used to shorten its full name. These are the Church's preferred identifiers.

4. Mormon congregations are known as branches or wards, depending on their size. The congregational leader for a branch is known as a branch president and a ward congregational leader is known as a bishop. The roles are voluntary and unpaid. Most congregations in Ireland are branches, due to their small size.

5. A stake and a district are different types of administrative regions within the Church. Each ward or branch will fall under one of these. Like wards and branches, often the key difference between the two is based on the size of the membership in each region.

6. All missionaries are referred to as sister (female) or elder (male) for the entirety of their time on their mission. Missionaries can be called to serve anywhere in the world, and typically serve a two-year (men) or eighteen-month (women) mission, with various "mission companions." Not knowing much about missionary life before I began this project, I was stunned to learn that missionary companions should spend all their time together, except when visiting the bathroom. Some missionaries take this very seriously indeed. On one occasion after Sacrament meeting my conversation with a sister missionary was abruptly cut short as she ran out of the room to follow her companion, whom she had spotted walking away. Though most missionaries are aged between eighteen and twenty-five, Elder and Sister McGuire in this book were senior missionaries. Senior missionaries are often elderly couples who go on a mission together in their retirement.

7. Individuals interested in joining the Church are commonly called "investigators" to reflect that they are investigating the Church with a view to joining. I have always considered the term to be ironic as I have found that new members often join the Church after a very short period of investigation and do not seem to have detailed knowledge about the Church, its history, or its doctrine.

8. Every first Sunday of the month, a Fast and Testimony Sacrament meeting is held. Members fast for part of the day and make a "fast offering" to the Church. During Sacrament meeting, in lieu of the typical three talks given by members, any member can approach the lectern to offer a testimony of faith. I always enjoyed these meetings, with their regular flow of people approaching the lectern to speak unscripted. As a researcher I often found people's testimonies to be useful and revealing as it allowed me to spot patterns in people's thematic discussions or to hear people divulge details about their lives that I may have been unaware of.

9. My fieldwork took place before recent changes to the length of Sunday church meetings.

10. To assist with protecting participants' privacy and anonymity in the context of researching a small community, I generally refer to those participants who come from outside of Ireland only by the general region and not by their specific nationality. This is also why I have chosen not to provide any supplementary material on participants in an appendix. Providing details such as occupation, marital status,

age, nationality, gender, and other information in one location may be informative for the reader; however, to protect participants it is important that only information relevant to the context of their narrative is provided as and when needed. For similar reasons, pseudonyms are used throughout this book for all participants and any people they refer to in their narratives.

Chapter 1. Religion in Contemporary Ireland

1. As Kenny (2004, p. 15) notes, "Ireland's population fell by one-third because of the famine: one million people died and two million more emigrated."

2. See the work of scholars such as Davie (2000), Sakaranaho (2003, 2006, 2011, 2015), Casanova (2004), Geaves (2009), Cox (2015), and Day & Mia (2015).

3. There has been criticism of Hervieu-Léger's ideas, such as Ron Geaves (2009), who has used the example of Prem Rawat, his teachings, and his followers to argue that there is no universality to Hervieu-Léger's theory of modern religious change, and to suggest that it is too Christian-centric in its focus. Sakaranaho (2011) also acknowledges that both Halbwachs and Hervieu-Léger predominantly rely on Judaism and Christianity to make their claims, and so we can question if this perspective on religion is more broadly applicable. Rather than seeing Hervieu-Léger's ideas as being a universal theory of religion I prefer to view it as a "working tool" (Hervieu-Léger, 2000, p. 69) with which to analyze changes under way in the sphere of Irish religion.

Chapter 2. The Challenges of Belonging in Modern Mormonism

1. The "gathering" of Mormon adherents in the valley of the Great Salt Lake in Utah throughout the nineteenth century involved the mass migration of early followers from other parts of the United States and from Europe to Utah. There, the Church aimed to create a Mormon Zion—a kingdom of God on earth (Phillips & Cragun, 2013; Woods, 2018).

2. Given that the Church does not remove inactive members from their records it is likely that "literally millions of people who are claimed to be Mormon by the church do not self-identify as such" (Cragun & Lawson, 2010, p. 366). Despite these inaccuracies, we can nonetheless be confident that the majority of Church membership now lies outside of the United States.

3. It should be noted here that the term NRM is contested. Sociologist Eileen Barker defines NRM as "a religion with a predominantly first generation membership" (Barker, 2013, p. 2). Hervieu-Léger (2000) argues that it is "is an umbrella for a wide range of phenomena" including "cults and sects that have recently come into competition with traditional churches (dominant or historic minorities)" (2000, p. 32). In Ireland, Cosgrove et al. argue that what defines an NRM is "its lack of relative power, rather than any inherent characteristic" (2011, p. 11), noting that the "key

feature in the rise of NRMs in twenty-first-century Ireland has undoubtedly been the collapsing power of established religion" (2011, p. 11).

4. The Plan of Salvation is a Church doctrine that outlines the purpose of life and what is necessary for salvation in the afterlife (Church of Jesus Christ of Latter Day Saints, 2008). It outlines why we are here, what God's purpose is for us, and what will happen to us when we die.

Chapter 3. They All Seem Very Nice but It's a Bit Weird Isn't It?

1. Mormons are asked to contribute 10 percent of their earnings to the Church. Tithing is a sign of an active and "worthy" member and is used as a criterion of entry to the temple, the most sacred Mormon space. Though tithing is between members and their bishop/branch president, their access to temple serves as a way of knowing that that person is a full tithe-payer. Thus, the words of Leone still have relevance for us now in the twenty-first century: "within the Mormon community, among the hierarchs who run the church and also among one's neighbors, the quality of the tithe is one of the marks of the Saint" (Leone, 1979, p. 54).

2. Individuals interested in the Church attend a number of introductory lessons with missionaries as they learn about the Church.

3. The missionary's badge must be worn at all times in public and states the missionary's name and the name of the Church.

4. First Communion is a Catholic rite of passage for children of about seven years of age during which the child first receives the Eucharist.

5. In Ireland, opposition to religion is often a response to the darker history of the dominance of the Catholic Church in Irish society, including but not limited to the involvement of the Catholic Church in Ireland's era of institutionalization in the twentieth century. This involved the institutionalization of women, children, the poor, and the vulnerable in Magdalene laundries, mother and baby homes, and industrial and reformatory schools. There was widespread physical, sexual, and emotional abuse throughout these institutions, evidenced in the findings of various investigations into this era such as the Report of the Commission to Enquire into Child Abuse (2009), which uncovered widespread child abuse along with a culture of secrecy and protection of perpetrators.

6. I had read the *Book of Mormon* and some of Doctrine and Covenants and had also been attending Sunday School each week. I think what Marilyn might be referring to here is my openness with her and others that I was not religious and would not read scripture for anything other than professional purposes.

7. Marilyn left the Church for many years and had recently returned to attending regularly after an encounter with missionaries. However, she was still not fully "worthy" in the eyes of the Church as she struggled to give up cigarettes and alcohol and freely admitted she was not fully adherent.

8. Senior missionary couples are retired married couples, often from the United States, on a year's missionary work. Appleby has received a number of these senior couples.

Chapter 5. Irish-Irish and Mormon-Irish

1. At the time of this conversation, Michael and Mackey had recently traveled together for a branch trip to visit the temple in the United Kingdom. The incident at airport security he referred to relates to this trip.

2. "Buggy" is a word used in Ireland for what is often referred to as a "stroller" in American English.

Chapter 6. We Preach That Culture

1. An equivalent term in American English for this Irish turn of phrase might be to "rib" someone—to tease.

2. Mary was inactive for a time, no longer regularly attending church or living to Mormon standards.

3. Church manuals that guide members and leadership in their running of their congregation, and that provide lesson plans for meetings each week.

4. Based in Utah, the Quorum of the Twelve is a group encompassing the Church's most senior leaders, considered to be God's prophets on earth. They are all male, all over sixty years of age (many are in their eighties and nineties), almost all are White, and with the exception of one German and one Brazilian, they are all American.

Bibliography

Allen, J. B. (1990). When our enemies are also Saints: Response to Claudia W. Harris's "Mormons on the Warfront." *BYU Studies Quarterly, 30*(4), 21–26. http://scholarsarchive.byu.edu/cgi/viewcontent.cgi?article=2684&context=byusq.

Allen, J. B. (1992). On becoming a universal church: Some historical perspectives. *Dialogue: A Journal of Mormon Thought, 25*(1), 13–36. https://www.dialoguejournal.com/wp-content/uploads/sbi/articles/Dialogue_V25N01_15.pdf.

Allen, J. K. (2017). *Danish but not Lutheran: The impact of Mormonism on Danish cultural identity, 1850–1920.* University of Utah Press.

Allen, J. K. (2019). Neither fairyland nor dystopia: Taking Western Europe seriously in Mormon studies. *Mormon Studies Review, 6,* 34–45. https://www.jstor.org/stable/10.18809/mormstudrevi.6.2019.0034#metadata_info_tab_contents.

Allen, J. K., & Östman, K. B. (2020). Mormons in the Nordic region. In Gordon Shepherd, Gary Shepherd, & R. T. Cragun (Eds.), *The Palgrave handbook of global Mormonism* (pp. 533–559). Palgrave Macmillan.

Ammerman, N. T. (1998). Culture and identity in the congregation. In N. T. Ammerman, J. W. Carroll, C. S. Dudley, & W. McKinney (Eds.), *Studying congregations: A new handbook* (pp. 78–104). Abingdon Press.

Ammerman, N. T. (2007). Observing modern religious lives. In N. T. Ammerman (Ed.), *Everyday religion: Observing modern religious lives* (pp. 3–21). 1st ed. Oxford University Press.

Anderson, K. (2012). Ireland in the twenty-first century: Secularization or religious vitality? In D. Pollack, O. Muller, & G. Pickel (Eds.), *Social significance of religion in the enlarged Europe: Secularization, individualization, and pluralization* (pp. 66–109). Ashgate Publishing.

Are you right there Father Ted? (1998, March 13). *Father Ted.* Channel 4.

Axner, M. (2015). Studying public religions: Visibility, authority, and the public/ private distinction. In T. Hjelm (Ed.), *Is God back?: Reconsidering the new visibility of religion* (pp. 19–32). Bloomsbury.

Barker, E. (2013). Revision and diversification in new religious movements: An introduction. In E. Barker (Ed.), *Revisionism and diversification in new religious movements* (pp. 1–15). Ashgate Publishing.

Barlow, B. A. (1968). *History of the Church of Jesus Christ of Latter-day Saints in Ireland since 1840* [Unpublished master's thesis]. Brigham Young University. http:// contentdm.lib.byu.edu/cdm/ref/collection/MTAF/id/15538.

Barlow, B. A. (2000). Ireland. In A. K. Garr, D. Q. Cannon, & R. O. Cowan (Eds.), *Encyclopedia of Latter-day Saint history*. Deseret Book Company. http://global mormonism.byu.edu/?page_id=103.

Becker, P. E. (1999). *Congregations in conflict: Cultural models of local religious life.* Cambridge University Press.

Beek, W. E. A. van (1996). Ethnization and accommodation: Dutch Mormons in twenty-first-century Europe. *Dialogue: A Journal of Mormon Thought, 29*(1), 119–138.

Beek, W. E. A. van (2005). Mormon Europeans or European Mormons? An "Afro-European" view on religious colonization. *Dialogue: A Journal of Mormon Thought, 38*(4), 3–36. https://openaccess.leidenuniv.nl/bitstream/handle /1887/9545/ASC_1241507_161.pdf?sequence=1.

Beek, W. E. A. van (2009). Mormonism, a global counter-church? *By Common Consent.* https://bycommonconsent.com/2009/06/18/mormonism-a-global-counter -church-i/.

Beek, W. E. A. van (2010). Meaning and authority in Mormon ritual. *International Journal of Mormon Studies, 2*(3), 17–40.

Beek, W. E. A. van, Decoo, E., & Decoo, W. (2020). Persisting in a secular environment: Mormonism in the Low Countries. In Gordon Shepherd, Gary Shepherd, & R. T. Cragun (Eds.), *The Palgrave handbook of global Mormonism* (pp. 503–533). Palgrave Macmillan.

Benally, M. (2017). Decolonizing the blossoming: Indigenous people's faith in a colonizing church. *Dialogue: A Journal of Mormon Thought, 50*(4), 71–78. https://www .dialoguejournal.com/archive/dialogue-premium-content/winter-2017/.

Bennion, L. C., & Young, L. A. (1996). The uncertain dynamics of LDS expansion, 1950–2020. *Dialogue: A Journal of Mormon Thought, 29*(1), 8–31. https://www .dialoguejournal.com/wp-content/uploads/sbi/articles/Dialogue_V29N01_14.pdf.

Berger, P. L. (1967). *The sacred canopy: Elements of a sociological theory of religion.* Anchor Books.

Berger, P. L. (2012). Further thoughts on religion and modernity. *Society, 49*(4), 313–316. doi: 10.1007/s12115-012-9551-y.

Black, K. L. (2016). *A sociology of Mormon kinship: The place of family within the Church of Jesus Christ of Latter-day Saints.* Edwin Mellon Press.

Bloxham, B. V., Moss, J. R., & Porter, L. C. (Eds.) (1987). *Truth will prevail: The rise of the Church of Jesus Christ of Latter-day Saints in the British Isles, 1837–1987*. Cambridge University Press.

Bourdieu, P. (1986). The forms of capital. In J. Richardson (Ed.), *Handbook of theory and research for the sociology of education* (pp. 241–258). Greenwood.

Bowman, M. (2012). *The Mormon people: The making of an American faith*. Random House.

Breen, M. J., & Reynolds, C. (2011). The rise of secularism and the decline of religiosity in Ireland: The pattern of religious change in Europe. *International Journal of Religion and Spirituality in Society, 1*. https://dspace.mic.ul.ie/bitstream/handle/10395/1800/.

Brooks, J. (2018). The possessive investment in rightness: White supremacy and the Mormon movement. *Dialogue: A Journal of Mormon Thought, 51*(3), 45–83. https://www.dialoguejournal.com/wp-content/uploads/sbi/articles/Dialogue_V51N03_3.pdf.

Bruce, S. (2002). *God is dead: Secularization in the West*. Blackwell.

Bruce, S. (2014). Late secularization and religion as alien. *Open Theology, 1*(1), 13–23. doi: 10.2478/opth-2014-0003.

Bruce, S. (2016). The sociology of late secularization: Social divisions and religiosity. *British Journal of Sociology, 67*(4), 613–631. doi: 10.1111/1468-4446.12219.

Buchanan, F. S. (1987). The ebb and flow of Mormonism in Scotland, 1840–1900. *BYU Studies Quarterly, 27*(1), 27–53. http://scholarsarchive.byu.edu/cgi/viewcontent.cgi?article=2477&context=byusq.

Buerger, D. J. (2001). The development of the Mormon temple Endowment ceremony. *Dialogue: A Journal of Mormon Thought, 34*(1/2), 75–122. https://www.jstor.org/stable/45226771.

Bush, L. Jr. (2018). Looking back, Looking forward: "Mormonism's Negro doctrine" forty-five years later. *Dialogue: A Journal of Mormon Thought, 51*(3), 1–29.

Bushman, C. L. (2006). *Contemporary Mormonism: Latter-day Saints in modern America*. Praeger.

Cadge, W., & Sigalo, E. (2013). Negotiating religious differences: The strategies of interfaith chaplains in healthcare. *Journal for the Scientific Study of Religion, 52*(1), 146–158. https://wendycadge.com/wp-content/uploads/2017/10/CadgeSigalo2013.pdf.

Cannell, F. (2013a). The blood of Abraham: Mormon redemptive physicality and American idioms of kinship. *Journal of the Royal Anthropological Institute*, pp. 77–94.

Cannell, F. (2013b). The re-enchantment of kinship. In F. Cannell & S. McKinnon (Eds.), *Vital relations: Modernity and the persistent life of kinship* (pp. 217–240). SAR Press.

Card, O. S. (1978). The Saints in Ireland. *Ensign*. https://www.lds.org/ensign/1978/02/the-saints-in-ireland?lang=eng.

Casanova, J. (2004). Religion, European secular identities, and European integration. *Transit, 27,* 1–17. doi: 10.1017/CBO9780511491917.004.

Central Statistics Office. (2000). *That was then, this is now: Change in Ireland, 1949–1999.* Government of Ireland. http://www.cso.ie/en/media/csoie/releases publications/documents/otherreleases/thatwasthenthisisnow.pdf.

Central Statistics Office. (2012). *Migration and diversity.* Government of Ireland. http://www.cso.ie/en/media/csoie/census/documents/census2011profile6 /Profile_6_Migration_and_Diversity_entire_doc.pdf.

Central Statistics Office. (2016a). *Measuring Ireland's progress 2014.* Government of Ireland. http://www.cso.ie/en/releasesandpublications/ep/p-mip/mip2014/.

Central Statistics Office. (2016b). *Vital statistics Q3 2016.* Government of Ireland. http://www.cso.ie/en/releasesandpublications/ep/p-vs/vitalstatisticsthird quarter2016/.

Central Statistics Office. (2017a). *Census of population 2016—Profile 8 Irish Travellers, ethnicity, and religion.* Government of Ireland. http://www.cso.ie/en /releasesandpublications/ep/p-cp8iter/p8iter/p8rnraa/.

Central Statistics Office. (2017b). Details of census. Government of Ireland. http:// www.cso.ie/en/csolatestnews/presspages/2017/census2016summaryresults-part 1/.

Central Statistics Office. (2020a). *Ireland's UN SDGs 2019—Report on Indicators for Goal 1 No Poverty.* Government of Ireland. https://www.cso.ie/en /releasesandpublications/ep/p-sdg1/irelandsunsdgs2019-reportonindicators forgoal1nopoverty/.

Central Statistics Office. (2020b). *Population and migration estimates.* Government of Ireland. https://www.cso.ie/en/releasesandpublications/er/pme/populationand migrationestimatesapril2020/.

Central Statistics Office. (2021). *Marriages 2020.* Government of Ireland. https://www .cso.ie/en/releasesandpublications/ep/p-mar/marriages2020/.

Charles, C. (2018). Mormon studies in France: An academic tradition. In I. E. Annus, D. M. Morris, & K. B. Östman (Eds.), *Mormonism in Europe: Historical and contemporary perspectives* (pp. 179–196). Americana Ebooks.

Church of Jesus Christ of Latter-day Saints. (2009). *The Plan of Salvation.* https:// www.lds.org/bc/content/ldsorg/content/english/manual/missionary/pdf/36950 _the-plan-of-salvation-eng.pdf?lang=eng.

Church of Jesus Christ of Latter-day Saints. (2014). *Mormonism is a Christ-centered, global faith.* https://youtu.be/Hg7OVOKqeQU.

Church of Jesus Christ of Latter-day Saints. (2016). *Teaching in the Savior's way.* https://www.churchofjesuschrist.org/study/manual/teaching-in-the-saviors -way?lang=eng.

Church of Jesus Christ of Latter-day Saints (2021). *Elder Jeffrey R. Holland urges BYU to embrace its uniqueness, stay true to the Savior.* https://newsroom.churchof jesuschrist.org/article/elder-jeffrey-r-holland-2021-byu-university-conference.

Church of Jesus Christ of Latter-day Saints. (n.d.-a). *Baptisms for the dead.* https:// www.lds.org/topics/baptisms-for-the-dead?lang=eng.

Church of Jesus Christ of Latter-day Saints. (n.d.-b). *Diversity and unity in the Church of Jesus Christ of Latter-day Saints, gospel topics.* https://www.churchof jesuschrist.org/study/manual/gospel-topics/diversity-and-unity?lang=eng.

Church of Jesus Christ of Latter-day Saints. (n.d.-c). *Facts and statistics: USA. Mormon Newsroom.* http://www.mormonnewsroom.ie/facts-and-statistics/country /united-states/.

Church of Jesus Christ of Latter-day Saints. (n.d.-d). *Facts and statistics: Worldwide statistics.* https://newsroom.churchofjesuschrist.org/facts-and-statistics.

Church of Jesus Christ of Latter-day Saints. (n.d.-e). *The guide to the scriptures: The Word of Wisdom.* https://www.lds.org/scriptures/gs/word-of-wisdom.

Church of Jesus Christ of Latter-day Saints. (n.d.-f). *What is Zion.* https://www.lds .org/youth/learn/yw/building-up-the-church/zion?lang=eng.

Cieslik, A., & Verkuyten, M. (2006). National, ethnic, and religious identities: Hybridity and the case of the Polish Tatars. *National Identities, 8*(2), 77–93. doi: 10.1080/14608940600703650.

Cleary, J. (2004). Postcolonial Ireland. In K. Kenny (Ed.), *Ireland and the British Empire* (pp. 251–289). Oxford University Press.

Colvin, G., & Brooks, J. (Eds.). (2018a). *Decolonizing Mormonism.* University of Utah Press.

Colvin, G., & Brooks, J. (2018b). Introduction: Approaching a postcolonial Zion. In G. Colvin. & J. Brooks (Eds.), *Decolonizing Mormonism: Approaching a postcolonial Zion* (pp. 1–25). University of Utah Press.

Commission to Enquire into Child Abuse. (2009). *Report of the Commission to Enquire into Child Abuse.* Government of Ireland. http://www.childabuse commission.ie/rpt/pdfs/.

Connor, P. (2014). *Immigrant faith: Patterns of immigrant religion in the United States, Canada, and Western Europe.* New York University Press.

Conway, B. (2013). Social correlates of church attendance in three European Catholic countries. *Review of Religious Research, 55*(1), 61–80. doi: 10.1007/s13644-012 -0086-x.

Conway, B. (2014). Religious public discourses and institutional structures: A cross-national analysis of Catholicism in Chile, Ireland, and Nigeria. *Sociological Perspectives, 57*(2), 149–166.

Corish, M. (1996). Aspects of the secularisation of Irish society 1958–1996. In E. Cassidy (Ed.), *Faith and culture in the Irish context* (pp. 138–173). Veritas Publications.

Cosgrove, O. (2013). *The experience of religious stigma and discrimination among religious minorities in Ireland: A multi-faith approach* [Unpublished doctoral dissertation]. University of Limerick. http://rian.ie/en/item/view/73067.html.

Cosgrove, O., Cox, L., Kuhling, C., & Mulholland, P. (2011). Understanding Ireland's new religious movements. In O. Cosgrove, L. Cox, C. Kuhling, & P. Mulholland (Eds.), *Ireland's new religious movements* (1–27). Cambridge Scholars Publishing.

Coulter, C. (2018). The end of Irish history? An introduction to the book. In C. Coulter & S. Coleman (Eds.), *The end of Irish history? Critical reflections on the Celtic tiger* (pp. 1–33). Manchester University Press. doi: 10.7765/9781526137715.00007.

Cox, J. (2015). Religious memory as a conveyor of authoritative tradition: The necessary and essential component in a definition of religion. *Journal of the Irish Society for the Academic Study of Religions, 2*(1), 23–34. https://jkapalo.files.wordpress.com/2015/04/religious-memory-as-a-conveyor-of-authoritative-tradition-the-necessary-and-essential-component-in-a-definition-of-religion-pdfl.pdf.

Cragun, R. T. (2017). The declining significance of religion: Secularization in Ireland. In M. J. Breen (Ed.), *Values and identities in Europe: Evidence from the European Social Survey* (pp. 17–35). Routledge.

Cragun, R. T. (2020). Summing up: Problems and prospects for a global church in the twenty-first century. In Gordon Shepherd, Gary Shepherd, & R. T. Cragun (Eds.), *The Palgrave handbook of global Mormonism* (pp. 817–851). Palgrave Macmillan.

Cragun, R. T., & Lawson, R. (2010). The secular transition: The worldwide growth of Mormons, Jehovah's Witnesses, and Seventh-Day Adventists. *Sociology of Religion: A Quarterly Review, 71*(3), 349–373. doi: 10.1093/socrel/srq022.

Cuthbert, D. A. (1987). Church growth in the British Isles. *BYU Studies Quarterly, 27*(2), 13–27. doi: 10.1007/s13398-014-0173-7.2.

Davie, G. (1990). "An ordinary god": The paradox of religion in contemporary Britain. *British Journal of Sociology, 41*(3), 395–421. doi: 10.2307/590965.

Davie, G. (1994). *Religion in Britain since 1945: Believing without belonging.* Blackwell.

Davie, G. (2000). *Religion in Europe: A memory mutates.* Oxford University Press.

Davie, G. (2005). From obligation to consumption: A framework for reflection in northern Europe. *Political Theology, 6*(3), 281–301. doi: 10.1558/poth.6.3.281.66128.

Davie, G. (2006). Religion in Europe in the 21st century: The factors to take into account. *European Journal of Sociology, 47*(2), 271–296. doi: 10.1017/S0003975606000099.

Davie, G. (2007). Vicarious religion: A methodological challenge. In N. T. Ammerman (Ed.), *Everyday religion: Observing modern religious lives* (pp. 21–37). Oxford University Press.

Davie, G. (2014). Managing pluralism: The European case. *Society, 51*(6), 613–622. doi: 10.1007/s12115-014-9834-6.

Davies, D. J. (2000). *The Mormon culture of salvation.* Ashgate Publishing.

Davies, D. J. (2003). *An introduction to Mormonism.* Cambridge University Press. doi: 10.1017/CBO9780511610028.

Davies, D. J. (2007). The invention of sacred tradition: Mormonism. In J. R. Lewis & O. Hammer (Eds.), *The invention of sacred tradition* (pp. 56–74). Cambridge University Press. doi: 10.1017/CBO9780511488450.004.

Davies, D. J. (2010). *Joseph Smith, Jesus, and satanic opposition: Atonement, evil, and the Mormon vision.* Ashgate Publishing.

Davies D. J. (2011). *Emotion, identity, and religion: Hope, reciprocity, and otherness.* Oxford University Press.

Day, A., & Mia, L. (Eds.). (2015). *Modernities, memory, and mutations: Grace Davie and the study of religion*. Ashgate Publishing.

Daynes, K. M. (2015). Celestial marriage (eternal and plural). In T. L. Givens & P. L. Barlow (Eds.), *The Oxford handbook of Mormonism* (pp. 334–349). Oxford University Press.

de Cléir, S. (2017). *Popular Catholicism in 20th-century Ireland: Locality, identity, and culture*. Bloomsbury.

Decoo, W. (1981). Mormonism in a European Catholic region: A contribution to the social psychology of LDS converts. *BYU Studies Quarterly, 24*(1), 61–77. http://scholarsarchive.byu.edu/byusq/vol24/iss1/6.

Decoo, W. (1996). Feeding the fleeing flock: Reflections on the struggle to retain Church members in Europe. *Dialogue: A Journal of Mormon Thought, 29*(1), 97–118. https://www.dialoguejournal.com/wp-content/uploads/sbi/issues/V29N01.pdf.

Decoo, W. (2013a). "As our two faiths have worked together"—Catholicism and Mormonism on human life ethics and same-sex marriage. *Dialogue: A Journal of Mormon Thought, 46*(3), 1–44. https://www.dialoguejournal.com/wp-content/uploads/sbi/articles/Dialogue_V46N03_wd.pdf.

Decoo, W. (2013b). In search of Mormon identity: Mormon culture, gospel culture, and an American worldwide church. *International Journal of Mormon Studies, 6*. https://www.academia.edu/12167273/GOSPEL_CULTURE_AND_AN_AMERICAN_WORLDWIDE.

Decoo, W. (2015). Mormons in Europe. In T. L. Givens & P. L. Barlow (Eds.), *The Oxford handbook of Mormonism* (pp. 543–559). Oxford University Press.

Decoo-Vanwelkenhuysen, C. (2016). Mormon women in Europe: A look at gender norms. In K. Holbrook & M. Bowman (Eds.), *Women and Mormonism: Historical and contemporary perspectives* (pp. 213–230). University of Utah Press.

Department of Education. (2013). *Diversity of school patronage*. Government of Ireland. http://www.education.ie/en/Schools-Colleges/Information/Diversity-of-Patronage/.

Donnelly, S., & Inglis, T. (2010). The media and the Catholic Church in Ireland: Reporting clerical child sex abuse. *Journal of Contemporary Religion, 25*(1), 1–19. doi: 10.1080/13537900903416788.

Duke, J. T. (1998). Cultural continuity and tension: A test of Stark's theory of church growth. In J. T. Duke (Ed.), *Latter-day Saint social life: Social research on the LDS Church and its members* (pp. 71–104). Religious Studies Center, Brigham Young University. http://rsc.byu.edu/archived/latter-day-saint-social-life-social-research-lds-church-and-its-members/3-cultural.

Durkheim, E. (1915). *Elementary forms of the religious life*. Macmillan.

Dursteler, E. R. (2018). One hundred years of solitude: Mormonism in Italy, 1867–1964. In I. E. Annus, D. M. Morris, & K. B. Östman (Eds.), *Mormonism in Europe: Historical and contemporary perspectives* (pp. 91–115). Americana Ebooks.

Dy, A. C. (2014). The Virgin Mary as mazu or guanyin: The syncretic nature of Chinese religion in the Philippines. *Philippine Sociological Review, 62*, 41–63. https://www.jstor.org/stable/43486492.

Educate Together. (2005). *What is an Educate Together National School.* http://www
.educatetogether.ie/sites/default/files/wiaets_2006_en_small-copy.pdf.

Eliason, E. A. (2002). The cultural dynamics of historical self-fashioning: LDS pioneer
nostalgia, American culture, and the international Church. *Journal of Mormon
History, 28*(2), 140–174. http://digitalcommons.usu.edu/mormonhistory/vol28
/iss2/1.

Embry, J. L. (2000). LDS ethnic wards and branches in the United States: The
advantages and disadvantages of language congregations. *Deseret Language and
Linguistic Society Symposium, 26*(1), 45–50. https://scholarsarchive.byu.edu/dlls
/vol26/iss1/6.

Es, M. A. van (2019). Muslim women as "ambassadors" of Islam: Breaking stereotypes
in everyday life. *Identities, 26*(4), 375–392. doi: 10.1080/1070289X.2017.1346985.

Faulconer, J. E. (2006). Why a Mormon won't drink coffee but might have a Coke:
The atheological character of the Church of Jesus Christ of Latter-day Saints.
Element, 2(2), 21–37. http://libojs2.uncg.edu/index.php/element/article/view/20.

Faulconer, J. E. (2015). The Mormon temple and Mormon ritual. In T. L. Givens &
P. L. Barlow (Eds.), *The Oxford handbook of Mormonism* (pp. 196–209). Oxford
University Press.

Fentress, C., & Wickham, W. (1992). *Social memory.* Blackwell.

Fielding Smith, J. (1950). *Essentials in Church history.* Deseret Book Company.
http://www.josephsmithfoundation.org/sources/family_history/essentials
_church_history.pdf.

Frankenburg, R. (1993). *White women, race matters: The social construction of Whiteness.* Routledge.

Frawley, O. (2011a). Towards a theory of cultural memory in an Irish postcolonial
context. In O. Frawley (Ed.), *Memory Ireland: History and modernity* (pp. 18–37).
Syracuse University Press.

Frawley, O. (Ed.) (2011b). *Memory Ireland: History and modernity.* New York: Syracuse University Press.

Frawley, O. (Ed.) (2021). *Women and the decade of commemorations.* Indiana University Press.

Ganiel, G. (2016a). A charismatic church in a post-Catholic Ireland: Negotiating
diversity at Abundant Life in Limerick City. *Irish Journal of Sociology, 24*(3),
293–315. doi: 10.1177/0791603515627050.

Ganiel, G. (2016b). *Transforming post-Catholic Ireland: Religious practice in late
modernity.* Oxford University Press.

García, I. M. (2017). Thoughts on Latino Mormons, their afterlife, and the need
for a new historical paradigm for Saints of color. *Dialogue: A Journal of Mormon Thought, 50*(4), 1–29. https://www.dialoguejournal.com/archive/dialogue
-premium-content/winter-2017/.

García, I. M. (2018). Empowering Latino Saints to transcend historical racialism: A
bishop's tale. In G. Colvin & J. Brooks (Eds.), *Decolonizing Mormonism: Approaching a postcolonial Zion* (pp. 139–161). University of Utah Press.

Garner, S. (2005). Guests of the nation. *Irish Review, 33*, 78–84.

Gay and Lesbian Equality Network. (2013). *Dáil and Seanad debates on decriminalisation of homosexuality June 1993*. http://www.glen.ie/attachments/Decriminalisation_1993_-_GLEN_Extract_of_Dail_and_Seanad_Debates.PDF.

Geaves, R. (2009). Forget transmitted memory: The de-traditionalised "religion" of Prem Rawat. *Journal of Contemporary Religion, 24*(1), 19–33. doi: 10.1080/13537900802630471.

Gedicks, F. M. (2011). Mormonism in western society: Three futures. *Dialogue: A Journal of Mormon Thought, 44*(4), 144–162. http://www.dialoguejournal.com/wp-content/uploads/2011/12/Dialogue_V44N04_148.pdf.

Givens, T. L. (2007). *People of paradox: A history of Mormon culture*. Oxford University Press.

Givens, T. L. (2016). The global Church. In M. A. Goodman & M. Properzi (Eds.), *The worldwide Church: Mormonism as a global religion* (425–442). Religious Studies Center, Brigham Young University. http://ldseuroseminar.org/wp-content/uploads/2017/02/Hansen_Noot_Mema_Churchs-cultural-challenges-in-Europe_2015.pdf.

Grant, B. J. (1992). The Church in the British Isles. In D. H. Ludlow (Ed.), *The encyclopedia of Mormonism* (pp. 227–232). Macmillan.

Grover, M. L. (2015). Mormons in Latin America. In T. L. Givens & P. L. Barlow (Eds.), *The Oxford handbook of Mormonism* (pp. 515–529). Oxford University Press.

Grow, M. J. (2004). The Whore of Babylon and the Abomination of Abominations: Catholic and Mormon mutual perceptions and religious identity. *Church History, 73*(1), 139–167. doi: 10.1017/S0009640700097869.

Haar, G. ter (1998). *Halfway to paradise: African Christians in Europe*. Cardiff Academic Press.

Haight, D. B. (1990, April). Filling the whole earth. *LDS General Conference*. Church of Jesus Christ of Latter-day Saints. https://www.lds.org/general-conference/1990/04/filling-the-whole-earth?lang=eng.

Halbwachs, M. (1992). *On collective memory* (L. A. Coser, Trans.). University of Chicago Press.

Halford, A. (2020). Women's gender roles and Mormonism in England. In A. Hoyt & T. G. Petrey (Eds.), *The Routledge handbook of Mormonism and gender* (pp. 392–405). Routledge.

Halford, A., & O' Brien, H. (2020). Contemporary issues for the Church of Jesus Christ of Latter-day Saints in Ireland and the United Kingdom. In Gordon Shepherd, Gary Shepherd, & R. T. Cragun (Eds.), *The Palgrave handbook of global Mormonism* (pp. 475–501). Palgrave Macmillan.

Halikiopoulou, D. (2008). *The changing dynamics of religion and national identity: Greece and the Republic of Ireland in a comparative perspective* [Unpublished doctoral dissertation]. London School of Economics and Political Science. doi: 10.1163/187489208X336551.

Halman, L., & Draulans, V. (2006). How secular is Europe? *British Journal of Sociology, 57*(2), 263–288. doi: 10.1111/j.1468-4446.2006.00109.x.

Hanciles, J. J. (2015). "Would that all God's people were prophets": Mormonism and the new shape of global Christianity. *Journal of Mormon History, 41*(2), 35–68. https://www.jstor.org/stable/10.5406/jmormhist.41.2.35.

Hansen, G. Jr., Noot, H., & Mema, M. (2016). The Church's cultural challenges in Europe. In M. A. Goodman & M. Properzi (Eds.), *The worldwide Church: Mormonism as a global religion* (pp. 309–330). Religious Studies Center, Brigham Young University. http://ldseuroseminar.org/wp-content/uploads/2017/02/Hansen_Noot_Mema_Churchs-cultural-challenges-in-Europe_2015.pdf.

Haroldsen, E. O. (1995, August). Good and evil spoken of. *Ensign*. https://www.lds.org/ensign/1995/08/good-and-evil-spoken-of?lang=eng.

Harris, C. W. (1984). Making sense of the senseless: An Irish education. *Dialogue: A Journal of Mormon Thought, 17*(4), 83–102. https://www.dialoguejournal.com/wp-content/uploads/sbi/issues/V17N04.pdf.

Harris, C. W. (1990). Mormons on the warfront: The Protestant Mormons and Catholic Mormons of Northern Ireland. *BYU Studies Quarterly, 30*(4), 7–19. http://scholarsarchive.byu.edu/byusq/vol30/iss4/2.

Haws, J. B. (2013). *The Mormon image in the American mind*. Oxford University Press.

Healy, A. E., & Breen, M. (2014). Religiosity in times of insecurity: An analysis of Irish, Spanish, and Portuguese European social survey data, 2002–12. *Irish Journal of Sociology, 22*(2), 4–29. doi: 10.7227/IJS.22.2.2.

Heaton, T. B., Albrecht, S. L., & Johnson, J. R. (1987). The making of British Saints in historical perspective. *BYU Studies Quarterly, 27*(2), 119–136. https://scholarsarchive.byu.edu/byusq/vol27/iss2/10

Hendrix-Komoto, A., & Stuart, J. R. (2020). Race and gender in Mormonism. In A. Hoyt & T. G. Petrey (Eds.), *The Routledge handbook of Mormonism and gender* (pp. 26–38). Routledge.

Hervieu-Léger, D. (2000). *Religion as a chain of memory*. Polity Press.

Hervieu-Léger, D. (2003). The role of religion in establishing social cohesion. *Religion in the New Europe*, (May), 45–63. https://books.openedition.org/ceup/1275.

Hjelm, T. (Ed.) (2015). *Is God back?: Reconsidering the new visibility of religion*. Bloomsbury.

Holman, T. B. (1996). Commitment making: Mate selection processes among active Mormon American couples. In D. J. Davies (Ed.), *Mormon identities in transition* (pp. 125–132). Cassell.

Howe, S. (2000). *Ireland and empire: Colonial legacies in Irish history and culture*. Oxford University Press.

Hwang Chen, C. (2014). Diverse yet hegemonic: Expressions of motherhood in "I'm a Mormon" ads. *Journal of Media and Religion, 13*(1), 31–47. doi: 10.1080/15348423.2014.871973.

Inglis, T. (1998). *Moral monopoly: The rise and fall of the Catholic Church in modern Ireland*. UCD Press.

Inglis, T. (2004). *Catholic identity, habitus, and practice in contemporary Ireland.* ISSC Discussion Paper WP2004/13. http://www.ucd.ie/geary/publications/2004/isscwp2004-13.pdf.

Inglis, T. (2007). Catholic identity in contemporary Ireland: Belief and belonging to tradition. *Journal of Contemporary Religion, 22*(2), 205–220. doi: 10.1080/13537900701331064.

Inglis, T. (2010). *Local belonging, identities, and sense of place in contemporary Ireland.* IBIS Discussion Paper: Politics and Identity, 4. https://researchrepository.ucd.ie/handle/10197/2414.

Inglis, T., & MacKeogh, C. (2012). The double bind: Women, honour, and sexuality in contemporary Ireland. *Media, Culture, and Society, 34*(1), 68–82. doi: 10.1177/0163443711427200.

Inouye, M. W. (2014). The oak and the banyan: The "glocalization" of Mormon studies. *Mormon Studies Review, 1*, 70–79. https://publications.mi.byu.edu/fullscreen/?pub=2402&index=7.

Irish Catholic Bishops Conference (2014). *Recent trends in ordained and professed people in the Catholic Church in Ireland.* http://www.catholicbishops.ie/wp-content/uploads/2014/07/Recent-trends-in-ordained-and-professed-people-in-the-Catholic-Church-in-Ireland-3-July-2014.pdf.

Jackson Noble, R. (2011). The changing face of Irish Christianity: The evangelical Christian movement in the Republic. In O. Cosgrove, L. Cox, C. Kuhling, & P. Mulholland (Eds.), *Ireland's new religious movements* (pp. 131–147). Cambridge Scholars Publishing.

James, C. P. (1997). Cead mile failte? Ireland welcomes divorce: The 1995 divorce referendum and the Family (Divorce) Act of 1996. *Duke Journal of Comparative and International Law, 8*, 175–228. http://scholarship.law.duke.edu/cgi/viewcontent.cgi?article=1277&context=djcil.

Johnson, J. (2019). *Mormons, musical theater, and belonging in America.* University of Illinois Press.

Joseph, E. (2018). Whiteness and racism: Examining the racial order in Ireland. *Irish Journal of Sociology, 26*(1), 46–70. doi: 10.1177/0791603517737282.

Joshi, K. Y. (2020). *White Christian privilege: The illusion of religious equality in America.* New York University Press.

Kenny, K. (2004). Ireland and the British Empire: An introduction. In K. Kenny (Ed.), *Ireland and the British Empire* (pp. 1–26). Oxford University Press.

Keohane, K., & Kuhling, C. (2004). *Collison culture: Transformations in everyday life in Ireland.* Liffey Press.

Kline, C. (2020). Finding peace, claiming place: Black South African women navigating the Church of Jesus Christ of Latter-day Saints. In Gordon Shepherd, Gary Shepherd, & R. T. Cragun (Eds.), *The Palgrave handbook of global Mormonism* (pp. 607–635). Palgrave Macmillan.

Kmec, V. (2014). Religion as a response to the crisis of modernity: Perspectives of immigrants in Ireland. In G. Ganiel, H. Winkel, & C. Monnot (Eds.), *Religion in times of crisis* (pp. 1–16). Brill.

Kmec, V. (2017). Transnational and local: Multiple functions of religious communities of EU migrants in Dublin. *Journal of the Irish Society for the Academic Study of Religions, 5*, 20–39. https://jisasr.org/current-issue-volume-5-2017.

Knowlton, D. C. (1996). Mormonism in Latin America: Towards the twenty-first century. *Dialogue: A Journal of Mormon Thought, 29*(1), 159–176. https://www.dialoguejournal.com/wp-content/uploads/sbi/issues/V29N01.pdf.

Kuhling, C., & Keohane, K. (2007). *Cosmopolitan Ireland: Globalisation and quality of life*. Pluto Press.

Larsen, S. S. (1982). The two sides of the house: Identity and social organisation in Kilroney, Northern Ireland. In A. P. Cohen (Ed.), *Belonging: Identity and social organisation in British rural cultures* (pp. 131–165). Manchester University Press.

Lawson, R., & Cragun, R. T. (2012). Comparing the geographic distributions and growth of Mormons, Adventists, and Witnesses. *Journal for the Scientific Study of Religion, 51*(2), 220–240. doi: 10.1111/j.1468-5906.2012.01646.x.

Lentin, R. (2007). Ireland: Racial state and crisis racism. *Ethnic and Racial Studies, 30*(4), 610–627. doi: 10.1080/01419870701356023.

Leone, M. P. (1979). *Roots of modern Mormonism*. Harvard University Press.

Lobb, C. G. (2000). Mormon membership trends in Europe among people of color: Present and future assessment. *Dialogue: A Journal of Mormon Thought, 33*(4), 55–68. https://www.dialoguejournal.com/wp-content/uploads/sbi/articles/Dialogue_V33N04_65.pdf.

Lövheim, M. (2007). Virtually boundless? Youth negotiating tradition in cyberspace. In N. T. Ammerman (Ed.), *Everyday religion: Observing modern religious lives* (pp. 83–103). Oxford University Press.

Lövheim, M., & Linderman, A. (2015). Religion, media, and modernity: Editorials and religion in Swedish daily press. In T. Hjelm (Ed.) *Is God back?: Reconsidering the new visibility of religion* (pp. 32–46). Bloomsbury.

Loyal, S. (2003). Welcome to the Celtic tiger: Racism, immigration, and the state. In C. Coulter, (Ed.), *The end of Irish history? Reflections on the Celtic tiger* (pp. 112–136). Manchester University Press.

Maffly-Kipp, L. (2017). The clock and the compass: Mormon culture in motion. *Journal of Mormon History, 43*(2), 1–19. https://www.jstor.org/stable/10.5406/jmormhist.43.2.0001.

Malesevic, V. (2010). Ireland and neo-secularisation theory. *Irish Journal of Sociology, 18*(1), 22–42. doi: 10.7227/IJS.18.1.2.

Martin, D. (2011, May 2). Homily at Liturgy Spring Seminar. *Spring Seminar Dublin Diocese*. http://www.dublindiocese.ie/522011-homily-at-liturgy-spring-seminar/.

Martin, D. (2013, April 24). Catholic Ireland, past, present, and future. *The Russo family lecture*. http://www.dublindiocese.ie/2442013-fordham-addresscatholic-irelandpast-present-future/.

Martinich, M. (2020). Mormons in North America, Latin America, the South Pacific, Europe, Africa, and Asia: An overview. In Gordon Shepherd, Gary Shepherd, & R. T. Cragun (Eds.), *The Palgrave handbook of global Mormonism* (pp. 323–343). Palgrave Macmillan.

Mason, P. Q. (2016). Introduction. In P. Q. Mason & J. G. Turner (Eds.), *Out of obscurity: Mormonism since 1945* (pp. 4–14). Oxford University Press. doi: 10.1093/acprof:oso/9780199358212.001.0001.

Mason, P. Q., & Turner, J. G. (Eds.). (2016). *Out of obscurity: Mormonism since 1945.* Oxford University Press. doi: 10.1093/acprof:oso/9780199358212.001.0001.

Mauss, A. L. (1989). Assimilation and ambivalence: The Mormon reaction to Americanization. *Dialogue: A Journal of Mormon Thought, 22*(1), 30–67. http://www.dialoguejournal.com/wp-content/uploads/sbi/articles/Dialogue_V22N01_32.pdf.

Mauss, A. L. (1994a). Refuge and retrenchment: The Mormon quest for identity. In M. Cornwall, T. B. Heaton, & L. A. Young (Eds.), *Contemporary Mormonism: Social science perspectives* (pp. 24–42). University of Illinois Press.

Mauss, A. L. (1994b). The Mormon struggle with assimilation and identity: Trends and developments. *Dialogue: A Journal of Mormon Thought, 27*(1), 129–149. https://www.dialoguejournal.com/wp-content/uploads/sbi/articles/Dialogue_V27N01_141.pdf.

Mauss, A. L. (1996a). Identity and boundary maintenance: International prospects for Mormonism at the dawn of the twenty-first century. In D. J. Davies (Ed.), *Mormon identities in transition* (pp. 9–20). Cassell.

Mauss, A. L. (1996b). Introduction to Mormons and Mormonism in the twenty-first century. *Dialogue: A Journal of Mormon Thought, 29*(1), 1–8. https://www.dialoguejournal.com/wp-content/uploads/sbi/articles/Dialogue_V29N01_4.pdf.

Mauss, A. L. (2008). Seeking a "second harvest": Controlling the costs of LDS membership in Europe. *Dialogue: A Journal of Mormon Thought, 41*(4), 1–54. https://www.dialoguejournal.com/wp-content/uploads/sbi/issues/V41N04.pdf.

Mauss, A. L. (2011). Rethinking retrenchment: Course corrections in the ongoing campaign for respectability. *Dialogue: A Journal of Mormon Thought, 44*(4), 1–42. https://www.dialoguejournal.com/store/premium-digital-articles-2/premium-digital-articles-vol-44-num-4-winter-2011/#_am.

McGonigle, L. (2012). "Doesn't Mary have a lovely bottom?": Gender, sexuality, and Catholic ideology in *Father Ted. Etudes Irelandaises, 37*(1), 89–102.

McGuire, M. B. (2008). *Lived religion: Faith and practice in everyday life.* Oxford University Press.

Menig, D. W. (1965). The Mormon Culture Region: Strategies and patterns in the geography of the American West, 1847–1964. *Annals of the Association of American Geographers, 55*(2), 191–220.

Mitchell, H. (2001). "Being there": British Mormons and the history trail. *Anthropology Today, 17*(2), 9–14.

Mitchell, J. P., and Mitchell, H. J. (2008). For belief: Embodiment and immanence in Catholicism and Mormonism. *Social Analysis, 52*(1), 79–94. doi: 10.3167/sa.2008.520105.

Moane, G. (2014). Postcolonial legacies and the Irish psyche. In T. Inglis (Ed.), *Are the Irish different?* (pp. 121–133). Manchester University Press.

Mulholland, P. (2019). *Love's betrayal: The decline of Catholicism and the rise of new religions in Ireland.* Peter Lang.

Murray, D. (1996). Faith and culture: A complex relationship. In E. Cassidy (Ed.), *Faith and culture in the Irish context* (pp. 16–35). Veritas.

Newton, M. (1991). "Almost like us": The American socialization of Australian converts. *Dialogue: A Journal of Mormon Thought, 24*(3), 9–20. https://www.dialoguejournal.com/wp-content/uploads/sbi/articles/Dialogue_V24N03_11.pdf.

Nuttall, D. (2015). Keeping their heads down: Shame and pride in the stories of Protestants in the Irish Republic. *Journal of the Irish Society for the Academic Study of Religions, 2*(1), 47–72. https://jkapalo.files.wordpress.com/2015/04/keeping-their-heads-down-shame-and-pride-in-the-stories-of-protestants-in-the-irish-republic-pdf1.pdf.

Oaks, D. H. (2010). The Gospel culture. The Church of Jesus Christ of Latter-day Saints. https://www.churchofjesuschrist.org/study/ensign/2012/03/the-gospel-culture?lang=eng.

O'Caollaí, É., & Hilliard, M. (2015, May 24). Ireland becomes first country to approve same-sex marriage by popular vote. *Irish Times.* http://www.irishtimes.com/news/politics/ireland-becomes-first-country-to-approve-same-sex-marriage-by-popular-vote-1.2223646.

O'Connell, P. J., Collins, M., Creighton, M. J., & da Silva Pedroso, M. (2019). *Irish social attitudes in 2018–19: Topline results from round 9 of the European Social Survey.* Dublin. https://www.ucd.ie/geary/static/ess/ESS_Geary_Round9.pdf.

O'Hearn, D. (2014). Just another bubble economy? In T. Inglis (Ed.), *Are the Irish different?* (pp. 34–44). Manchester University Press.

Olick, J. K., Vinitzky-Seroussi, V., & Levy, D. (Eds.) (2011). *The collective memory reader.* Oxford University Press.

O'Mahony, E. (2010). *Religious practice and values in Ireland: A summary of European Values Study 4th wave data.* Irish Catholic Bishops' Conference. https://www.catholicbishops.ie/wp-content/uploads/images/stories/cco_publications/researchanddevelopment/evs_4th_wave_report.pdf.

Östman, K. B. (2002). "The other" in the limelight: One perspective on the publicity surrounding the new LDS temple in Finland. *Dialogue: A Journal of Mormon Thought, 40*(4), 71–106. https://www.jstor.org/stable/10.5406/dialjmormthou.40.4.0071.

Otterstrom, S. M. (2008). Genealogy as religious ritual: The doctrine and practice of family history in the Church of Jesus Christ of Latter-day Saints. In T. J. Dallen & J. K. Guelke (Eds.), *Geography and genealogy: Locating personal pasts* (pp. 137–152). Ashgate Publishing. doi: 10.1017/CBO9781107415324.004.

Pandian, J. (2006). Syncretism in religion. *Anthropos,* 229–233. https://www.jstor.org/stable/40466631.

Patterson, S. M. (2016). Everyone can be a pioneer. In P. Q. Mason & J. G. Turner (Eds.), *Out of obscurity: Mormonism since 1945* (pp. 302–318). Oxford University Press. doi: 10.1093/acprof:oso/9780199358212.001.0001.

Petrey, T. G. (2020). *Tabernacles of clay: Sexuality and gender in modern Mormonism.* University of North Carolina Press.

Pew Research Center (2018). *Being Christian in Western Europe*. https://www
.pewresearch.org/religion/2018/05/29/being-christian-in-western-europe/.

Phillips, R. (2008). "De facto congregationalism" and Mormon missionary outreach:
An ethnographic case study. *Journal for the Scientific Study of Religion, 47*(4),
628–643. doi: 10.1111/j.1468-5906.2008.00431.x.

Phillips, R., & Cragun, R. T. (2013). Contemporary Mormon religiosity and the legacy
of "gathering." *Nova Religio: The Journal of Alternative and Emergent Religions,*
16(3), 77–94. doi: 10.1525/nr.2013.16.3.77.

Pine, E. (2011). *The politics of Irish memory: Performing remembrance in contemporary
Irish culture*. Palgrave Macmillan.

Powell, A. J. (2016). Covenant cloaks: Mormon temple garments in the light of
identity theory. *Material Religion, 12*(4), 457–475. doi: 10.1080/17432200.2016
.1227642.

Properzi, M. (2010). The religious 'Other': Reflecting upon Mormon perceptions.
International Journal of Mormon Studies, 3, 41–55.

Rasmussen, M. L. (2016). *Mormonism and the making of a British Zion*. University
of Utah Press.

Reeve, W. P. (2015). The Mormon Church in Utah. In T. L. Givens & P. L. Barlow
(Eds.), *The Oxford handbook of Mormonism* (pp. 38–55). Oxford University Press.

Riain, O. (2014). Where is Ireland in the worlds of capitalism? In T. Inglis (Ed.), *Are
the Irish different?* (pp. 22–33). Manchester University Press.

Riess, J. (2018, October 20). The name "Mormon": Why all the fuss, and why now?
Religion News Service. https://religionnews.com/2018/10/20/the-name-mormon
-why-all-the-fuss-and-why-now/.

Riess, J. (2019). *The next Mormons: How millennials are changing the LDS Church*.
Oxford University Press.

Riess, J. (2021, August 25). Elder Holland's BYU speech is for a university of yesteryear.
Religion News Service. https://religionnews.com/2021/08/25/elder-hollands-byu
-speech-is-for-a-university-of-yesteryear/.

Rigal-Cellard, B. (2018). Inculturation of Mormonism in France. In I. E. Annus, D. M.
Morris, & K. B. Östman (Eds.), *Mormonism in Europe: Historical and contemporary
perspectives* (pp. 196–208). Americana Ebooks.

Ritter, C. S., & Kmec, V. (2017). Religious practices and networks of belonging
in an immigrant congregation: The German-speaking Lutheran congregation in Dublin. *Journal of Contemporary Religion, 32*(2), 269–281. doi: 10.1080
/13537903.2017.1298907.

Romanello, B. (2020). Multiculturalism as resistance: Latina migrants navigate US
Mormon spaces. *Dialogue: A Journal of Mormon Thought, 53*(1), 5–31. doi: 10.5406/
dialjmormthou.53.1.0005.

Roudometof, V. (2018). Glocal religions: An introduction. *Religions, 9* (294), 1–9.
doi: 10.3390/rel9100294.

Ruane, J. (2010). Ethnicity, religion, and peoplehood: Protestants in France and in
Ireland. *Ethnopolitics, 9*(1), 121–135. doi: 10.1080/17449050903557500.

Ruane, J., & Todd, J. (2009). Protestant minorities in European states and nations. *National Identities, 11*(1), 1–8. doi: 10.1080/14608940802680953.

Rutherford, T. F. (2016). The internationalisation of Mormonism. In P. Q. Mason & J. G. Turner (Eds.), *Out of obscurity: Mormonism since 1945* (pp. 37–60). Oxford University Press. doi: 10.1093/acprof:oso/9780199358212.003.0003.

Rutter Strickling, L. (2018). *On fire in Baltimore*. Greg Koffard Books.

Ryan, L. (2011). Multiculturalization and Irish national memory. In O. Frawley (Ed.), *Memory Ireland: History and modernity* (pp. 207–221). Syracuse University Press.

Sakaranaho, T. (2003). Les rhétoriques de la continuité: Les femmes, l'Islam et l'héritage Catholique en Irlande. *Social Compass, 50*(1), 71–84.

Sakaranaho, T. (2006). *Religious freedom, multiculturalism, Islam: Cross-reading Finland and Ireland*. Brill.

Sakaranaho, T. (2011). Religion and the study of social memory. *Temenos—Nordic Journal of Comparative Religion, 47*(2), 135–158. doi: 10.33356/temenos.5151.

Sakaranaho, T. (2015). A memory that mutates. In A. Day & L. Mia (Eds.), *Modernities, memory, and mutations: Grace Davie and the study of religion* (pp. 31–43). Ashgate Publishing. https://www.vlebooks.com/vleweb/Product/Index/569362?page=0.

Scanlon, L. A., & Satish Kumar, M. (2019). Ireland and Irishness: The contextuality of postcolonial identity. *Annals of the American Association of Geographers, 109*(1), 202–222. doi: 10.1080/24694452.2018.1507812.

Scharbrodt, O. (2015). Being Irish, being Muslim. In O. Scharbrodt, T. Sakaranaho, A. H. Khan, Y. Shanneik, & V. Ibrahim (Eds.), *Muslims in Ireland: Past and present* (pp. 216–229). Edinburgh University Press. http://www.jstor.org/stable/10.3366/j.ctt14brwn5.13%0AJSTOR.

Scharbrodt, O., & Sakaranaho, T. (2011). Islam and Muslims in the Republic of Ireland: An introduction to the special issue. *Journal of Muslim Minority Affairs, 31*(4), 469–485. doi: 10.1080/13602004.2011.630857.

Schwadel, P. (2010). Jewish teenagers' syncretism. *Review of Religious Research, 51*(3), 324–332.

Sen, M. (2011). Memory, modernity, and the sacred. In O. Frawley (Ed.), *Memory Ireland: History and modernity* (pp. 101–115). Syracuse University Press.

Shanneik, Y. (2015). Muslim women in Ireland. In O. Scharbrodt, T. Sakaranaho, A. H. Khan, Y. Shanneik, & V. Ibrahim (Eds.), *Muslims in Ireland: Past and present* (pp. 193–215). Edinburgh University Press. http://www.jstor.org/stable/10.3366/j.ctt14brwn5.12.

Share, P., & Corcoran, M. P. (2010). From enchantment to disillusion. In P. Share & M. P. Corcoran (Eds.), *Ireland of the illusions: A sociological chronicle 2007–2008*. Institute of Public Administration.

Shepherd, Gordon, Shepherd, Gary, & Cragun, R. T. (Eds.). (2020). *The Palgrave handbook of global Mormonism*. Palgrave Macmillan. doi: 10.1080/19376529.2014.950158.

Sherlock, I. (2018). The LDS Church in Flanders: Their way, our way, or their way in our own way. In G. Colvin & J. Brooks (Eds.), *Decolonizing Mormonism: Approaching a postcolonial Zion* (pp. 186–201). University of Utah Press.

Shipps, J. (2006). *Sojourner in the promised land: Forty years among the Mormons.* University of Illinois Press.

Simmel, G. (1971). The stranger. In D. N. Levine (Ed.), *On individuality and social forms* (pp. 324–339). University of Chicago Press.

Stark, R. (1984) The rise of a new world faith. *Review of Religious Research, 26*(1), 18–27. doi: 10.2307/3511039.

Starrs, P. F. (2010). Meetinghouses in the Mormon mind: Ideology, architecture, and turbulent streams of an expanding church. *Geographical Review, 99*(3), 323–355. doi: 10.1111/j.1931-0846.2009.tb00436.x.

Stewart, D. G. J. (2020a). The dynamics of LDS growth in the twenty-first century. In Gordon Shepherd, Gary Shepherd, & R. T. Cragun (Eds.), *The Palgrave handbook of global Mormonism* (pp. 163–205). Palgrave Macmillan.

Stewart, D. G. J. (2020b). The LDS Church in Eastern Europe, Russia, and Central Asia. In Gordon Shepherd, Gary Shepherd, & R. T. Cragun (Eds.), *The Palgrave handbook of global Mormonism* (pp. 559–585). Palgrave Macmillan.

Stewart, D. G. J. (2017). *Statistical Profile: Northern Ireland, Cumorah.* https://www.cumorah.com/countries/viewStats/UnitedKingdom/333/UK- Northern Ireland.

Stewart, D. G. J., & Martinich, M. (n.d.). *Reaching the nations: Ireland, Cumorah.* http://www.cumorah.com/countries/reachingNations/Ireland.

Storm, I. (2011). Ethnic nominalism and civic religiosity: Christianity and national identity in Britain. *Sociological Review, 59*(4), 828–846 doi: 10.1111/j.1467-954X.2011.02040.x.

Storm, I. (2013). "Christianity is not just about religion": Religious and national identities in a northern English town. *Secularism and Nonreligion, 2*, 21–38. doi: 10.5334/snr.aj.

Suiter, J., & Reidy, T. (2015, May 21). Why Ireland's holding a same-sex marriage referendum. *BBC News.* https://www.bbc.com/news/world-europe-32809355.

Thomas, M. S. (1987). The influence of traditional British social patterns on LDS Church growth in southwest Britain. *BYU Studies Quarterly, 27*(1), 107–118. http://scholarsarchive.byu.edu/byusq/vol27/iss2/9.

Turpin, H. (2019). Leaving Roman Catholicism. In D. Enstedt, G. Larsson, & T. T. Mantsinem (Eds.), *Handbook of leaving religion* (pp. 186–200). Brill.

Tweed, T. (2014). Beyond "surreptitious staring": Migration, missions, and the generativity of Mormonism for the comparative and translocative study of religion. *Mormon Studies Review, 1*, 17–29.

Ugba, A. (2009) *Shades of belonging: African Pentecostals in twenty-first-century Ireland.* Africa World Press.

Uluave-Hafoka, M. (2017). To be young, Mormon, and Tongan. *Dialogue: A Journal of Mormon Thought, 50*(4), 99–104. https://www.dialoguejournal.com/archive/dialogue-premium-content/winter-2017/.

Upton, D. (2005). What the Mormon cultural landscape can tell us. *Journal of Mormon History, 31*(2), 1–30. http://digitalcommons.usu.edu/mormonhistory/vol31/iss2/1.

Vertovec, S. (2004). Religion and diaspora. In P. Antes, A. W. Geertz, & R. R. Warne, (Eds.), *New approaches to the study of religion* (pp. 275–305). Walter De Gruyter.

Vial, T. (2016). *Modern religion, modern race.* Oxford University Press. doi: 10.1558/bar.35775.

Walsh, T. (2015). Learning from minority: Exploring Irish Protestant experience. *Journal of the Irish Society for the Academic Study of Religions, 2*(1), 73–93. https://jkapalo.files.wordpress.com/2015/04/learning-from-minority-exploring-irish-protestant-experience-pdf.pdf.

Werbner, P. (1997). Introduction: The dialectics of cultural hybridity, In P. Werbner & T. Modood (Eds.), *Debating cultural hybridity: Multicultural identities and the politics of anti-racism* (pp. 1–29). Zed Books.

Werbner, P. (2004). Theorising complex diasporas: Purity and hybridity in the South Asian public sphere in Britain. *Journal of Ethnic and Migration Studies, 30*(5), 895–911. doi: 10.1080/1369183042000245606.

Whitehead, A., Perry, S., & Baker, J. O. (2018). Make America Christian again: Christian nationalism and voting for Donald Trump in the 2016 presidential election. *Sociology of Religion, 79*(2), 147–171. doi: https://doi.org/10.1093/socrel/srx070.

Whyte, J. H. (1976). *Church and state in modern Ireland 1923–1979.* 2nd ed. Gill and Macmillan.

Widtsoe, J. A. (1988, April). Why are the Latter-day Saints a peculiar people? *Ensign.* https://www.churchofjesuschrist.org/study/ensign/1988/04/i-have-a-question/why-are-the-latter-day-saints-a-peculiar-people?lang=eng.

Wilson, B. (1966). *Religion in secular society.* Penguin.

Wilson, B. (1982). *Religion in sociological perspective.* Oxford University Press.

Woods, F. E. (2018). Gathering the European Saints to America in the nineteenth century. In I. E. Annus, D. M. Morris, & K. B. Östman (Eds.), *Mormonism in Europe: Historical and contemporary perspectives* (pp. 115–132). Americana Ebooks.

Worldometer (2021). *Europe population. Worldometer.* Retrieved September 28, 2021, from https://www.worldometers.info/world-population/europe-population/.

Yang, F., & Ebaugh, H. R. (2001). Transformations in new immigrant religions and their global implications. *American Sociological Review, 66*(2), 269–288. http://www.jstor.org/stable/2657418.

Yorgason, E., & Chen, C. H. (2008). "Kingdom come": Representing Mormonism through a geopolitical frame. *Political Geography, 27*(4), 478–500. doi: 10.1016/j.polgeo.2008.03.005.

Yorgason, E., & Robertson, D. B. (2006). Mormonism's raveling and unraveling of a geopolitical thread. *Geopolitics, 11*(2), 256–279. doi: 10.1080/14650040600598528.

Young, M. B., & Gray, D. A. (2015). Mormons and race. In T. L. Givens & P. L. Barlow (Eds.), *The Oxford handbook of Mormonism* (pp. 363–386). Oxford University Press.

Yukich, G., & Edgell, P. (Eds.). (2020). *Religion is raced.* New York University Press.

Index

Africans: church near Appleby building, 9; and conversion efforts, 62–64, 71–72; East Africans, 104, 165–68; and family conversions, 106; and global Mormonism, 156; and immigration, 33; interviewees, 16–17; and place-based difference, 138–41; responsibilities as Black Mormon in Ireland, 120, 179

agnostic, 36, 42

alcohol, 10, 16, 49, 67, 75–79, 82; pubs, 75, 79, 154

Americanism, 7, 48, 52, 60–61

Asians, 53, 63, 156–58; Southeast Asians, 18–19, 113, 125–28, 131–33, 158

atheist, 20–21, 36, 42–43, 85, 180

Ballard, M. Russell, 159–62

baptism: church statistics, 8, 44; convert, 72, 94–95, 156; for the dead (posthumous), 91–99, 104, 111, 173–74; in decline, 54, 63–64; Roman Catholic, 1

Belgium, 56–57

Berger, Peter, 34, 134, 138

Bible, 12, 49, 72–73, 121

Black people: investigator, 72; and the Mormon racial restriction, 62; Mormons, 120, 167, 179; Pentecostal, 9, 120; South Africans, 139

Book of Mormon: and Americentrism, 48; and missionary work, 72; and Mormon visibility, 75; in Mormon worship services, 12; and race, 62; role in conversion, 105, 166

branch president, 10–11, 97, 118, 122–29, 173

Brigham Young University (BYU), 50, 58, 110, 135, 176

British: colonial control, 25–26, 40; and Easter Rising, 118; empire, 5; Mormonism in, 27, 51–53; Protestantism of, 26, 28, 41

Brooks, Joanna, 5, 60, 62, 152

Buddhism, 4, 50, 136, 140

callings, 123–25, 149–51, 176

children: childrearing, 58, 87–88, 175; education, 80–86; and genealogy, 174; of God, 89–91, 147; and immigration, 114; and meetinghouses, 7, 11, 130; in Mormon beliefs, 49, 89–91, 96, 101–8, 11; Mormon children, 64; and patriotism, 132–33, 146–47; Primary organization, 12

Christianity: and Britishness, 41; global, 49–50; in Latin America, 54; Mormon, 60, 179; Orthodox, 37; and visible religious identity, 121

Church of Ireland, 3, 118–19, 131

Church of Jesus Christ of Latter-day Saints: debates over naming, 4, 49–50

collective memory: and adaptation, 168; and Irishness, 7, 133; and Irish religion, 22, 25, 38–45, 163; and Mormonism, 45–46, 65, 107, 137, 162, 171; and tradition, 44–45, 133

colonialism: and Ireland, 6, 25–29, 40; and Mormonism, 5, 60–63, 125, 137; postcolonial societies, 50

colonization, 5, 26
Colvin, Gina, 5, 60, 62, 152
conversion: and adaptation of Catholicism to Mormonism, 46, 169–170; and Africans, 63; Americanness as incentive, 60; from Catholicism to Mormonism, 19, 23, 28, 39, 42, 81, 94–95, 115; chain of belief, 38, 43–45, 87, 94, 98, 137, 162, 165, 168, 174; from Church of Ireland, 131; and exclusion, 118; and family relationships, 57, 87–88, 94–95, 103–5, 166–67, 171; and gathering, 25; and Irishness, 42–43, 70–71, 77; and lived religion, 146; and marriage, 139; from Pentecostalism, 120; as pioneers, 159; retention of, 55; and temples, 111; and visibility, 116–20. *See also* Missionaries

Davie, Grace, 34–35, 41–43, 56–57, 83, 179
Davies, Douglas, 48–51, 89–97, 107, 173
Denmark, 52–53, 56

education: bilingualism, 114; Catholic schools, 1, 37, 81–85, 139–40; Mormonism and schools, 49, 81–86, 139–40; and patriotism, 133, 146; Protestant, 165; state institutions, 178–79; university (third-level), 67, 135, 180. *See also* Brigham Young University (BYU); Sunday School
Elders Quorum, 12, 21
emotions, 23, 68, 160–61; crying, 12, 94, 102, 105, 107, 160
ethnicity: and diversity, 124, 158; and identity, 89, 178; and Ireland, 1–4, 43, 157–58; in Mormon congregations, 123–28, 157, 167, 179–80; and Mormon Irishness, 7, 23, 133, 139–40, 145; and race, 62–65; and religion, 37–38, 57; and religious diversity, 83; and unity, 159
Europe: and Americanism, 60–61, 152, 159; assimilation of European Mormons, 58–60; belonging in European Mormonism, 55–56; conversions to Mormonism and family tragedy, 87–89, 167, 169; and family norms, 32–34; isolation and European Mormonism, 56–57, 77, 111, 134; lived Mormonism in, 22, 49, 139; Mormon growth in, 8, 25–26, 54, 180; Mormon marriage challenge, 174; and Mormon membership's activity, 7; and public religious practice, 74; and racialized religion, 2; and religion, 47,

83; and religious decline, 5; and religious pluralism, 179; stigmatization of Mormonism, 30; secularization, 35–37, 43; study demographics, 16–17; and tithing, 68; Whiteness, 63–66
European Union (EU), 5, 32–33

family: conversion as tragedy, 57, 87–88, 94–95, 103–5, 166–67, 171; Daddy-Daughter/Son Day, 90; eternal, 89–91, 98–109, 176; exaltation and family destiny, 91, 96–97; Family Home Evening, 49; kinship, 87–92, 97–102, 106, 111–12, 173–74; parents, 93–94, 102–9, 122, 132, 142, 149, 165, 175; part-member, 88, 95, 103–10; theology, 87, 91, 95–103, 106–11, 173–74. *See also* baptism: for the dead (posthumous); children; temple: sealing
Fast and Testimony Sacrament meetings, 14, 18, 76, 103–7, 110, 177
Father Ted, 3–4
Finland, 43, 56, 61
France, 33–34, 37, 43, 57
Francis (Pope), 140

Ganiel, Gladys, 34–35, 39, 169
garments, 99–101
gender: and Catholicism, 94; equality, 58; and identity, 40; and Latinas, 63; in marriage, 127; in Mormon beliefs, 124, 145, 173; in Mormon worship practices, 12–13, 173; and Tongans, 65; and worthiness, 150
genealogy, 45, 49, 91–96, 99, 111, 174
Germany, 152, 157
global: Christianity, 49–50; globalization, 5–6, 31, 49, 57, 64; Global South, 55, 57, 156, 178; Mormonism, 5, 47, 49, 53, 58, 65, 125, 129, 133, 145, 148–52, 162–63, 171–77
God: and callings, 123; and Catholic dis/beliefs, 42, 78; and family, 89–91, 147; Irish belief in, 37; and Joseph Smith's First Vision, 20, 107; in Mormon ritual, 44, 96; personal relationships with, 41, 73, 141–42, 150; and prophets, 159–61; and revelation on race, 62. *See also* Heavenly Father

Hanciles, Jehu, 5, 49–50, 57, 176
Heavenly Father, 98, 101, 123–24, 129, 167, 173; humans as children of, 89–91

Hervieu-Leger, Daniele, 41–44, 88, 98–99, 111, 133, 137, 162, 168, 174. *See also* collective memory; identity: fragmentation
Hinduism, 45, 50, 136
Holland, Jeffrey R., 58
Holy Spirit, 105, 107, 155

Iceland, 56
identity: American national, 7, 48–52, 57, 60–62, 73, 132, 137, 152–62, 175; congregational, 23, 121–29; cultural, 29, 42, 52; fragmentation of, 5, 42–46, 88, 134, 168; racial, 2. *See also* collective memory
immigrants: and assimilation, 114; and conversion, 85; and cultural difference, 127; and Ireland, 23, 33, 53, 180; Mormon, 7; and Mormonism in Europe, 22; and religious diversity, 1–2, 36–38, 54, 63–64; and xenophobia, 153
India, 50, 156
Inglis, Tom, 35, 37, 41–42, 57, 70
Inouye, Melissa, 53, 177
interviewee demographics, 16–17
Ireland: and abortion, 32–33; and the army, 116, 178; attitudes toward Mormonism, 85; and Catholic identity, 1–2, 7, 39, 42–43, 46, 57, 95, 115–16, 170, 175–79; Celtic Tiger period, 1, 3, 26, 31, 180; Easter Uprising, 118–19; emigration, 26, 31, 111–12, 174; idealization of Mormonism and Utah, 23, 48, 154; independence, 26–30, 56, 117–18; Irish-Irish designation, 23, 118–19; liberalization of family norms, 1, 32–34; national anthem, 132–33; patriotism, 29, 116–18, 127–28; potato famine, 26; World War II (the Emergency), 30. *See also* Irish (national identity); St. Patrick's Day
Irish (national identity): and Catholicism, 1–2, 7, 29, 39–43, 70–71, 170; and conversion to Mormonism, 23, 46, 77, 95, 115–16, 145, 175–79; and Mormonism in Europe, 57; and race, 133, 139–40
Islam: BYU courses on, 135; conversion to Protestantism, 165; in Ireland, 4, 36–37, 43; Irish knowledge of, 33; and migrant populations, 2; racialized, 83, 120–21, 139; as world religion, 50

Jehovah's Witnesses, 55, 80
Jesus Christ: abandoned faith in, 136; atonement of, 59; as brother, 89; close to

prayers, 18–20; imagery, 45, 49; leaders viewed as representative, 122, 129; love of, 104; and missionaries, 71–73; in Mormon beliefs, 71, 80, 124, 169; testimonies of, 12
Judaism, 4, 33, 135

Latin America, 54–55
LGBTQ+: and Catholicism, 172; civil partnership, 32; homosexuality criminalized in Ireland, 32; Mormon support of same-sex marriage, 141–42; Mormon teachings on, 45, 58, 163. *See also* Marriage: same-sex

Maffly-Kipp, Laurie, 6
Marriage: and caste, 50; and dowry, 139; heterosexual, 91, 141; in Ireland, 32; marrying within Mormonism, 98, 107–11, 146, 171, 174–76; and Mormonism, 49, 58–59; Mormons voted to legalize same-sex, 141; premarital, 67–68; same-sex, 32, 58, 94, 109, 141–42, 163, 172–76; and stereotypes of Mormons, 75; temple, 96, 98, 101, 104–10
Mauss, Armand, 53–62
minority religions: and Catholicism, 2–4, 30, 37, 139–40, 179; in Denmark, 52; and family relationships, 56–58; in Finland, 61; and immigration, 38, 63–64; knowledge of, 33; Mormonism in Ireland, 7, 22, 69, 75–76, 80, 86, 115, 120, 129–34, 170, 179; perform religion, 35, 82–83; racialization of, 167
missionaries: American, 51–52, 61, 153, 155; badges, 72, 74; and conversion, 20; and correlation, 156; investigators, 11–12, 15, 67–72, 100; early Irish missions to, 27–30; Eastern European, 54; in fieldwork, 11–12; and immigrants, 63; Ireland Dublin Mission, 8; and local Mormonism, 52, 143–44, 177; and Mormon culture, 49; Mormon mission daily life, 69–74, 85; and Mormon religiosity, 58; non-Mormon religions and, 55; payment for, 67–68; president, 156; raising children to serve, 101; reactions to Irish perceptions, 46; senior missionaries, 10; stereotyping, 74–75; training of, 177–78; US bias, 60; and visibility, 74–80; and the Word of Wisdom, 150–51

Mormon Culture Region: and cultural capital, 53, 171, 178; distance from, 134; likened to Irish Catholic influence, 158; and marriage, 176; and Mormonism's international presence, 22, 161–62; and race, 65; and social outlets, 175; White American worldview, 50, 57

Mormonism: and Americanism, 7, 48, 52, 60–61; "Church Americans," 155; Church culture, 23, 48–50, 137, 145–55, 162–63, 167, 174–76; and Church guidance, 139, 142–45, 172; correlation, 48, 60–61, 137–40, 145, 156, 162, 175; as cult, 57, 76; dating, 58, 108; and exclusion, 6, 22–23, 38, 46, 52, 58, 88, 96, 118–19, 150, 167, 177, 179; as foreign, 3, 22, 25, 61, 71, 110, 115, 174, 179; growth outside US, 5, 8, 47–48, 53–55, 59–63, 156–58, 170; and hierarchy, 30, 48, 50, 54, 63, 122, 128–29, 173; as insiders and outsiders, 18–22; Latinas and Latinos, 63, 65, 157; localization, 51; as master identity, 79–80; "Molly Mormon" stereotype, 58–59, 135; myths of, 146, 152, 158; and optimum conflict, 59–60; performance of religiosity, 35, 78–80; peripheries, 6, 50–53, 176; Pioneer Day, 152–53, 177; pioneers, 5, 58–59, 95, 158–59; priesthood, 12–13, 36, 44, 62, 97, 126, 151; racialized as people of color, 120; social class, 68, 118; stereotypes, 51, 58, 69, 74–75, 81, 136, 153, 159, 173–74, 179; visibility, 7–8, 50, 58, 61, 74–80, 83–84, 120, 162; worldview, 23, 69, 88–93, 96, 102, 124, 136–37, 150, 159, 175–77

music, 21, 53, 82, 105, 127–32

Netherlands, the, 56–57, 156
New Age, 4, 37
new religious movements (NRMs), 2, 4, 25, 37–38, 57, 117, 140
Nigeria, 71, 117, 139, 157
North American Mormonism: and Americanism, 73, 132, 137, 152–62; missionaries, 69–70, 78; and Mormon culture, 23, 125, 130, 145, 154–61, 176–77; and Mormonism in the workplace, 81–82; and multiculturalism, 119; study demographics, 16
Northern Ireland: Belfast, 160–61; and colonialism, 26; and Mormonism, 27–29, 161; and religious division, 145–46; and religious identity, 41, 121
Norway, 56

Pentecostalism, 4, 9, 36, 120
Philippines, the, 156–57
Plan of Salvation, 59, 71–72, 89–93, 98, 101, 104, 147–48
pluralism, 83, 163, 179
prayer: Angelus, 37; in Ballard meeting, 160–61; and callings, 123–25; Catholic, 78, 82, 140; and conversion, 108, 166; daily, 49, 68; in Irish, 117, 176; Joseph Smith and, 107; Mormon modes of, 18–20, 90; temple as space to pray, 98; and visibility, 72
priesthood: Mormon, 12–13, 44, 62, 97, 126, 151; Roman Catholic, 36
primary (organization). See children
Protestantism: and anti-Mormonism, 28; Britain, 26, 29; connection to Mormonism, 116, 121, 145; conversion to, 54–55, 165; European, 37, 43; Irish, 28–29, 116–17, 121, 145

race: Blood of Israel, 55, 63; and global Christianity, 49; and immigration, 33, 117, 124; and Irishness, 40; and Mormon culture, 62–66, 123, 127, 129, 140, 156–159; Mormons racialized, 120, 167, 178–79; pioneer stock, 158–59; racialized religion, 2–4, 7, 38, 180; represented in media, 157–59; and worthiness, 62, 150. See also Black people; Whiteness
Relief Society: activity, 113; lesson comments, 76, 105, 135; and Mormon worship, 11–14, 138; president, 122, 130
revelation, 62, 123–24, 150
Roman Catholic Church: decline of, 1–5, 34–39, 43, 54–55, 169–70; First Communion, 73, 94; healthcare, 35; as Irishness, 1–2, 7, 29, 39, 40–43, 46, 57, 95, 115–16, 170, 175–79; in Latin America, 54–55; Mormon bias against, 29; nonpracticing, 70, 107; older generations, 42, 70; Pope-Watch, 84; sacrament, 1, 79, 82, 94; sexual abuse crisis, 37; St. Anthony, 1; St. Bridget, 131
Rutherford, Taunalyn, 50–51, 138, 177

Sacrament (Mormon): cups, 68; and the Easter Uprising, 118–19; meetings, 12; Mormon ritual, 44–45, 144; talks, 89–96, 99, 140. *See also* Fast and Testimony Sacrament meeting

Scientology, 57

Scotland, 8, 29

scripture, 20, 49, 68, 76. *See also* Bible; *Book of Mormon*

secularization: defined, 34–35; in Europe, 22, 43; in Ireland, 5–6, 25–26, 34–38, 129, 170–73; in Mormonism, 5–6, 52, 55; religious decline, 1–5, 8, 34–39, 43, 51, 54, 169–70; workplace as secular, 81

Seventh-day Adventists, 55

sex: abuse crisis, 37; education, 58; heterosexual, 91, 141, 143; norms, 32, 175; pornography, 144; premarital, 67, 77, 94; and "straying" from Mormonism, 149

Smith, Joseph, 20, 27, 72, 107, 159; First Vision, 20, 107

Social life of Mormons: Christmas, 15–16, 75, 105–7, 140; Halloween, 15–16; male only, 14–15, 21; Mormons Having Fun, 15; Same Ten People (STP), 15. *See also* St. Patrick's Day

South America: and cultural differences, 127; in field study sample, 16–17; and Mormon culture, 119, 145–51; Mormon growth in, 156; and racialization, 179; and racial restriction revelation, 62; and temples, 97–98

St. Patrick's Day, 15–16, 127–30, 179

Sunday School, 12, 90–93, 124, 158, 168; Gospel Principles, 12, 72

Sweden, 56, 162

temple, Mormon: attendance, 49; endowment, 50, 96, 99–100; and family theology, 87, 91, 95–103, 106–11, 173–74; and Finish media coverage, 61; liturgy, 62; and marriage in the USA, 146; racial restriction, 62; rituals, 61, 71, 73, 84, 87, 91–103, 111, 173–74; in sacrament meeting talks, 90; sealing, 96–98, 101–2, 107, 111, 173–74; as symbol, 160–61; and Utah, 155. *See also* baptism: for the dead (posthumous)

tithing, 49, 68

Tonga, 64–65

Unification Church (Moonies), 57

Utah: and Americanism, 48, 62, 175; anti-Mormonism, 81; gathering to, 51, 95; idealized, 174; and Mormonism, 4–7, 23, 53, 137, 171, 177; Tongan communities in, 64

Whiteness: Catholicism constructed as white, 3; defined, 19, 62; and global Christianity, 49; and Irishness, 2–5, 25, 40, 121, 133, 179; majority White congregation, 9; missionaries, 69, 72; and Mormon culture, 23, 50, 62–65, 137, 150, 155–59; Mormon demographics in Ireland, 30, 69, 119; and Mormon leadership, 123–27, 176; Mormons as insiders and outsiders to, 22, 76; Mormonism constructed as white, 65; Mormon relationship to White Irish Catholicism, 7, 178–79; Mormons racialized as nonwhites, 120; and religious visibility, 83, 139–40; study demographics, 16; supremacy, 46

Word of Wisdom: coffee, 49, 79, 115, 143–44; Mormon health code, 79, 143; personal interpretation, 143–44; policed by non-Mormon Irish, 79; public expression of faith, 144; tea, 49, 79, 143–44; and temple worthiness, 97; and tobacco, 49, 77. *See also* alcohol

Young Men's groups, 12

Young Women's groups, 12

HAZEL O'BRIEN is a lecturer in sociology at
South East Technological University.

The University of Illinois Press
is a founding member of the
Association of University Presses.

———————————————

University of Illinois Press
1325 South Oak Street
Champaign, IL 61820-6903
www.press.uillinois.edu